The New New World

The re-emerging market in South America

Gilbert Le Gras

REUTERS

Published by **Pearson Education**

London · New York · San Francisco · Toronto · Sydney
Tokyo · Singapore · Hong Kong · Cape Town · Madrid
Paris · Milan · Munich · Amsterdam

PEARSON EDUCATION LIMITED

Head Office
Edinburgh Gate
Harlow CM20 2JE
Tel: +44 (0)1279 623623
Fax: +44 (0)1279 431059

London Office:
128 Long Acre,
London WC2E 9AN
Tel: +44 (0)20 7447 2000
Fax: +44 (0)20 7240 5771
Website:www.business-minds.com

First published in Great Britain in 2002

ISBN 1 903 68405 6

British Library Cataloguing in Publication Data
A CIP catalogue record for this book can be obtained from the British Library

10 9 8 7 6 5 4 3 2 1

Typeset by Pantek Arts Ltd, Maidstone, Kent
Printed and bound in Great Britain by Biddles Ltd., Guildford and Kings Lynn

The Publishers' policy is to use paper manufactured from sustainable forests.

Acknowledgements

The New New World was written in the belief that South Americans are making a concerted effort to reinforce their democratic institutions and reform their economies to a model that will lead to sustainable growth.

My father's interest in Latin American affairs and insistence I learn Spanish set me on the path that has yielded this book while my mother's development work in Asia and the Caribbean showed me how much one person's efforts helped those communities.

My father's wife showed me that living in a foreign country that speaks another language is not as difficult as it may seem. I'd like to thank my brother and his wife for teaching me that 'when the going gets tough, the tough get going'. Thanks to my wife, Natalia, whose love, support and encouragement helped me turn the dream of this book into reality and her parents and sister for showing me the world through the eyes of South Americans.

I am also indebted to a number of my colleagues at Reuters who either assisted in gathering information, arranging interviews or served as sounding boards in the aim of setting as accurate a tone as possible in this book. In this acknowledgement, I would like to single out Guido Nejamkis in Buenos Aires, Shasta Darlington and Jeremy Smith in Rio de Janeiro, Marco Sibaja in Brasilia and Daniel Flynn in Caracas. I owe a special thanks to Hugh Bronstein and Genevieve Wilkinson on the emerging markets desk in New York and Sarah Edmonds who heads economics coverage in Washington as well as Martin Redrado, chief economist at Buenos Aires-based think tank Fundacion Capital and trade lawyer Carlos Alfaro whose insights proved invaluable.

There are many elements in the pages of this book that are the result of conversations with market analysts, diplomats and academics who preferred to remain anonymous and to who I am grateful for their guidance.

I also very much appreciate the assistance of everyone who worked with Pearson Education who took part in shepherding this project to completion.

A number of other people, too many to name here, deserve my gratitude for their contribution to my professional development in general and specifically for the roles they played in making this book a reality. Thanks also to Melvin Mencher, whose rigorous editing of my copy while at Columbia University's Graduate School of Journalism, taught me the power of reporting when practised with commitment, compassion and conscience.

It is my desire that *The New New World* both helps to dispel cliches and misconceptions about South America and serves as a risk-assessment tool for you in developing this region of the world further.

Contents

To Natalia

Introduction:
Rediscovering a land of promise

'The United States will export more to Latin America by 2007 than it does to the European Union and Japan combined,' said Rubens Barbosa, Brazil's ambassador to the United States, in his Washington office days before George W. Bush was sworn in as 43rd US president.[1] 'Like the United States, Latin America has not been a top priority for the European Union, but we are pleased the EU is willing to discuss all areas of trade.'

Why is US and European business spending more time, money and effort on the South American market? It's not enough to argue that the continent's 346 million potential consumers are the attraction. Nor does the region's vast amounts of energy, food and minerals explain the growing interest in South America, since these resources have always been there. So what has changed in this part of the world for it to re-emerge as a new marketplace for western goods, services and capital?

Stability

Renewed interest in this market probably stems most from recent and dramatic steps taken by many of the 12 South American republics to wrestle inflation under control. The renewal of democracy and relatively smooth transitions in government from Peru to Bolivia also go a long way to creating a stable and predictable environment in which business can make plans in at least the short to medium term. Those two factors alone are the reasons most often cited by investors, from the chairman of chemicals conglomerate DuPont, the European Union commissioners for trade and external affairs, to senior officials at the International Monetary Fund.

Add to that the fact the financial services sector in South America is consolidating, maturing and opening up to foreign banks and you have the reason why fewer Argentines, for example, pulled cash from their accounts at the height of the liquidity crisis of 2001 than did during the 1995 Tequila crisis – when Argentina saw one of the most intensive bank runs in the 20th Century.

Latin America is one of the few regions in the world with which the US enjoys a trade surplus, so if your business is based in the United States, you can probably count on some form of government support if you want to launch a venture down there.

Growth

South America has a relatively young population who are enjoying this unprecedented economic and political stability. There is evidence of a middle class emerging in these countries, although income distribution is still out of balance in comparison with developed nations. Their political leaders are making tangible efforts to co-operate for the improvement of the region as a whole by means of a continental infrastructure, energy and telecommunications investment plan. The governments of South America hope these public works will stimulate economic development, attract more foreign direct investment and add pesos to their people's pockets.

Competition

South Americans, Europeans and Americans may have different interpretations of globalization but they are all competing for the same thing: a bigger slice of the world market. Many of the South Americans talk about closing ranks to form a Latin front in trade talks. Their two main regional blocs, the Andean Community of Nations and the Common Market of the South (Mercosur), are gradually drawing the continent together into one economy. In that process, they are forging common markets along the lines of World Trade Organization (WTO) rules that make them more predictable and understandable to outside investors like you and your company. That doesn't mean all the holdovers of the import-substitution era have been swept away or that legal loopholes and changes to concession contracts no longer occur. But South American governments are learning that these 'surprises' are counterproductive.

Let's face it, South America at the dawn of the 21st century is not in the same position as the Asian Tigers of the 1980s. Everyone from the United Nations to central bankers to academics say that most countries there have relatively solid banking systems compared with other emerging markets. That explains in part why most of South America fared better than many expected during the Asian, Russian and Brazilian and Argentine financial crises between 1997 and 2001 and why Brazil recovered more quickly and more strongly than foreseen.

Latin Americans have no illusions about the US-sponsored Free Trade Area of the Americas initiative. Many argue that their re-emerging 'new' world is one focus of commercial competition between the globe's two economic superpowers. 'Since the fall of the Berlin Wall, the United States has been worried about the European Union expanding into Eastern Europe, so they want to do the same here,' said Jorge Lavopa, of the Argentine Council on International Relations (CARI).[2] There's no denying that rivalry when you consider the world produced $40.7 trillion worth of goods and services in 1999 and the US economy accounted for 23 per cent of that total, compared with the European Union's 20 per cent. The South American market generated almost 6 per cent of gross world product and the continent's two biggest economies, Brazil and Argentina, alone produced 3.5 per cent of global output in 1999.[3] The value of goods and services produced in those two countries is roughly equal to the size of Italy's economy, or about twice the size of Canada's output. By early July 2001, the European Union had made a unilateral, comprehensive offer to phase in free trade with Mercosur over the next decade on the condition the South Americans matched their offer. Then, on 4 September 2001, US Trade Representative Robert Zoellick and the foreign ministers of Mercosur agreed to begin preliminary, exploratory talks on free trade. 'We believe that the financial reforms should be accompanied by a broad-based trade liberalization policy and we are trying to accomplish that globally, regionally and in the context of the four plus one (Mercosur countries plus United States),' Zoellick said.

Explanations that try to go beyond a purely cost-benefit analysis of what the new South America has to offer the global marketplace will surely fuel long and complex debates. What is certain is that Latin America attracted the largest amount of foreign direct investment of any emerging market region for the first time ever in 1999. Then, in the year 2000, the region drew its lowest level of aid loans since 1994 from the Inter-American Development Bank, borrowing only $5.2 billion thanks to market stability and government policies which 'are moving forward with a process of sound economic management.'[4]

This book aims to help you, your business and your clients understand the risks and rewards that can be reaped in this part of the world. To do that, this overview is divided into 10 chapters. The first chapter is a summary of the region's economic evolution since the Opec oil crisis of the 1970s, through the 1980s' debt crises and the macroeconomic readjustment initiatives during the 1990s. The next chapter explains the mechanics of Mercosur, the regional trade bloc that is the principal magnet drawing overseas business and investors, and briefly describes the Andean Community of Nations. Then you can analyze the demographic and market profiles of each of South America's 12 republics to gain a better appreciation of whom you are trying to sell to, buy from or assess before advising investors on what to do with their portfolio. The fourth chapter distils the rules of engagement in Mercosur and the Andean Community from dispute settlement to anti-trust rules and foreign investment policy to intellectual property. Chapter Five looks at the labour and business conditions, including controls on capital flows and shareholder rights. Chapter Six provides you with an inventory of the area's raw materials and commodities, from minerals to foodstuffs to energy, and forecasts trends in those sectors. The next chapter explains how to move your goods or services around this part of the world and what plans are under way to improve transportation. Chapter Eight explains the Mercosur nations' version of the EU Maastricht Treaty which aims to synchronize their key economic vital signs so that the Southern Cone countries converge into one relatively seamless regional market. Academics are already talking about the possible creation of a common currency. Then Chapter Nine explains the political goals of South American leaders, from Venezuela's enigmatic Hugo Chavez to Chile's pragmatic Ricardo Lagos and the geopolitical ambitions of Brazil's Fernando Henrique Cardoso. Finally, Chapter 10 distils these trends into a summary of where this region is likely to be heading in the coming years. Table 1 provides a snapshot of the region's key economic indicators since 1997.

The purpose of this book is to serve as a risk assessment tool. In evaluating the dangers and opportunities you may face, there have been two underlying assumptions. First, given that the Southern Cone of South America accounts for more than 50 per cent of continental gross domestic product (GDP), it will continue to be the primary focus of your company's attention. Second, civil war in Colombia has been a major impediment to investment in that country and may be an increasingly relevant

Table 1 Latin American and Caribbean economic indicators (Percentage change unless otherwise indicated)

	1997	1998	1999	2000	2001
Real GDP	4.5	2.0	0.4	4.2	2.5
Inflation	10.2	8.6	8.6	7.8	6.1
Public sector balance (ratio to GDP)	–2.8	–4.1	–4.9	–2.6	–3.4
Investment (ratio to GDP)	22.5	21.9	20.3	20.1	20.5
National savings (ratio to GDP)	19.7	18.1	17.2	17.9	17.8
External current account (ratio to GDP)	–2.8	–3.9	–3.1	–2.2	–2.7
Gross Domestic Product (US$ billions)	1969.0	1978.2	1744.3	1930.2	1953.5

Source: International Monetary Fund (*www.imf.org*) 10 August 2001

concern to neighbouring nations, depending on how the controversial Plan Colombia initiative unfolds. Now the arrival of populist Hugo Chavez in Venezuela is another point of concern for business and diplomats. Who is this man, and what does he really want? An exclusive interview with Chavez with excerpts distributed throughout this book tries to answer those questions.

So, what is the basis of these assumptions? Brazil alone attracted more foreign direct investment than any other developing economy apart from China in 1999, and was fourth overall after the United States and Britain. The six countries that are partners or associates of Mercosur (Brazil, Argentina, Uruguay, Paraguay and associates Chile and Bolivia) represent 233 million people producing about $1.17 trillion in goods and services each year. Put another way, Mercosur has less than half the population of the Association of South East Asian Nations (Asean has about 500 million people), but almost twice its combined gross domestic product of $737 billion. Eastern Asia attracted $108.9 billion in foreign direct investment in 1999 compared with $66.9 billion in 1994, but Asean's share dropped to 14.9 per cent of that from 30.5 per cent. 'We in Asia are nowhere near the level of European regionalism. We may not want to follow their brand of regionalism … But we cannot afford not to start working on a model of our own,' said Yeo Cheow Tong, Singapore's minister for communications.[5] The Andean Community consists of more than 109 million people who produce $620 billion in goods and services and the leaders of those countries (Bolivia, Colombia, Ecuador, Peru and Venezuela) intend to negotiate a free trade agreement with their Mercosur counterparts.

'The underlying trend is ... (towards) ... a general improvement in the quality of macroeconomic policy and structural reforms. There's been a fundamental change in the quality of policymakers with a better understanding of the benefits of good macroeconomic policies and structural reforms,' said Claudio Loser, director of the Western Hemisphere for the International Monetary Fund.[6]

Trade negotiators from other parts of the world have changed their view of Mercosur from that of yet another Latin American attempt to erect a commercial fortress to perceiving it as a genuine attempt to make trade a more meaningful part of the regional economies. Like other developing nations, countries in South America want more time to prepare their industries for global trade and to face a world with fewer tariff and regulatory restrictions. South American economies have come a long way in opening up to the outside world in the past decade. In 1988, Brazil maintained import tariffs of 51 per cent, while in 1989 Argentina's import tariffs were about 30 per cent, according to World Trade Organization figures. Now they and the two other full members of Mercosur have a common external tariff that averages 12.5 per cent. On top of that achievement, the four member nations and two Mercosur associates (Chile and Bolivia) have agreed to keep inflation below 5 per cent per year between 2002 and 2005 while limiting their federal government deficits to no more than 5 per cent of gross domestic product in 2002. All six governments agreed that debt as a proportion of GDP should not exceed 40 per cent from 2010. It's true that Mercosur is the world's third-largest trade bloc after the North American Free Trade Agreement (Nafta) and the European Union. But if you look at it another way, it is also the leading effort at economic integration among developing nations. Political and business leaders inside and outside Latin America are aware that Mercosur is an example other developing regions are studying. 'There are a range of areas where the outcome of previous multilateral negotiations have been weighted against the developing countries. This is not only restrictive of our development but will soon also be a restraint on the continued growth and prosperity of the world economy,' South African President Thabo Mbeki told his South American counterparts at a Mercosur summit in Florianopolis, Brazil, to which he had been invited as an observer.[7]

The jury is still out on how much trade is diverted within Mercosur rather than created by the fledgling trade group. But one thing everyone agrees on is that the regional bloc has been importing an ever increasing amount over the past decade. US exports to Mercosur reached $20.3 billion in 1998 compared with EU shipments of $22.1 billion, an EU report found. The world's two biggest economic blocs are almost neck and neck in their exports to this region so it is no wonder they are both pushing their own free trade agendas to take the lead. The United States calls Mercosur an 'ally' in its efforts to create a free trade area spanning two continents, uniting North and South America and running through Central America and the Caribbean (with the exception of Cuba). The Americans want this completed by 2005 but the Brazilians say they prefer to take the time needed to negotiate properly. Whether the Americans or European like it, Brazil is the linchpin. The EU held three rounds of free trade talks with Mercosur in 2000 and both trade commissioner Pascal Lamy and external affairs commissioner Chris Patten said Mercosur's 'Little Maastricht' plan had given the region a competitive edge in attracting foreign investment.[8] The insurance that both Argentina and Brazil stay the course on fiscal prudence that is so vital to your confidence in making long-term investments there is the fact that they have both received multi-billion-dollar aid packages from the International Monetary Fund in return for fundamental improvements in how they run their economies.

The idea behind the Mercosur Maastricht plan was first suggested in June 1999 after Brazil's devaluation threw the tightly knit regional trade flows out of kilter and worsened the recessions of neighbouring countries. Brazil's real now floats freely on currency markets, while Argentina's peso remains fixed at par to the US dollar through a currency board system, and Chile's central bank maintains a wide currency band. Whether the six nations want to or will be able to forge a common currency will depend on political will and is something everyone agrees will be a long-term project. Chapter Eight explores this longer-term scenario in greater detail. But for now, South American central bankers have said price stability is the solution to harmonizing their poles-apart foreign exchange regimes and a step towards creating an EU-like common market. While Brazil's devaluation raised howls of protest from Argentine industry, which used to enjoy a currency exchange advantage exporting into that market, Brazilian inflation has been gradually reintroducing equilibrium between the prices on products from both countries.

The ascendancy of Mexican president Vicente Fox after 71 years of rule by the Institutional Revolutionary Party (PRI) may ease commercial relations between Latin America's two largest economies (Brazil and Mexico) but only time will tell. Venezuela's president Hugo Chavez, meanwhile, has talked of closer commercial ties between the north and the south of the continent.

'The key issue for Mercosur, both economically and politically, is the resolution of the debate about deepening or widening,' said Riordan Roett, director of Latin American studies at Johns Hopkins University, in Washington DC. 'To deepen means stronger institutional mechanisms to resolve disputes, etc. To widen and bring in more members is a dangerous alternative. My sense is that Brazil is slowly coming to the realization that deepening is preferable.'[9]

If the United States wants to successfully shepherd its western hemisphere neighbours into creating the world's largest free trade zone it will have to proceed without being too overbearingly interventionist, especially in military terms. Late in 2000, political think-tank Inter-American Dialogue urged the incoming Bush administration to work more closely with Brazil. 'On many of the most important issues in hemispheric affairs, the US simply will not be able to make much headway without the backing of Brazil. If Brazil and the US find common ground, free trade in the Americas is inevitable; if they cannot, it is impossible,' the group's year-end report said. It also warned against the dangers of the most significant US military assistance in the western hemisphere since the end of the cold war, in the form of $1.3 billion in mostly military backing for Plan Colombia. 'Like some US opponents of military aid to Colombia, several governments fear a Vietnam-style debacle. The US must show that it understands Colombia's problems need to be addressed multilaterally – and that it is prepared to work co-operatively with other countries and to accept a common agenda of building peace and achieving reconciliation in Colombia. Washington must leave no doubt that it supports the peace negotiations of the Colombian government and that US troops will not be used in combat,' said Inter-American Dialogue.

Colombia's four decades old conflict has taken on a new facet of the domestic sovereignty issue with the introduction of Plan Colombia. 'There is a fear in this region of the world that the United States can deny them economic sovereignty. Colombia's civil war has become an integral part of Colombian government policy. There are few Colombian presidents who haven't been suspected of profiting from the drug trade,' said human rights consultant Christophe Swinarski.[10]

Venezuelan president Hugo Chavez said he did not like the military facet of Plan Colombia but that his nation was ready to co-operate in fighting drug trafficking and organized crime. One commercial casualty of Colombia's ongoing conflict is physical integration of the Andean Community. That process took a step backwards in 2000 when Chavez decided to suspend trans-shipments of goods by truck across the country's border with Colombia. The Andean Community's General Secretariat ordered Venezuela to lift the ban but it has refused to do so, one of the first times in the trade bloc's history that a national government has failed to comply with a Community order. 'We didn't break the accord. It states that there should be equality of conditions, and circumstances are not the same in our countries. Venezuelan truckers are getting killed in Colombia. Safety in Colombia won't impede integration but it makes it more difficult', said Chavez.[11]

This book attempts to explain to you why your business should care about or even support economic integration in South America. Does integration make a meaningful difference to your business operations? The case studies you will read in these pages illustrate examples of companies in various sectors for whom integration makes doing business in the region simpler. It is not only harmonized regional regulations that will help but also plans to create a common market where inflation is low and relatively uniform across multiple borders in order to lower the country risk ratings and interest rates.

In Chapter Seven, a director of ACBL Hidrovias S.A., a unit of American Commercial Barge Line Co., explains that the differences in river barge regulations between Argentina, Bolivia, Brazil, Paraguay and Uruguay are a headache but work is under way to standardize these norms. Chapter One cites the example of Banco Santander Central Hispano's expansion in the financial services sector and what it expects this part of the world to look like in the coming 10 to 15 years. Then in Chapter Three you can see how Brazilian brewer AmBev is betting on population trends and growth in discretionary income in its South American expansion strategy. Volkswagen Argentina's president, Viktor Klima, argues in Chapter Two that freer trade with other countries is the key to boosting production, while in Chapter Five, Alan Hill, of Barrick Gold Corp. predicts the improving business climate in the region will attract many mining companies to invest heavily in the coming years. Meanwhile, natural gas exploration and exploitation firm Canadian Hunter International Ltd. in Chapter Six is counting on Brazil's power deficit to fuel demand for its production out of the Neuquen basin, the 'West Texas' of Argentina.

Take Anglo-Dutch consumer products giant Unilever Plc/NV as an example. That conglomerate plans to evenly split $340 million in new investments in Brazil and Argentina in 2001 to increase productivity and marketing. The company plans to divide its regional plants into specialities: Argentina will manufacture aerosol products for all of Latin America; Brazil will concentrate on toothpaste; and Mexico will make facial cream. The point is that in a regional marketplace it is unlikely that industry would need to duplicate production of the same goods in several countries. Instead, factories in each major market could specialize in certain products destined for the region as a whole. Put another way, will it make sense for Argentina to have eight carmakers after 2006, when car tariffs within Mercosur are intended to be removed, given that assemblers are making the same platforms in nearby Sao Paulo, Brazil? Probably not.

The decline of one industry in a country always sets the stage for a political battlefield and those governments truly committed to integration will have their resolve put to the test. Their best defence will be a well-planned economic diversification strategy. One facet of economic diversification is taking advantage of economies of scale to develop a resource that in a domestic market may not be commercially viable, such as natural gas in Bolivia for use in Brazil. This book attempts to tell you where South America has come from and tries to forecast where it is heading in order to serve as a useful guide to you and your business.

Notes

[1]Barbosa, Rubens, Brazilian ambassador to the United States, interview in Washington, D.C., 12 January 2001.

[2]Lavopa, Jorge (2000) 'External Relations of Mercosur', seminar given at Universidad del Salvador, Buenos Aires, 5 December 2000.

[3]Office of the Director of Central Intelligence (2000) *The World Fact Book 2000*, Central Intelligence Agency (*www.odci.gov.cia/publications/factbook/geos/xx.html*).

[4]Iglesias, Enrique, president, Inter-American Development Bank, press statement, 27 December 2000.

[5]Cheow Tong, Yeo, Singapore Minister for Communications, interview published in the *Financial Times*, 11 January 2001, page 6.

[6]Loser, Claudio, director of the western hemisphere, International Monetary Fund, interview in Washington, D.C., 12 January 2001.

[7]Mbeki, Thabo, president of South Africa, address to Mercosur presidential summit, 15 December 2000.

[8]Lamy, Pascal, European Union trade commissioner, and Patten, Chris, European Union external affairs commissioner, interviews in Buenos Aires, 29 September 2000 and 8 November 2000.

[9]Roett, Riordan, Sarita and Don Johnson professor and director, Western Hemisphere Program, The Paul H. Nitze School of Advanced International Studies, Johns Hopkins University, interview, 27 July 2000.

[10]Swinarski, Christophe, human rights consultant and former human rights observer of the International Committee of the Red Cross to Argentina, Brazil, Uruguay and Paraguay (1987 to 1991) as well as Bolivia and Chile (1989 to 1991), interview in Buenos Aires, 18 December 2000.

[11]Chavez, Hugo, president of Venezuela, interview in Puerto Ordaz, Venezuela, 20 January 2001.

1

A wild ride since the 1960s

For much of the past generation, Latin America has been in the grip of a die hard debt which has turned back the clock on development in some countries while limiting the evolution of others. Sky-high interest rates diverted government spending to debt service payments and dominated the economic agendas of South America's 12 republics. In times of crisis these countries typically cut imports and try to boost exports to build up the foreign reserves necessary to pay back their crippling debts. Living beyond their means and finding themselves at the mercy of volatile emerging debt markets has been a painful lesson for South Americans. But pain is often the best teacher and no one in the region wants to learn the hyperinflation lesson of the 1980s again. There are varying degrees of willingness to take the steps necessary to ensure economic circumstances don't unravel, with perhaps Ecuador dragging its heels the most. Others simply have the resources to avoid the dreaded 'IMF handshake'.

'Borrowing money from the International Monetary Fund is like dealing your soul to the devil,' said Venezuelan president Hugo Chavez.[1]

Over the course of the past generation the International Monetary Fund has been widely vilified as badgering regional nations into responsible fiscal policies at the expense of social development. Former World Bank chief economist Joseph Stiglitz resigned late in 2000 complaining that the IMF 'one size fits all' solution to the developing world's economic dilemmas ignored the particularities of individual countries. This chapter will describe those particularities, country by country, and the struggle to contain inflation so that you have a better understanding of the kind of market volatility you may be dealing with in whichever of those markets you may invest in.

Hard luck history

The idea that easy money and a good living were up for the taking in South America dates back to the time of the Spanish conquistadores. While it is true the New World has a vast and varied array of wealth, it has never easily been up for grabs. The legend of El Dorado, or the 'gilded man', lured thousands of colonizers from the Old World to scour this continent. What they found was the world's fourth-largest continent, a major source of minerals and food and later oil and now natural gas.

Brazil has become one of the world's nine largest economies and one of the globe's most industrialized developing nations. Latin America's largest economy produces everything from regional aircraft and internet services to tropical beverages such as coffee and cocoa. But South America also poses formidable physical and fiscal obstacles. Regional leaders are only now taking their destiny in their own hands and confronting both of these challenges.

Geographical obstacles

South America's more than 346 million people are separated by some of the highest mountains in the world, dense Amazonian jungles and a wide network of rivers. The mountains and hills that dot the Brazilian coastline mean most rivers in that country flow inland. The Amazon and Hidrovia river networks, akin to the Mississippi in the United States or the Danube in Europe, link Brazil to almost every other nation on the continent. In Chapter Seven you will be able to assess the development projects proposed to turn these waterways, and Venezuela's Orinoco, into alternative routes for cargo traffic. The Hidrovia waterway is already supplying and shipping commodities out of five countries, but the tonnage it handles could almost triple to

15 million tonnes in 2003 from 6 million tonnes in 1999 with the help of a minimal amount of dredging and a new signalling system. Barge transport today accounts for less than 10 per cent of cargo movement in the region, but riverside development plans could change that.

Roughly 80 per cent of goods are hauled by truck in this part of the world and while highways linking Sao Paulo to Buenos Aires and on to Santiago are in good shape, alternative routes, especially those through Bolivia leading to Pacific ports, are in decrepit condition. Rail transport is one of the least common forms of shipping here because of differences in track width within and between countries, let alone the logistical challenges involved in hauling freight over some of the highest mountain passes in the world. Air cargo tonnage has been growing since the mid-1990s and expected airline consolidation could make the movement of goods by air that much more efficient. In September 2000 Germany's Lufthansa Cargo integrated its air freight activities into a common flight network with Brazil's leading airline, Varig.

Whichever way your business chooses to deliver a product to a customer or ship equipment to a branch office, freight forwarders agree there has been a dramatic reduction in red tape at border checks between Mercosur nations since the customs union began its evolution in 1995. That means products that took as much as two to three weeks to arrive in Buenos Aires from Sao Paulo now take about four days to be delivered. That's partly thanks to a computerized customs pre-clearance system and more efficient border control as well as a change in border guards' attitudes, shippers say. However, customs clearance elsewhere leaves a lot to be desired and the objective of Free Trade Area of the Americas (FTAA) talks to set a six-hour clearance period on express shipments has yet to be realized.

> **“Rail transport is one of the least common forms of shipping here because of differences in track width within and between countries, let alone the logistical challenges”**

Financial obstacles

Raising capital locally to finance a business is another challenge. The gross domestic savings ratio for Latin America is 17.3 per cent compared with 31.8 per cent in Asia.[2] Years of inflation and banking sector turmoil have marked a generation with a deep mistrust of local financial institutions. But consolidation over the past decade and deeper penetration by foreign banks in the domestic market, most notably in Argentina, have created a home-grown safe haven for business and personal account holders. The banking sectors in most of these countries have consolidated considerably in the past two decades so that there is a higher concentration of financial services in fewer hands, which means your loans, deposits and transfers are at less risk of a bank failing. The advent of private pension schemes has also attracted more savings into the financial services system and shifted government and corporate debt financing reliance increasingly onto the domestic market. A case study of Spanish bank Banco Santander Central Hispano at the end of this chapter will serve to illustrate the evolution of South America's financial services sector over the past decade.

'In Latin America as a whole, about a third of its people live on $2 per day or less, and income inequality is worse than in any other region. Justice systems, while improving, remain inefficient and unresponsive in many countries. Corruption, though decreasing, remains a problem. Education, while under reform, remains unequal in quality or unavailable to the poor and isolated rural communities,' said US State Department deputy assistant for western hemisphere affairs William Brownfield.[3] 'International economic integration gives both consumers and producers lower prices, greater choices and expanded services. It encourages more efficient production and stimulates innovation. It creates more jobs and better quality jobs in all countries.'

With the exception of some mainly isolated Native American subsistence farmers on the Andean high plains or semi-nomadic tribes in the Brazilian Amazon, South America has largely embraced market economics as the way to develop its economies. The dream of pan-Latin integration dates back to the time of Simón Bolívar (1783–1830) whose call for an 'American Union' at the 1826 Panama Congress was the first expression of continental, supranational unity. Born in Caracas, Bolivar was one of South America's most important revolutionaries and statesmen, leading campaigns against the Spaniards from 1812 to 1824. Venezuela's Hugo Chavez has dusted off Bolivar's cause and given it a 21st-century spin during multiple marathon speeches to his citizens, emphasizing a 'multipolar' geopolitical landscape which includes a Latin American front. What happened between Bolivar and Chavez was a continuation of geopolitical tutelage from colonial rule under Spain and Portugual to the Monroe Doctrine of the United States of America.

Latin American resistance to US involvement in their domestic affairs dates back to 1823 when US president James Monroe (1758–1831) warned the Old World not to interfere in the region. Now, Brazil is trying to position itself as the leader of a counterweight to the view that South America is a US dominion and if there is any kind of unifying thread in the thin concept of pan-Latin unity it is in how Latin Americans define themselves as being opposed to US political interference in their affairs. It is true that the region's largest nation is significantly distinct from every other country in Latin American in terms of history, culture and business practices. But the differences that distinguish Brazil from its Latin cousins are minimal if you compare them to those that separate the member nations of Asean or the European Union. Brazil is the only Latin American nation that separated from its colonizer, Portugal, without a struggle and consequently it enjoyed a smoother transition to independence. Almost everywhere else on the continent armed conflict before and after liberation stalled development.

Bolívar in the north and José Francisco de San Martin (1778–1850) in the south waged campaigns to oust the Spaniards which ended when the two military leaders joined forces in 1821 in Peru and scored decisive victories in Junín and Ayacucho in 1824 that broke the remnants of Spain's hold of South America. Burdened by racial and class conflict, lack of public education and economic development, the new republics of South America were controlled for much of the next century either by military dictators or by the authoritarian elite which ruled under the guise of committees called 'caudillos' while the vast majority of people lived in poverty and without land.

In an attempt to develop their economies, Latin American nations borrowed heavily in the 1920s on low interest rates and easy terms. When US interest rates began rising in 1928 and 1929 in a consumer bubble that preceded the Great Crash, the Latin American borrowers tried to trim imports and boost exports to earn hard currency – a policy they repeated during the debt crises of the 1980s. So, when global trade collapsed between 1929 and 1932, the Latin American leaders imposed import restrictions and devalued many of their currencies. Most could still not avoid insolvency. Bolivia was the first to stop servicing its debt and by 1933 all but Haiti and Argentina had defaulted too. But even Argentina felt the strain, which set the stage for the arrival of populist leader Juan Domingo Perón (1895–1975) who predicted that by the year 2000 South America would either be united or dominated.

Latin American leaders' initial attempts at uniting in the 20th century resulted in trading fortresses. The Treaty of Montevideo (18 February 1960) gave birth to the Latin American Free Trade Area (ALALC). The 11 Latin American republics (Argentina, Bolivia, Brazil, Chile, Colombia, Ecuador, Mexico, Paraguay, Peru, Uruguay and Venezuela) that signed the ALALC deal formed a defensive trade group whose economic development policies relied on high tariff barriers to force industry to establish a domestic presence by making it economically prohibitive to import. The group was created in accordance with Article 24 of the WTO's predecessor, the General Agreement on Tariffs and Trade (GATT), and the ALALC nations granted each other most favoured nation (MFN) status and shared a list of common irrevocable products. That project failed. Then the 1979 Tokyo Round of the GATT only granted one exception to developing countries that did not want to extend MFN status to developed countries.

That is why another Treaty of Montevideo (12 August 1980) was signed involving the same 11 countries, plus Cuba later on, and was called the Association of Latin American Trade Partners (ALADI). In this case the idea is to create a common Latin American market through a gradual process of regional integration and preferential tariffs. It has a council of ministers who meet periodically to evaluate progress towards integration and has a secretary general entrusted with its administration. In the meantime, South America has pursued two separate projects: the Andean Community of Nations and the Common Market of the South.[4] Colombia and Venezuela are also phasing into the Group of Three free trade area with Mexico. Venezuela also formally asked in June 2001 to be admitted into Mercosur and a response was expected at the next Mercosur summit.

'We want to advance in creating a greater economic area in South America. The priority is to implement a free trade area between Mercosur and the Andean Community no later than January 2002,' Brazilian president Fernando Henrique Cardoso told his South American counterparts on 31st August 2000 when opening the first summit of South American presidents in Brasilia. 'We want to actively take part in global decision making regarding the reorganization of the international financial architecture. We don't want to be barely kept informed of the decisions of the G7 or G8.'

'While viewed with initial suspicion by US trade officials as yet another regional attempt to set up a fortress-like barrier to commerce, Mercosur has since been lauded by both European Union and US political and business leaders as a concerted effort to stabilize and open the region's economies to the world market.[5]

The 'Brady' Bunch

Debt is the single biggest threat to economic stability in the nascent democracies of South America. Now many of these nations have strict loan agreements with the International Monetary Fund that underpin their market reform programmes and act as insurance that those governments will go through with reforms that open their markets to you, the foreign investor. Unlike the 1920s when sovereign borrowing ran out of control and created the economic conditions that eventually contributed to world war, multilateral lenders were created during the presidency of Harry Truman to keep nations from the brink of financial disaster. Some South American economists lament that the IMF was not set up under English economist John Maynard Keynes' vision where creditor nations would have had to make the effort to buy more exports from troubled debtor nations. A number of academics claim the IMF and World Bank failed in their duties and allowed Latin American governments to yet again go on a borrowing binge in the 1970s. Rather than shoulder their share of the responsibility, these academics say, the IMF and World Bank deflected the blame entirely onto Latin American governments when the region was broadsided by the spike in world crude oil prices in 1973 that sent interest rates up and economic growth down. Of course, these governments got themselves into this mess in the first place, but resentment that the global financial traffic cops didn't pull these borrowers over sooner partly explains why there are a number of national and regional development banks in the region that answer to a South American agenda rather than that set by Washington. The United States is the single largest stakeholder in the IMF with a 17.6 per cent share of the vote on the executive board. Now those regional development banks are behind an ambitious series of projects described in Chapter Seven.

Whichever interpretation you take of what the IMF and World Bank did or did not do, the fact is that what followed the Opec oil crisis was inflation and economic stagnation which fed Latin America's growing debt – by 1985 Latin American debt topped $376.6 billion, a more than five-fold increase within a decade from $68.5 billion in 1975. A second rise in oil prices in 1979 fuelled interest rates even more, pushing Mexico into crisis in mid-1982, which scared foreign banks and investors away from Latin America over the following years. There are a number of Latin Americans who remain sharply critical of the role of the IMF and World Bank, and Stiglitz's resignation as World Bank chief economist in 2000 has added credibility to their arguments that some adjustment programmes are sometimes ill suited to particular national needs.

Given this mushrooming debt, investors like you were increasingly reluctant to earmark funds for this region during the hyperinflation days of the 1980s because of concerns that the purchasing power of that capital would be diminished once it was repayed. That meant lenders demanded ever higher interest rates on bonds, which fed the debt spiral further. Consequently, Brazil, Mexico, Argentina, Venezuela, Peru, Ecuador, Uruguay and others had to have their principal, interest and interest arrears reduced under a debt restructuring plan named after then-US Treasury secretary Nicholas Brady. Along with the IMF and World Bank, Brady sponsored the reorganizing of outstanding sovereign loans and interest payment arrears into liquid debt instruments called 'Brady bonds'. Mexico and Venezuela, among others, linked their par and discount Brady bonds to warrants granting bondholders the right to recoup part of their debt or debt service reduction if their ability to service that debt improved. That's why some are called oil warrants, because they are tied to oil export prices and the foreign exchange revenues they generate.

“by 1985 Latin American debt topped $376.6 billion, a more than fivefold increase within a decade”

Brady bonds relieved the pressure on South America by rescheduling the debt payments over a longer time period, but inflation remained a top concern. Export earnings continue to be a key indicator analysts watch since much of the outstanding debt of most countries on the continent is still held offshore and in foreign currencies, principally the dollar, the euro and the yen – with Brazil and Chile being the exceptions. Other countries are in the process of swapping their Brady bonds for global bonds in order to extend their amortizations and at the same time induce the development of domestic capital markets by opening up their pension schemes to private fund managers.

Wrestling the inflation monster

Brazil

Brazil struggled through high inflation in the 1980s and early 1990s. That crippled economic activity and hindered investment, cutting growth and development. Latin America's largest economy imposed an inflation-busting programme called 'Plan Real' in 1994 which pegged the country's currency, the real, to the US dollar. It succeeded in reigning in inflation to single digits, but not fast enough to keep the prices of domestic goods and services from overshooting those of imports. The result was a flood of cheaper imports into that market as Brazilian products became increasingly expensive, which added to the nation's current account deficits – the balance of its flows in goods, services income and unilateral transfers.

Then came the Asian financial crisis of 1997, followed by Russia's de facto bond default in August 1998, and jittery international capital markets turned their attention to Brazil's increasingly precarious current account balance and wondered how it could maintain its currency policy. In a move aimed at staving off a potential financial crisis, Brazil received $41.5 billion in IMF-led aid in November 1998 once it had established a fiscal adjustment programme and promised to make structural reforms to its economy. But the multilateral package wasn't enough to cap the flight of emerging market capital and on 13 January 1999 the Brazilian Central Bank stopped defending the currency's trading bands. The real fell as much as 42 per cent against the greenback in 1999, but the devaluation stemmed Brazil's economic downturn that year and helped the South American nation beat the IMF's prescribed debt-to-GDP ratio. It also met its public sector surplus goal for 2000 with about $71 million to spare on the IMF's primary budget surplus target of $19.3 billion. That surplus was equal to 3.56 per cent of GDP.

In 2001 Brazil must post a surplus of 3.35 per cent of GDP under the 1998 IMF deal. Credit rating agency Moody's Investors Services upgraded Brazil's foreign-exchange debt ceiling in late December 2000 to B1 from B2. Standard & Poors followed in the first week of 2001, boosting the government's foreign bond rating to 'BB-', in line with the ratings of Peruvian government foreign bonds because of Brazil's narrowing budget deficit and expanding economy. Finance Minister Pedro Malan said on 7 August 2001 the Brazilian government would cut spending and tighten its fiscal targets in order to secure a new $15 billion loan from the IMF in order to weather the emerging market financial storm unleashed by its cash-strapped neighbour Argentina. Brazil raised its primary public sector budget surplus objective – a measure of fiscal excess that excludes debt payments – to 3.5 per cent of GDP in 2002 from 3 per cent. By the time of Malan's August 2001 announcement Brazil had already met its IMF-set fiscal targets for the past 11 consecutive quarters. Malan said GDP should grow 2.7. per cent in 2001 and 3.5 per cent in 2001. (For more details on Brazil's budget please visit *www.stn.fazenda.gov.br.*)

Argentina

Argentina saw monthly inflation peak at about 200 per cent in 1989, so its counter-inflationary measure was to implement a currency board system in 1991. The way this stopped inflation dead in its tracks was by limiting growth in the money supply by law to the growth in reserves of US dollars, effectively pegging the peso at par to the greenback. The monetary policy of South America's second-largest economy has withstood the emerging market capital flights caused by the 1995 Mexican peso devaluation, or 'Tequila' crisis, the 1997 and 1998 Asian and Russian financial crises, not to mention Brazil's devaluation. Result: the proportion of pesos, personal savings and term deposits to the size of Argentina's economy had grown to 33 per cent by mid-2000 from 7 per cent in 1989. Economists call this measure of the money supply M2 and in the US it is equal to 49.3 per cent of the economy, compared with 40 per cent in Brazil and 45.7 per cent in Chile. Analysts see more room for growth in Argentina's financial sector. Private domestic pension funds now manage more than $19.8 billion in investments, much of which is government debt, up from $8 billion in 1994 and growing at an annual rate of 1.5 per cent to GDP.[6] But many economists blame Argentina's depression from 1999 to 2001 on the peso's high level compared to that of its top trading partner, Brazil. By mid-2001 Argentina's Congress passed a law that would peg the peso to the intra-day 50-50 average of the dollar and the euro, due to come into effect when the euro reaches parity to the greenback. Some economists called this a 'controlled devaluation'. Economy Minister Domingo Cavallo said it would make Argentine exports more competitive.

Market liquidity, meanwhile, continued to evaporate throughout 2000 leading to fears Argentina might not be able to meet its billions in local and foreign debt obligations coming due in the following years. So as in Brazil two years earlier, the IMF and other lenders cobbled together $39.7 billion in cash aid in December 2000 over the next three years aimed at reassuring markets and reining in Argentine interest rates. But the politically weak and indecisive coalition government of President Fernando de la Rua failed to reel in chronic overspending. By the first quarter of 2001 Argentina had overshot its IMF deficit target by $1 billion. Argentina tried pushing its mammoth debt bulge further out into the future through the end of 2005. Then, at the end of July it passed a zero-deficit law and swapped $1.32 billion in domestic Treasury bills but by then Argentines feared for the worst and in that one month alone had pulled more than $5 billion from their bank accounts. Central Bank vicepresident Mario Blejer, who worked for the IMF for 21 years and helped broker a new $8 billion IMF aid package in August, said the run on banks had stopped shortly after the deal was announced on 21 August 2001. From the end of June to that date, total bank deposits had fallen 11 per cent and international reserves had plunged almost 30 per cent. While mass withdrawals often precipitate devaluations or debt defaults, the soundness of Argentina's financial sector was widely credited with helping the nation avoid a disaster. Bank withdrawals ocurred at a far lesser rate than during the 1995 Tequila crisis when deposits fell 21 per cent in three months, one of the steepest bank runs any country in the world experienced in the 20th Century. The 1995 crisis led Argentina's Central Bank to raise its reserve requirements well beyond Bank of International Settlements standards and subsequent consolidation and foreign penetration of the financial sector created a kind of domestic banking safe haven. Now, Argentina has one of Latin America's highest concentrations of foreign banks. (For more details on Argentina's official economic outlook, please visit: *www.mecon.gov.ar*.)

Chile

Even investment-grade Chile felt the combined effects of the Asian, Russia and Brazilian crises which in 1999 pushed its economy into recession for the first time in 15 years. Real growth in GDP averaged 8 per cent between 1991 and 1997 thanks to deeper economic reforms pursued by the country's first democratic president, Patricio Aylwin, since the end of General Augusto Pinochet's repressive regime. Chile's banking sector began consolidating in 1996 as foreign banks acquired domestic financial institutions and market share tilted from 69 per cent held by local banks then to 54 per cent held by foreign banks in 2000.[7] The fact that foreign banks have such a substantial presence in Chile's domestic market means there is a local safe haven for account holders and foreign businesses like yours. The shift towards private pension schemes has also reduced Chile's reliance on international capital markets to finance any budget gap. President Ricardo Lagos took over from Eduardo Frei in March 2000, maintaining the presidency in the hands of Chile's centre-left Concertacion coalition that has ruled since the return of civilian rule in 1990. After Mexico, Chile has the most open of Latin American economies, with trade accounting for about 25 per cent of GDP. This is a country that has skillfully adapted from heavy reliance on one export commodity (nitrates in the Atacama desert) to another (copper). Chile had successfully parlayed increasing foreign investment ($10.6 billion in 1999 from $1.5 billion in 1990) to diversify its exports between mining (45 per cent), industry (43 per cent) and to a lesser extent agriculture and forestry (11 per cent) and others by 1999.[8]

"Colombia's biggest impediment to attracting foreign investment is not the state of its solvency but rather the basic issue of public safety."

Colombia

Colombia also suffered a severe recession in 1999 when its economy shrank 4.3 per cent and unemployment shot up to a record 20 per cent. But unlike most other South American nations, Colombia's biggest impediment to attracting foreign investment is not the state of its solvency but rather the basic issue of public safety. A four-decades-old campaign to overthrow the government has escalated since 1990 as guerillas fund themselves through the growth, processing and export of coca leaves and cocaine, not to mention ransoms held for foreign workers taken hostage in the countryside. Since 1990 more than 35,000 civilians have died as a result of the conflict and more than 2 million people have been displaced. Police said 3,162 people were kidnapped in 2000, beating 1999's record of 2,959 and making Colombia once again the kidnapping capital of the world.

Public finances are another casualty of Colombia's civil war. The total external debt was estimated at $35 billion by the end of 1998, the year Columbia lost its investment grade status. By the end of 1999 Colombia had signed a $2.7 billion belt-tightening deal with the IMF where it cut its 2000 fiscal deficit to 3.6 per cent of GDP and is scheduled to cut it further to 2.8 per cent in 2001 and 1.5 per cent in 2002. The public pension scheme of about $87 billion is equal to at least half of the country's economic output and is the target of more government cuts, as are transfers to the nation's indebted provinces and municipalities. If and when president Andres Pastrana's Plan Colombia is able to yield a negotiated peace settlement with the left-wing Revolutionary Armed Forces of Colombia (FARC) and right-wing guerrillas, then the oil and coffee-rich nation will be in dire need of infrastructure investment but its ability to finance those works will be minimal.

Venezuela

Venezuela, like Chile, has an economy that is heavily dependent on one export commodity, oil. Its economy shrank 7.2 per cent in 1999 on the steep downturn in crude prices the year before to about $8 per barrel. The oil sector accounts for about a third of Venezuela's GDP and roughly 80 per cent of its export earnings and about half of government operating revenues. One consequence of the massive inflow of foreign currencies into the world's third-largest oil producer is an overvalued bolivar currency. That makes it difficult for local companies to compete efficiently against foreign imports. Wild market swings have rippled through Venezuela's finances in the past and translated into civil unrest. Riots and looting over steep price rises left hundreds dead in the capital Caracas in 1989 and military officers staged two bloody coup attempts in 1992, the first led by current president Hugo Chavez. The nation's total external debt was $32 billion in 1999 and the government needed to raise funds to rebuild $15 billion to $20 billion worth of infrastructure damaged during massive floods and landslides in December of that year.

Some investors are hesitant to direct funds to this economy because of uncertainty regarding the reform agenda of Chavez, a former paratrooper who transformed himself into a populist politician once he was released from jail in 1994 and won his first presidency in 1998. Since then, Chavez has increased the role of the military, nurtured ties with Cuba and China, as well as pushing through a new constitution. Chavez also raised minimum wages 20 per cent in 2000. Nine out of 10 Venezuelan business leaders said they feared for democracy under the Chavez presidency, but six out of 10 of the 319 companies surveyed by the Venezuelan-American Chamber of Commerce in January 2001 said they would continue to invest in the country. (For more information on Venezuela, please see *www.mre.gov.ve.*)

Peru

In the 10 years that Alberto Fujimori ruled Peru (from 1990 to 2000), the Andean nation rid itself of much of its Shining Path Maoist and Tupac Amaru guerrillas, privatized a number of state-owned enterprises and instituted sweeping market reforms. The result: strong growth between 1994 and 1997, with inflation wrestled under control. But just like all the other South American nations fronting the Pacific Ocean, 1998's El Nino weather phenomenon wreaked significant damage to Peru's agriculture while the Asian and Russian financial crises sapped emerging market capital from its economy. 1999 proved no better as Brazil's crisis added to the region's woes, but Peru successfully completed negotiations with the IMF for an Extended Fund Facility in June of that year. Those targets ended up being renegotiated later.

Flawed elections in April and May 2000 were followed by a corruption scandal involving Fujimori's spy chief, Vladimiro Montesinos, which eventually led to Fujimori's resignation in November. He then sought asylum in Japan, leaving a caretaker government in charge so many investors chose to sit out the ensuing uncertainty until after a new president was elected the following year. Fujimori's rival, a former shoeshine boy turned World Bank economist, Alejandro Toledo, was elected after a run-off vote pitted him against Alan Garcia, who had served as president before Fujimori. Shortly after that, Montesinos was apprehended in Venezuela and returned to Peru in June 2001 for questioning.

Ecuador

To the north is Ecuador, which has the distinction of being the only country in the world to have defaulted on its Brady bond payments, in October 1999. The default was preceded by the collapse of Ecuador's banking sector earlier that year, with 15 of 35 banks being taken over by the government and many personal savings accounts being frozen.

Ecuador relies on exports of oil, bananas and shrimp to earn the foreign currency it needs to pay off its debt The Andean Community member sustained two major blows in 1997–1998 when El Nino significantly damaged its agriculture and aquaculture and world crude oil prices slumped to about $8 a barrel, cutting down export earnings on a significant source of government operating revenues. With the economy in free fall during 1999, inflation topped 60 per cent while the sucre currency shed two-thirds of its value. Ecuador's total external debt had reached $15.3 billion by the end of 1999 while its economy produced $54.4 billion in goods and services.

Harvard-educated president Jamil Mahuad proposed junking the sucre and adopting the dollar, but he was deposed by peasants and a rebel army unit in a 'proto-coup' in January 2000. However, his vice president and successor, Gustavo Noboa, forged ahead and the greenback was adopted as the national currency in April of that year. Ecuador joined Panama, which has used the US dollar for almost a century, and Argentina, whose peso has been at par to the greenback since 1991, in dollarizing its economy. El Salvador adopted the dollar in 2001, adding to the Latin American dollarization debate which you can read about in Chapter Eight.

Uruguay

Uruguay, while also relying significantly on commodity exports for both economic growth and as a source of net foreign currency inflows, is one of three Latin American nations (along with Chile and Mexico) that enjoy investment-grade status. But Uruguay's weakness is its heavy reliance on its neighbours for trade – half of its exports go to Brazil or Argentina, so devaluation in one market and recession in the other resulted in a 2.5 per cent contraction in its tiny economy in 1999.

The Uruguayans are positioning themselves as the storage place for vast amounts of natural gas being explored and exploited in the Southern Cone to feed energy-deficient Brazil and its booming industry in Sao Paulo.

Bolivia

Bolivia's challenge, in contrast, is not to diversify its trade partners but rather more basic: being able to ship its goods out of the country. The landlocked nation is one of the poorest in the western hemisphere, so domestic resources to build up its decrepit infrastructure are scarce.

Inflation is now in the single digits after ranking as one of the highest in the world when it reached 23,500 per cent in 1985. Despite Bolivia's severe poverty and relatively heavy debt it has benefited from debt pardons including a pioneering debt-for-nature swap where it created a national reserve in exchange for debt relief. Bolivia also has the good fortune of being located in the heart of South America, serving as a crossroads of the future for trade among Chile, Peru, Brazil, Paraguay and Argentina, all of which are keen to access the rivers and oceans of the others.

Projects to improve overland cargo transport were a key item on the agenda of the first ever summit of all of South America's presidents in Brasilia on 31 August 2000 and Bolivia is likely to be a major beneficiary of any such regional investment. Chapter Seven describes the highest priority projects for the continent. Bolivia's massive $500-million San Cristobal silver mine, one of the world's largest, will require heavy truck routes to Chilean Pacific ports.

Paraguay

Paraguay serves as another kind of continental trade crossroads, but in smuggled goods. It is estimated that the landlocked nation's informal sector may as much as equal the $19.9 billion value of the formal sector. Behind these numbers is a sordid story of weak democratic institutions, political violence and coup attempts. Like Bolivia's Altiplano dwellers, and to a much lesser extent some semi-nomadic tribes of Brazil's Amazon jungle, a number of Paraguayans live as landless subsistence farmers. Some human rights observers believe this disenfranchized group could one day become a political force. Paraguay's total external debt was $2.7 billion by the end of 1999.

Other than being a significant exporter of soybeans, cotton and meat, Paraguay is home to two of some of the largest hydroelectric dams in the world, which are a short distance from Brazil's industrial south, a net importer of energy. In Chapter Six you can read a description of South America's energy production and consumption profile. Paraguay is arguably one of the continent's weakest democracies and diplomats believe that if the large number of landless peasants were to find a strong political voice, the delicate circumstances there could easily be upset.

Neither Guyana nor Suriname are members or associates of either Mercosur or the Andean Community of Nations, and French Guiana is a department of France. *Guyana's* total external debt was $1.4 billion by the end of 1998 and the nation the size of Idaho produced $1.86 billion in goods and services, exporting sugar, gold and bauxite, a clay-like substance combining alumina and iron. *Suriname's* external debt totalled $175.6 million in 1998. Bauxite, accounts for more than 15 per cent of Suriname's GDP and 70 per cent of its exports. Suriname is preparing to open up its off-shore oil reserves to private foreign investors.

What do all these numbers and facts add up to? In Brazil's case you might conclude its ability to service its debt is limited by the fact that it is one of the world's most closed economies, where exports account for only 7 per cent of GDP,[9] but it borrows more from its domestic market, which helps shelter it from external shocks and its own currency devaluation. This lesson has not been lost on Argentina, Latin America's largest foreign borrower. Aware of its vulnerability to volatile international capital markets, Argentina has nurtured one of South America's strongest banking systems over the past decade and is following Chile in establishing a private pension system capable of meeting more of the government's needs. The long-term effects of high interest rates, hyperinflation and chronic budget deficits are a sobering thought when you consider that Argentina's economy was roughly double that of Brazil's around 1900, about equal in 1950, and now less than half.

“Aware of its vulnerability to volatile international capital markets, Argentina has nurtured one of South America's strongest banking systems over the past decade”

Stabilizing South America's biggest economies

Depending on whether you are a fund manager or an investment banker as opposed to a manufacturer or service provider, you are likely to hone in on different variables when it's time to decide whether you will invest in this part of the world and by how much. Bankers will focus on the debt-service ratio of the individual countries. You can calculate that by taking a nation's interest payments and payments of principal on its foreign debt and comparing this to export earnings to assess whether it is at a sustainable level. That's why financiers, service providers and manufacturers applauded news in

December 2000 when the Mercosur leaders agreed to macroeconomic convergence targets. As Table 1.1 shows, most economic indicators were at comparable levels in 1999. Starting in 2002, fiscal deficits will have to be no more than 3 per cent of gross domestic product. Annual inflation can be no more than 5 per cent in the 2002 to 2005 period. Total public debt cannot exceed 40 per cent of GDP by 2010.

Table 1.1 Mercosur economic indicators 1999

Country	GDP per cap (USD)	Inflation	Deficit	Current account deficit
Argentina	$8,671	–1.8 pct	1.7 pct	4.3 pct
Brazil	$3,790	8.9 pct	10.0 pct	4.4 pct
Chile	$4,448	2.3 pct	3.6 pct	0.0 pct
Paraguay	$1,951	5.4 pct	–2.2 pct	1.6 pct
Uruguay	$6,685	4.2 pct	3.7 pct	2.9 pct

Source: Mercosur Secretariate and IMF estimates

'The bottom line is that it's creating some macroeconomic predictability for the region. That will only benefit these countries in foreign direct investment and lower spreads in international bond markets,' said Doug Smith, head of Latin American strategy at IDEA Global in New York, on 13 December 2000 after the targets had been announced.

These same six countries started issuing common quarterly economic indicators on 31 October 2000 that can be found on the website *http://gmm.mecon.gov.ar*. Macroeconomic convergence is important because relatively stable consumer prices have been the basis for the growth in regional trade. Consumer prices grew by 347.4 per cent in Brazil between 1990 and 1998 and 7.8 per cent in Argentina.([10]) But Brazil's inflation was below 10 per cent by 1999 as its economy grew 1 per cent, while Argentina's deflation was 1.8 per cent during its 3.2 per cent economic contraction that year. Chile, which enjoys an investment-grade debt rating, saw inflation of 2.3 per cent during 1999's 1.1 per cent economic contraction.

You must understand what a remarkable achievement it is that a region which saw runaway hyperinflation less than two decades ago (Bolivian inflation of 23,500 per cent in 1985 and Argentine inflation of almost 5,000 per cent in 1989) can boast price stability now. In that context, a common market in spite of rows over trade in cars, farm products and clothing seems to be a realistic goal among countries with comparable legal, cultural and historical roots. Chapter Eight discusses macroeconomic indicators in greater detail.

'Price stability as the fundamental basis for a common market is the vision of (Brazilian economy minister) Pedro Malan. This is about competitiveness. Our countries are victims of import substitution. High tariffs to protect and nurture the development of our industries in the 1970s and 1980s made sense then, but now high tariffs harm our competitiveness and the domestic consumer,' said Luis Fernando Panelli César, minister councillor in charge of political affairs at the Brazilian Embassy in Buenos Aires.[11] 'We have cultural uniformity, we have no problems with territorial expansionism and we're all capitalist economies, albeit weak capitalist economies. It's unthinkable of having a common market between India and Pakistan or China and Japan. We're young democracies, but no one can imagine any more coups in Brazil or Argentina and this for foreign investors is important, and even more important is the integration process.'

Manufacturers and service providers need to be kept abreast of the ups and downs of these macroeconomic indicators to make sound investment decisions. Now that you see how most South American countries have managed to more or less stabilize their economies, you will also need to know how their population growth rates compare to economic growth, which countries are showing signs of a growing middle class, such as Chile and Brazil, and where the middle class is in peril of shrinking, like Argentina. That's the subject of Chapter Three. You need to know the levels of value added tax and corporate tax as well as what anti-trust rules you must abide by, all of which is explained in Chapters Four and Five. But first, let's examine the case of a provider of financial services that is playing an expanding role in South America.

CASE STUDY

Banco Santander Central Hispano

Spain's top bank, Banco Santander Central Hispano (BSCH), is the second leading bank in the euro zone and has quickly become one of the top banking franchise in Latin America, acquiring stakes in Brazil's Banco Meridional and Banco do Estado de Sao Paulo (Banespa) as well as Mexico's Grupo Financiero Serfin in 2000 after first gaining significant market share in Argentina. About 80 per cent of BSCH sales come from retail banking operations in Europe and Latin America. Grupo Santander banks held about 10 per cent of all Latin American deposits by the end of 2000.

The financial group is not only present in Latin America's three largest economies, Brazil, Mexico and Argentina, but in virtually every major country in South America, except Ecuador. The bank is betting that Latin America will follow the same path as the Spanish market in recent decades where the emergence of a middle class helped fuel the growth in the Spanish financial services sector. As you will see in Chapter Three, some United Nations officials acknowledge that there are signs of growth in the middle class in some South American countries, most notably Brazil, which accounts for more than half the continent's population. For this reason Grupo Santander reckons now is an ideal time to acquire assets on the cheap in Latin America. From the point of view of this financial group the region's 'controlled instability', where macroeconomic indicators are more volatile than in the Group of Seven industrialized nations (Canada, France, Germany, Italy, Japan, the UK and the US) but not off the scale as in some of the least developed countries, means higher interest rates and therefore higher profit margins. South America is a higher risk but it also represents higher rewards in the short term and probably a maturing market in the medium term.

'When you consider how Spain's banking system has evolved from the 1960s to now and how it has narrowed the gap with Germany in that time you understand why Santander has been investing in Latin America, committing itself to these markets. Spain was a country with a low gross domestic savings ratio 20 years ago compared to where it is today. This isn't a financial operation, it's a strategic positioning. About 20 to 25 per cent of Latin Americans have set foot in a bank, so there's room to grow. You can't expect to show up in 15 or 20 years when more people have deposits and be a major player,' said Ignacio Carballeira, finance manager at Banco Rio de la Plata S.A., an Argentine unit in which Grupo Santander acquired a controlling stake in 1997.[12]

BSCH reinforced its position in South America in November 2000 when it acquired a stake in Sao Paulo state bank Banespa. Brazil's seventh-largest bank was considered the plum pick of the country's state banks. Analysts believe that if Brazil grows 5 per cent per year for the next five years, demand for financial services there will expand significantly. It is also conceivable that in 15 to 20 years' time, if Mercosur is more fully integrated as a common market with harmonized banking regulations, Sao Paulo could serve as the continental nerve centre of South America's financial sector, taking advantage of economies of scale to offer competitively priced services in a more mature multi-country market in addition to the traditional deposits and loans portfolios.

BSCH was formed by the merger in 1999 of Banco Santander and Banco Central Hispanoamericano (BCH), two banks with a long Latin American history. A group of businessmen founded Banco Santander in 1857 to finance Latin American trade. Spanish banks avoided the worst of the Great Depression since their country was relatively isolated from the world economy and shunned the gold standard, but the Spanish civil war was a drain. Banco Santander expanded into Madrid in the 1940s and into other major cities where it merged with some of its rivals. The bank concentrated on expanding its branch network and investments in Latin America during the 1950s and 1960s when the dictatorship of Francisco Franco halted mergers and slapped controls on interest rates. Those controls were eased in the 1970s after Franco's death and, despite global recession, Banco Santander continued to invest in Latin America through to the mid-1980s. The bank focused on the Spanish market in the 1990s, kickstarting competition in 1989 when it introduced Spain's first high-interest account. After failing to woo

Banco Hispano Americano it acquired a 60 per cent stake in the ailing Banco Espanol de Credito (Banesto), which became a wholly owned unit in 1998. The emerging market crises hit Banco Santander's Latin American profit margins in 1998, prior to its merging with Banco Central Hispanoamericano in 1999.

BCH was the result of the 1991 merger of Banco Central and Banco Hispano Americano (BHA). BHA was created in 1900 by investors in Latin America and Banco Central was formed in 1919. The two banks offered commercial and investment banking and funded industrialization and investment in Latin America. They became two of the largest Spanish banks after Spain's civil war. BHA sold its Latin American assets after the civil war, while Banco Central expanded across Spain through mergers and acquisitions. Under Franco's rule the two banks focused on overseas investments and domestic branch growth. Competition at home and abroad intensified after Franco's death and BHA struggled with the costs of its purchases in the 1980s. Banco Central enjoyed major stakes in almost every industry and proved more resistant to economic volatility. Banco Central bought BHA in 1991 to be competitive when Spain entered the European Economic Community in 1992. BCH concentrated on Latin America and bought small stakes in small banks before merging with Banco Santander in 1999. (For more information on Banco Santander Central Hispano please see the following websites: *www.schinvestment.com*; *www.banesto.es*; *www.americaeconomia.com*.)

Notes

[1]Chavez, Hugo, president of Venezuela, interview in Puerto Ordaz, 20 January 2001.

[2]Leme, Paulo, head of emerging markets debt research at Goldman Sachs, speech to World Economic Forum conference on Mercosur at Rio de Janeiro, 8 May 2000.

[3]Brownfield, William, deputy assistant for western hemisphere affairs at the US Department of State, speech to a business conference in Montevideo, 25 September 2000.

[4]Baneo Villegas, Eduardo, lecture on Mercosur foreign relations at Universidad del Salvador, Buenos Aires, 11 October 2000.

[5]Campbell, Jorge, former chief trade negotiator for Argentina 1986–88 and 1989–1999, interview on Mercosur trade relations, Buenos Aires, 27 September 2000.

[6]Seoane, Raul, strategic analysis manager at Banco Galicia, interview in Buenos Aires, 19 November 2000.

[7]Morande, Felipe G., director of research and chief economist, Central Bank of Chile, presentation to Jornadas Bancarias y Monterias seminar hosted by the Central Bank of the Republic of Argentina in Buenos Aires, 24 August 2000.

[8]Chilean Central Bank, Foreign Investment Committee data presented to the September 25–26 PricewaterhouseCoopers-US State Department conference in Montevideo 'Doing business between Mercosur and the United States'.

[9]2000 World Bank Atlas.

[10]Ibid.

[11]Panelli, Luis, minister councillor in charge of political affairs at the Brazilian Embassy in Argentina, interview in Buenos Aires, 11 December 2000.

[12]Carballeira, Ignacio, finance manager at Banco Rio de la Plata S.A., an Argentine unit of Grupo Santander, interview in Buenos Aires, 28 February 2001.

2

Embracing neighbours and the world

Latin America has undergone profound economic and structural changes in the past decade as a result of the debt crises of the 1980s. Most of the region's republics have concentrated on macroeconomic and balance of payments adjustments, as well as privatized once publicly owned enterprises. These are the kinds of changes that can be executed relatively quickly and yield tangible results in little time. The next stage of reforms involves overhauling these countries' legal and regulatory frameworks to make it easier for you as foreign investors to invest there. That is a much more time-consuming task but one that a number of these nations are beginning to tackle. Essentially that is the core of what Mercosur and the Andean Community of Nations are about and what puts the trade blocs in the vanguard of market-friendly reforms in this region.

The Andeans have developed a much greater regional administrative machine since the trade bloc was created in 1969 and have advanced further in liberalizing the trade in services than their southern neighbours. But in other ways Mercosur has quickly become a much more economically dynamic subregional bloc. This chapter provides you with a brief description of the history behind the creation of Mercosur and the evolution of the Andean Community. You will also find an explanation of how Mercosur's institutions function as well as summaries of the major trade relationships in which the South Americans are engaged.

A tale of two trade blocs

The first step towards creating Mercosur was the Declaration of Iguazu on 30 November 1985. The document was signed by Brazil's Jose Sarney and Argentina's Raul Alfonsin, the first democratically elected presidents of South America's two largest economies after military dictators stepped down in 1985 and 1983 in each of those nations, respectively. The two leaders moved quickly to put an end to the military, commercial and diplomatic rivalries of the past at a time when all the major Latin American nations, save Cuba, started moving towards representative democracies. Their goals were as much political as economic: to mutually assure each other's democratic institutions and to impose the fiscal discipline that was lacking before and during the military juntas.

'Mercosur is our passport to history. It will generate the conditions by which we can negotiate and exert greater trade pressure and assure our survival. The viability of Latin America depends on Mercosur's consolidation and its expansion in Latin America,' said Universidad de Brasilia professor Helio Jaguaribe.[1]

The rapprochement among regional nations today compared with less than a generation ago is palpable. There remains a certain level of mistrust, but this is far from being an openly hostile environment. The thaw in regional relations perhaps began when Alfonsin invited Sarney to visit an Argentine secret nuclear fuel project in 1985 which closed the door on old suspicions between the two countries and eventually led to the signing of a nuclear co-operation treaty in 1986. Between then and 1989 the two countries signed 24 bilateral accords. To put things in their proper context you need to understand what was pulling and pushing these two countries into each other's arms.

- The desire to mutually assure the viability of each other's young democracies.
- The decision to set aside old geopolitical rivalries.

- The need to band together to confront Latin America's economic crises of the 1980s.
- The recognition that both nations needed to open up their economies to foreign trade.
- A worldwide movement to create regional trade blocs such as that between the United States and Canada, the world's largest trading partnership. They signed a free trade agreement in 1988 and were later joined by Mexico in 1992 and the Asia-Pacific Economic Cooperation group of nations that was constituted in 1989.[2]

In 1988, Brazil and Argentina signed the Treaty of Integration, Cooperation and Development which established the intention to form common economic grounds within the next 10 years via trade liberalization policies rather than import substitution. Liberalizing trade between the neighbouring nations did not appear to be such an easy task, but the political will of both governments ensured that this did indeed happen. In 1988, Brazil had import tariffs of 51 per cent while in 1989 Argentina's import tariffs were about 30 per cent, according to World Trade Organization data. At that time South America's two largest economies were the only nations that had signed the Treaty, which was sanctioned by their respective legislatures in August 1989. Then, on 6 July 1990, both nations agreed to set 31 December 1994 as the deadline for a definitive formation of a customs union between them. One month later, Paraguay and Uruguay joined their two neighbours in trade liberalization talks. All four countries signed the Treaty of Asuncion on 26 March 1991 for the creation of a 'Mercado Comun del Sur' which was ratified on 17 December 1994 with the signing of the Ouro Preto Protocol.

The Treaty of Asuncion gave the signatories until 31 December 1994 to align their import tariffs into a Common External Tariff (CET). This proved to be an awesome task for the Mercosur members, so what emerged on 1 January 1995 was an 'imperfect' customs union where some countries had higher import tariffs than others while key industries such as the car sector or sugar producers either struck their own side deals or remained exempt from the trade bloc. The common external tariff varies from one product to another between 0 to 35 per cent on about 85 per cent of the goods, or 9,000 categories, coming into the region. By 1998, trade within Mercosur had already quadrupled in value to $20 billion from $5 billion in 1995 by lowering tariffs on imports from neighbouring countries and attracting foreign multinationals to set up shop within its tariff bloc to fall within the umbrella of its manufacturing rules of origin. Mercosur was created after the 1979 'Tokyo Round' of the GATT where many world leaders decided to liberalize global trade and create the now familiar most favoured nation concept in trade law. In practical terms, what the Tokyo Round did was limit the time a country had to shelter industries from foreign competition. But it gave developing countries that formed trade blocs an exemption from granting MFN status to developed countries for a finite period of time. Trade inside the Mercosur zone, an area about the size of continental Europe, slumped in 1999 as most member nations fell into recessions that were exacerbated by Brazil's steep currency devaluation. The result was a series of trade rows that erupted mid-year after Argentina invoked Mercosur's safeguard clause to protect its industries. Most of the disputes were resolved by the end of 2000 when leaders from the four nations heralded the relaunching of Mercosur and end of 'Mercopesimismo', akin to the EU's Europessimism of the 1970s. Trade within Mercosur recovered in 2000, rising 16.8 per cent from 1999, and accounted for 41 per cent of the $43.2 billion in goods and services exchanged between the 12 ALADI nations – Argentina, Bolivia, Brazil, Chile, Colombia, Cuba, Ecuador, Mexico, Paraguay, Peru, Uruguay and Venezuela.[3]

“Trade inside the Mercosur zone, an area about the size of continental Europe, slumped in 1999 as most member nations fell into recessions that were exacerbated by Brazil's steep currency devaluation.”

The Andean Community of Nations was created in 1969 and has a General Secretariat based in Lima, Peru. Today the Community has a raft of bureaucratic agencies, but by far its most effective regional body is the Andean Development Corporation (Corporacion Andina de Fomento – CAF, *www.caf.com*). In many ways the Andean Community is considered by most people to be the mirror opposite of Mercosur: a bureaucratically integrated region but with less significant trade flows. Composed of more than 109 million people residing in Colombia, Venezuela, Ecuador, Peru and Bolivia the trade bloc had a purchasing power of $622.6 billion in 2000. The Andean countries share a common history, culture and region, but they are far from united in their integration efforts. In 1992, Community members approved Peru's request to remain on the sidelines of the Andean free trade zone. Then in 1997 they drafted a timetable by which Peru would be phased back into the free trade area, except for a limited number of products on which all restrictions are to be lifted by 2005. Peru had not adopted the Andean common external tariff by the end of 2000.

As part of a revitalization effort, the Andean Community in 1995 decided to set a common external tariff of 20 per cent. 'We're trying to improve the customs union so the Secretariat is drafting a new common external tariff since Peru has been outside for a long time and Ecuador and Bolivia have special treatment. This is fundamental in our international negotiations to join the FTAA in 2005,' said Sebastian Alegrett, secretary general of the Andean Community of Nations.[4] What's more of a concern respecting the functioning of this three-decades-old trade group is how since 1999 member nations have twice ignored rulings by the Andean Court of Justice. Both cases involved trade with Colombia. In the first dispute in March 1999 the Andean General Secretariat gave Ecuador 20 days in which to stop requiring import permits on Colombian sugar as well as stop failing to process those permits or cancel them without justification. Ecuador refused to comply so the General Secretariat started proceedings against that country which ended up before the Andean Court of Justice in September of the same year.

The court ordered Ecuador to scrap the import permits on Colombian sugar since the measure was in breach of community regulations, but the Ecuadorean government announced it would not comply with the ruling.

The other case began in May 1999 when Venezuela closed its border to Colombian trucks, forcing cargo to be transferred to national carriers instead. The decision violated one of the Andean Community's oldest agreements (Decision 399 on International Transport of Goods by Road) and the Andean Court of Justice dismissed arguments by the Venezuelans who said the measure was imposed because too many of their drivers were being killed in the lawless regions of war-torn Colombia. Venezuela has refused to comply with the Andean Court ruling. 'We're worried about what this does to our regulations. Last year (2000) commerce increased 42 per cent from Colombia to Venezuela despite this decision and less than 10 per cent from Venezuela to Colombia. This will eventually be resolved as business seeks more efficient ways of transporting goods,' Alegrett said. Diplomats concede there is some substance to the Venezuelans' public safety argument, based on exceptions defined in Decision 439 of the Community's regional legal code, but warn that both instances of ignored rulings augur badly for the Community's role in proving to foreign investors that it is able to enforce rulings made to resolve trade conflicts. It also casts some doubt on whether the Andean partners will go through with plans to gradually reduce barriers on a list of services defined in a regional inventory that are due to be completely liberalized by 2005.

The Andean Community is asymmetrical in that, like Mercosur's treatment of Paraguay and Uruguay in some products, it gives Bolivia and Ecuador more time and temporary exemptions to comply with their obligations in liberalizing their services sector, as laid out by Decision 439.[5] Some diplomats say Venezuela's enthusiasm for regional integration is strictly political and military under the leadership of president Hugo Chavez, a failed coup leader and former soldier who has shown less interest in trade and economics. What these observations underscore is the importance of political will as a prime mover behind regional integration. What is more, there are still no provisions for national treatment and market access for vehicles, goods, agriculture, rules of origin, unfair trade practices, safeguards, state enterprises and intellectual property between Colombia and Venezuela. It is not encouraging that these kinds of issues remain to be resolved within the Andean Community as it enters its fourth decade.

The Community's institutional structure; otherwise known as the Andean Integration System (SAI), is organized like this:

- the Andean Presidential Council is the highest-level body of the SAI;

- the Andean Council of Foreign Ministers and the Commission of the Andean Community are the policy-setting and decision-making bodies;
- the General Secretariat of the Andean Community is the executive body of the Andean Community;
- the Court of Justice of the Andean Community is the Community's judicial body;
- the Andean Parliament is the legislative body of the SAI;
- the Andean Development Corporation (CAF *www.caf.com*) and the Latin American Reserve Fund (FLAR, *www.flar.net*) are the Community's financial institutions;
- Hipolito Unanue Agreement and Simón Rodríguez Agreement are social institutions;
- Simón Bolívar Andean University is the educational institution of the Andean Community;
- the Andean Business Advisory Council and Andean Labor Advisory Council are the Community's two consultative institutions.

The mechanics of Mercosur

The 1991 Treaty of Asuncion, much like the 1957 Treaty of Rome in Europe, set the foundation for the nascent customs union by calling for:

- free circulation of goods, services, productive factors, people and capital by eliminating customs obstacles and non-tariff barriers;
- the adoption of a common external tariff with respect to imports from outside the four-nation group;
- the co-ordination of macroeconomic and sectoral policies;
- a schedule to co-ordinate domestic internal legislation of the member nations to promote free competition;
- a common rules of origin policy to avoid competition from products made outside Mercosur being treated as though they had been produced within the region;

- a trade dispute settlement mechanism to resolve litigations and controversies;
- a transitory system of safeguard clauses.

At the seventh meeting of what is called the Common Market Council in Ouro Preto, Brazil on 17 December 1994 the original Treaty of Asuncion was amended with a protocol that established the institutional framework of Mercosur which started functioning on 1 January 1995. There are six institutions that are charged with implementing Mercosur goals and policies.

- The *Common Market Council* (CMC) consists of the Foreign and Economy Ministers of each country who decide matters of common policy. This body meets once every six months when the rotating presidency of Mercosur is passed on to the next nation, in alphabetical order. The Council is Mercosur's top political institution and exercises a supervisory authority over all the other institutions. It has the power to issue decisions that are obligatory for the member nations' institutions. The Council negotiates and executes agreements with third parties, including international organizations. Although it has no permanent staff, in all other respects the Common Market Council of Mercosur resembles the European Union Council.
- The *Common Market Group* (CMG) is headed by trade negotiators from each Mercosur partner nation. These negotiators must include representatives from the central banks, economy and foreign ministries of each member nation. The group has the autonomy to create working subgroups to prepare for integration. It then recommends the findings of those subgroups to the Council. The CMG meets once every three months and is Mercosur's executive body. It exercises both policy-making and administrative responsibilities. It may adopt resolutions on financial and budgetary matters, based on the guidance of the Council, and may, if authorized by the Council, negotiate agreements on behalf of Mercosur with third parties. Among its administrative tasks, the group approves Mercosur's budget and the annual expenditures of Mercosur's Secretariat as well as

organizing Council meetings. The CMG can issue binding resolutions on member nations. Unlike its European counterpart, the European Union Commission, the group does not have a permanent staff and its role is more administrative than policy setting in nature.

- The *Commerce Commission* is responsible for calibrating Mercosur's common external tariff. It is responsible for ensuring Mercosur's common commercial policy is applied either through binding directives on the member nations or non-binding proposals. The commission is the first point of referral in the process to resolve trade disputes. The group meets once every month to hear commercial complaints. If it is unable to resolve the controversy on its own, it refers it to the Common Market Group. If the CMG cannot reach a unanimous decision on how to solve the dispute, it refers the matter to the Common Market Council. If the CMC is unable to reach concensus on the issue then a trade dispute resolution panel is convened. In the event that the Commission solves a trade row but the CMG disagrees with its ruling, the CMG can either refer the dispute to the Council or to a trade dispute resolution panel.[6]

- The *Joint Parliamentary Commission* is composed of an equal number of legislators from all the member nations who are studying the feasibility of creating a supranational legislative body, perhaps by 2006. The idea is for this body to assist in implementing Mercosur policies and to harmonize the legislation of the member nations. The Joint Parliamentary Commission has no decision-making powers and plays only an advisory role. It resembles the EU's original European Parliament as set out under the 1957 Treaty of Rome.

- The *Forum* is an advisory body of producers, consumers, workers and merchants who make non-binding recommendations regarding Mercosur policy. It is similar to the EU's Consultative Committee of the European Coal & Steel Community, the Economic and Social Committee of the European Economic Community, and Euratom.

- The *Secretariat* is a small administrative institution based in Montevideo, Uruguay that publishes regular bulletins on legislation that has been harmonized by all member nations. It is the only Mercosur institution with a permanent staff. It has no substantive decision-making powers. The Secretariat's director is appointed by the Common Market Group. The Secretariat is comparable to Nafta's Secretariat in that they both have a small permanent staff mainly mandated with administrative, logistical and technical support.

The working subgroups have made varying degrees of progress in their areas of expertise. They are as follows:

- Subgroup for commercial affairs.
- Subgroup for customs affairs.
- Subgroup for nomenclature and technical specifications.
- Subgroup for fiscal and monetary policies related to commerce.
- Subgroup for ground transportation.
- Subgroup for environmental policy.
- Subgroup for sea transportation.
- Subgroup for industrial and technological policies.
- Subgroup for agriculture policies.
- Subgroup for energy policies.
- Subgroup for the co-ordination of macroeconomic policies.
- Subgroup for labour affairs.
- Subgroup for air transportation.
- Subgroup for tourism.

The internal commercial liberalization programme scheduled by the Treaty of Asuncion calls for the gradual reduction of tariffs among Mercosur member nations. Under the agreement, the four full members concede each other greater preferences every six months until all tariffs are zeroed out. The majority of intra-regional trade has been free of tariffs since 1995.[7] Some sensitive goods have remained excluded from the free trade area and were supposed to be included by the end of 2001, but that has been delayed. Meanwhile capital goods, computers, software and telecommunications equipment are not yet included in the tariff regime.

Essentially, each country is allowed to charge its own duties on the exempted goods. Argentina and Brazil agreed to converge their capital goods tariffs at 14 per cent in January 2001, while Paraguay and Uruguay have until January 2006 to do so. In the case of computers, related software and telecommunications equipment, tariffs are scheduled to converge at 16 per cent for all countries by 2006.([8]) The car sector remains outside the subregional agreement although it accounts for as much as 30 per cent of trade within Mercosur. Argentina, Brazil and Uruguay ratified a new tariff regime among themselves on 14 December 2000 to regulate trade in vehicles and parts (you can find a more detailed summary of that deal at the end of this chapter). Paraguay, the only nation of the four full Mercosur members that has no car industry, signed a parallel accord in June 2001.

Sugar is another sensitive sector and a common policy has yet to be determined. See the final section of Chapter Six for more about Brazil's sugar cane subsidy programme and its consequences on world sugar prices and regional trade. Non-tariff barriers are another pivotal area in the regulation of trade between Mercosur members which range from phytosanitary rules to import quotas. Intentions are to ensure Mercosur norms comply with World Trade Organization rules and International Standards Organization (ISO) criteria to gain access to outside markets. International Monetary Fund (IMF) trade figures suggest that of all the trade blocs in the western hemisphere it is Mercosur that saw the most growth in intra-regional exports in percentage terms from 1991 to 1998. (see Table 2.1).

“The car sector remains outside the subregional agreement although it accounts for as much as 30 per cent of trade within Mercosur”

Table 2.1 Western hemisphere total and intra-regional exports and imports

	1991 (in mn of USD)	1998	Annual average growth 1991–1998
		Exports	
W. hem. ex Cuba			
Global exports	$686,560	$1,186,820	7.9 pct
Extra-hem.	$357,755	$494,462	4.7 pct
Intra-hem.	$328,805	$692,358	11.0 pct
Nafta			
Global exports	$590,603	$1,014,006	8.0 pct
Extra-Nafta	$341,128	$489,455	5.4 pct
Intra-Nafta	$249,474	$524,550	11.1 pct
Mercosur			
Global exports	$45,975	$81,435	7.2 pct
Extra-Mercosur	$40,872	$61,008	4.6 pct
Intra-Mercosur	$5,103	$20,427	22.1 pct
Group of Three (Colombia, Mexico and Venezuela)			
Global exports	$66,269	$155,496	14.7 pct
Extra-G3	$65,558	$151,303	14.6 pct
Intra-G3	$1,190	$4,193	19.0 pct
Andean Community			
Global exports:	$30,414	$45,370	4.6 pct
Extra-Andean	$28,645	$39,951	3.5 pct
Intra-Andean	$1,769	$5,419	19.4 pct
		Imports	
W. hem. ex Cuba			
Global imports	$764,816	$1,486,949	9.1 pct
Extra-hem.	$440,707	$809,026	7.9 pct
Intra-hem.	$324,109	$677,923	10.7 pct
Nafta			
Global imports	$679,619	$1,251,486	8.2 pct
Extra-Nafta	$439,296	$755,596	6.8 pct
Intra-Nafta	$240,323	$495,890	10.6 pct
Mercosur			
Global imports	$36,677	$103,423	16.0 pct
Extra-Mercosur	$31,229	$81,259	14.7 pct
Intra-Mercosur	$5,448	$22,164	22.2 pct
Group of Three (Colombia, Mexico and Venezuela)			
Global imports	$64,864	$137,443	16.0 pct
Extra-G3	$63,778	$133,018	15.9 pct
Intra-G3	$1,086	$4,426	23.2 pct
Andean Community			
Global imports	$20,865	$46,862	13.4 pct
Extra-Andean	$19,302	$41,216	12.6 pct
Intra-Andean	$1,563	$5,646	22.6 pct

Source: IMF, Direction of Trade Statistics, *www.imf.org*

The Commerce Commission is responsible for ensuring Mercosur's common external tariff is applied equally to third parties. In practice, the common external tariff may vary from one product to another and from one country to another because of the gradual synchronizing of those import tariffs that remains to be completed between the four full-member nations. The commission raised the CET by three per centage points in November 1997 to an average 14 per cent at Argentina's request since it feared an inflow of cheap Asian goods at the onset of the Asian financial crisis. The increase in the CET was scheduled to remain in place until 31 December 2000. Mercosur decided to cut the CET by half a percentage point effective from 1 January 2001 and intended it reduced by another one percentage point at the 20th meeting of the Common Market Council in Asuncion, Paraguay in June 2001 to 12.5 per cent.

This is why economists, analysts and trade officials often refer to Mercosur as an 'imperfect' customs union. Despite the significant achievement of setting common debt, deficit and inflation targets at the 19th meeting of the Common Market Council in Florianopolis, Brazil on 13 December 2000, you will also hear officials and observers complain that Mercosur has made little progress in 'institutional' integration. For example, the presidents are invited to the semesterly meetings of the CMC by their foreign and economy ministers, the joint parliament has yet to be set up, but most significantly legislation dealing with labour and tax issues as well as intellectual property has not been harmonized. That does not mean the labour and tax codes and other legislation of the four member nations are at polar opposites. In fact, the laws of Argentina, Brazil, Paraguay and Uruguay are all based on continental European legal systems owing to their common colonial past. Generally speaking, the legal systems of these countries are founded on Spanish, Italian, German and French legal reasoning, which means their logic flows from the general to the specific, as opposed to Anglo-Saxon law which is the sum of specific cases. That is why US business leaders find the South American legal system more foreign to them than do European executives.

There are also differences in constitutional law between the four countries regarding supranational institutions. Article 75 of the Argentine constitution requires both the Chamber of Deputies and the Senate to approve the creation of supranational bodies while neither the constitutions of Brazil nor Uruguay recognize supranational institutions. Article 145 of Paraguay's constitution allows for the creation of a supranational body dealing with human rights.[9] If these countries are serious about institutional integration they will have to address this issue sooner rather than later.

Latin trading: 'Abriendo caminos, rompiendo barreras' (Blazing trails, breaking barriers)

Trade among Latin American nations has certainly been on the rise in the past decade thanks to new trade deals and lower tariff barriers. Trade among Latin America's 12 ALADI member nations grew 24.2 per cent in 2000 to $43.2 billion from $34.8 billion in 1990. Table 2.2 details trade and terms of trade data for eight of Latin America's largest economies. The biggest increase in trade was between Mercosur and Mexico which saw trade jump by 43.9 per cent from 1999, largely thanks to rising Brazilian exports to Mexico. Overall, trade between Mexico and the Southern Cone Common Market accounted for only 7.1 per cent of ALADI member commerce in 2000, suggesting there is ample room for growth. Trade within the Andean Community of Nations (accounting for 12.2 per cent of the total) rose 32.2 per cent and Mercosur-Chile commerce (representing 13.3 per cent of the 2000 total) increased 31.8 per cent.[10]

Of course, part of the explanation for this dramatic increase is the region's economic recovery after stagnation and recession in 1999, but at the same time new trade relationships are being formed and expanded. Take the 'Group of Three' as an example. It combines the two largest economies of the Andean Community, Colombia and Venezuela, with Mexico. Those three countries entered a free trade agreement in 1995. Under the agreement, tariffs between Colombia and Mexico as well as between Venezuela and Mexico are being phased out by an annual 10 per cent to create a free trade area by 2005, the same deadline successive US administrations have set for the Free Trade Area of the Americas. As a result, bilateral trade between Colombia and Mexico rose 35 per cent between 1994 and 1999 to $625 million, and commerce between Venezuela and Mexico grew 60 per cent in the same period to $754 million.

Table 2.2 Foreign trade and terms of trade of eight Latin American economies 1998–1999 (percentage change over previous year)

	Exports						Imports						Terms of Trade		
	Volume		*Unit value*		*Value*		*Volume*		*Unit value*		*Value*				
Economy	'98	'99	'98	'99	'98	'99	'98	'99	'98	'99	'98	'99	'97	'98	'99
Argentina	9.9	–5.0	–9.0	–8.0	0.0	–12.6	8.1	–14.4	–4.6	–5.0	3.1	–18.6	0.4	–4.6	–3.2
Brazil	4.6	2.9	–8.0	–10.0	–3.8	–7.5	2.7	–13.0	–6.0	–2.0	–3.5	–14.7	5.7	–2.1	–8.2
Chile	8.0	11.3	–17.6	–7.0	–11.1	3.6	-0.2	–13.0	–4.6	–2.5	–4.7	–15.3	3.8	–13.6	–4.5
Colombia	7.1	6.3	–12.0	2.4	–5.8	9.0	–0.7	–28.0	–4.5	–2.5	–5.2	–29.8	9.8	–8.0	5.1
Ecuador	–5.5	0.4	–15.5	2.0	–20.1	2.4	17.2	–50.6	–5.0	–2.5	11.4	–51.8	2.1	–11.0	4.5
Mexico	10.8	13.1	–4.0	2.5	6.4	16.0	16.0	14.2	–1.6	–1.5	14.1	12.6	–0.8	–2.5	4.0
Peru	1.3	17.2	–17.1	–10	–16	5.6	0.4	-17.4	–4.6	–1.0	–4.1	–18.2	6.9	–13.1	–9.1
Venezuela	1.4	–5.7	–27.1	24.0	–26.0	16.9	9.5	–11.7	–1.5	–2.5	7.8	–14.0	–3.1	–25.9	27.1

Source: UNCTAD report September 2000, page 30, *www.unctad.org*

Another piece of the pan-American trade mosaic that could serve as a building block towards this free trade zone spanning North, Central and South America is the 1992 liberalization agreement in the commerce in goods between Chile and Mexico. Both countries enacted an expanded free trade deal in 1999 when most tariffs not eliminated under the original pact were immediately stripped away. The later agreement covered market access for goods, including cars, rules of origin, customs procedures, safeguards, sanitary and phytosanitary measures, and cross-border services such as telecommunications, air transport and the temporary entry of business people. This has freed up trade considerably, but these agreements are not comprehensive. For example, they do not cover government procurement, unfair trade practices and financial services. Still, two-way trade grew to $1.26 billion in 1999 from only $188 million in 1991, and trade between the two countries rose 30 per cent in 2000.

Mexico and Bolivia signed a free trade deal in 1994 which immediately cut tariffs on 97 per cent of Mexican shipments to Bolivia and 99 per cent of Bolivian exports to Mexico. About 98 per cent of products will change hands duty free by 2004 and the remaining 2 per cent will be completely liberalized by 2010. The consequence of this agreement has been an 18 per cent increase in the value of trade to $42.2 million in 1999 from $35.8 million in 1994.[11] What's more, these agreements also underscore the pivotal role Mexico could play in brokering free trade talks between South America and North America.

At the other end of the Americas you have Mercosur. Chile is an associate member which formalized its relationship with Mercosur in June 1996 at the 10th meeting of the Common Market Council in San Luis, Argentina. Bolivia was the next nation to join as an associate in December of the same year when it signed the Bolivian Economic Complementary Agreement in Fortaleza, Brazil at the 11th meeting of the CMC. Bolivia and Chile may be associates of Mercosur but they are by no means treated equally by Mercosur and that difference has proven to be an impediment to future additions of new nations to the customs union. The most notable achievement of the Mercosur-Chile Economic Complementary Agreement was the absence of a list of permanent exceptions to free trade between so-called 'Four plus One' negotiating parties. Many trade liberalization deals have a list of permanent exceptions but negotiators handling this agreement did everything they could to avoid any such permanent list. Mercosur was especially keen to gain unrestricted access to Chile's Pacific ports and the agreement includes a protocol on physical integration.

Meanwhile, negotiators for Mercosur and Bolivia had been reviewing the list of pre-existing bilateral agreements that would form the basis of the next 'Four plus One' free trade deal. What resulted was an agreement that covered about 95 per cent of product categories. What that really meant was only about 80 per cent of traded goods and services were covered by the 1996 deal because the most important products were excluded from the 10-year market liberalization schedule. The so-called 'especially sensitive products', most notably sugar and oilseeds, were given an 18-year phase-in period. Once again, the deal with Bolivia also included a protocol on physical integration. Bolivia is a landlocked nation nestled in the heart of South America but it borders five countries: Peru, Brazil, Paraguay, Argentina and Chile. Bolivia's vocation as a South American crossroads has yet to be realized owing to the decrepit state of its infrastructure, but physical integration was one of the top items on the agenda of the first meeting of all South American leaders in Brasilia on 31 August 2000. In signing a trade agreement with Bolivia, Mercosur proved that it was not only signing with big or rich countries but truly meant what it said about banding together in a common South American front in political and economic matters. Ironically, it was the very concept of 'especially sensitive products' that would later complicate Mercosur's attempts at reaching similar agreements with both the Andean Community of Nations and Mexico.

"In signing a trade agreement with Bolivia, Mercosur proved that it was not only signing with big or rich countries but truly meant what it said about banding together in a common South American front in political and economic matters"

Mercosur negotiators decided to take the same tack with the Andean Community of Nations as it had with Chile and try at all costs to avoid any permanent exceptions in free trade between the two blocs. Peru responded by temporarily suspending negotiations in 1998. But leaders from both trade groups agreed at the Brasilia summit to resume talks in the hopes of forging a free trade deal by January 2002. One Mercosur trade official said the Andean nations were not likely to settle for anything less than the concessions granted to Bolivia. 'Based on the advances we've made in bilateral Andean Community talks with Brazil and then Argentina, those are the building blocks toward a free trade zone with Mercosur. Now we're talking with Paraguay and Uruguay so I think it's possible to have an Andean Community-Mercosur free trade agreement by December 31 (2001),' said Andean Community secretary general Sebastian Algrett [12].

But not all Andean countries appear to be equal in their enthusiasm to open up their economies to Brazil and its southern neighbours, other trade negotiators have cautioned. 'It's a real challenge at this point. There are no specific differences, but individual Andean Community nations have different views. Venezuala is more inclined towards integration and free trade than Colombia. Ecuador is not in such good shape, so they're not as active as they could be. In Peru, there's been internal politics interfering with the process. In our case, there's a view that we'll have to partition the Brazilian market when we talk about specific markets and products. I don't think it's insurmountable, but it will take a lot of energy,' said Jose Alfredo Graça Lima, Brazil's undersecretary of trade and commercial affairs.[13]

According to ALADI estimates, Mercosur-Andean Community trade increased 27.3 per cent in 2000 from 1999. In the case of Mexico, ALADI asked the Mexicans to extend it the same trade preferences it had granted the United States and Canada to enter into the North American Free Trade Agreement. The Mexicans balked at that idea, so Mercosur negotiators decided that rather than offering to talk free trade they would review the list of pre-existing bilateral agreements between Mexico and each Mercosur nation, just as they had done with Bolivia. Another impediment to negotiations is the fact that Mexico and Brazil are in direct competition in the production and marketing of cars, a key industry in both economies. The ascension of Vicente Fox after 71 years of Mexican rule by the Institutional Revolutionary Party may change the dynamic of Mexico-Mercosur talks, but that has yet to be seen.

Other agreements of intention Mercosur has signed under its 'Four plus One' negotiating format are:

- 1991 agreement of intention on investment with the United States of America;
- 1995 agreement of co-operation in areas of mutual interest in economics, education, culture and investment with the European Union;
- 1998 agreement of intention on investment and to eliminate agriculture subsidies under the auspices of the Cairns Group with Canada (not yet in effect);
- 1998 agreement of co-operation with the Common Market of Central America;
- 1998 agreement to develop investment with the Andean Community of Nations;
- 1999 agreement to develop trade with Australia and New Zealand;
- 1999 agreement to develop trade with Guyana and Trinidad and Tobago.

None of these agreements of intention covers conflict resolution mechanisms. Trade dispute resolution will be covered more extensively in Chapter Four.

'O Mais Grande' (The biggest): Mercosur trade with the United States

Trade negotiators and economists have debated how much commerce is created rather than diverted within Mercosur, but one matter of which there is no doubt is the significant growth in imports into the Common Market of the South. Tariff and non-tariff barriers, as you can see in Table 2.3, decreased from 1985 to 1995. Despite the relative volatility this region saw in the 1990s, the concerted effort to reel in inflation has meant people living there have enjoyed a relatively stable level of purchasing power. That has freed up savings for the purchase of consumer goods and services from abroad. Only Paraguay's import tariff was lower than Mercosur's common external tariff before joining the trade bloc. Otherwise imports into Brazil faced a 51 per cent tariff in 1988 while duties on imports into Argentina were around 30 per cent in 1989. Uruguay's import tariff was more than 100 per cent at the end of the 1970s, according to WTO data. The average tariff levied by the four nations was 12.5 per cent by mid-2001.

Table 2.3 The growing openness of the Mercosur economies

	Average tariff barriers			Level of non-tariff barriers		
	expressed in percentages					
	1985	1991/2	1994/5	1985	1991/2	1994/5
Argentina	26.0	15.0	11.9	31.9	8.0	2.4
Brazil	80.0	21.1	12.3	35.3	10.0	2.0
Paraguay	71.7	16.0	10.2	9.9	0.0	0.0
Uruguay	32.0	12.0	10.5	14.1	0.0	0.4

Source: Instituto para la Integracion de America Latina y el Caribe *www.iadb.org/intal*

The ratcheting down of internal import tariffs since 1985 and greater macroeconomic stability in Brazil and Argentina in particular has been a boon to purchasing power, which has resulted in a dramatic growth in import demand into Mercosur. Between 1986 and 1995 imports of goods and services from North America and Europe and other sources into Mercosur grew 268 per cent versus exports out of the regional trade bloc which increased 129 per cent.[14]

Negotiations to create a free trade zone spanning the North and South American continents as well as Central America and the Caribbean have gained renewed confidence since Republican George W. Bush was confirmed as the 43rd president of the United States. While the Bush administration wants the FTAA ratified by 2003 rather than no later than 2005 as originally anticipated, that depends in part on Brazilian willingness to meet that schedule as well as whether or not the US trade representative wins 'fast track' authority by the end of 2001. Former president Bill Clinton tried to secure 'fast track' negotiating authority but the opposition-dominated Congress denied him the possibility of sending the legislature a take-it-or-leave-it trade deal. But the Mercosur nations do not agree with the Bush administration's desire to negotiate the FTAA country by country. Brazil and Argentina said they intended to negotiate their entry as a bloc rather than individual nations, and Brazilian foreign ministry officials have said they are more concerned about fair treatment in the deal than meeting any deadline.

Mercosur in general and Brazil in particular have enjoyed being courted simultaneously by the United States and the European Union on the trade front. Brazil has the world's ninth largest economy and it has long harboured dreams of being the voice of Latin America, if not the developing world. For Brazil, more than anything else, Mercosur is a political project of reinforcing its authority at negotiating tables, be they in Washington, Brussels or Geneva. That is why Brazil's foreign minister at the time, Luiz Felipe Lampreia, called it a 'stab in the back' when Chile announced on 29 November 2000 that it would negotiate a free trade agreement with the United States on its own. Brazil then suspended talks aimed at making Chile a full member of Mercosur that were supposed to begin at the following month's summit in Florianopolis, Brazil.

Two weeks later a jovial Brazilian president Fernando Henrique Cardoso called Chile's negotiations with the United States a 'fact of life'. Cardoso said Chile would lead Mercosur and South America forward into the FTAA negotiations just like the parade leader at Rio de Janeiro's annual carnival festivities heading out of the Sambodromo: guiding the group to the scene of the party. There was no doubt Brazil was upset by Chile's move and Cardoso made veiled references to 'bad experiences in the past' in dealing with the United States on trade matters, especially steel. 'We can fly higher together,' Cardoso told his Mercosur counterparts gathered in Florianopolis. 'I believe Mercosur can help Chile negotiate from a stronger position with the United States, if we do so together.' South American diplomats are eager to see how Chile, with an economy equal to about 1 per cent of US gross domestic product, will negotiate its entry into free trade with the United States.

'It's not that we are stronger or weaker. We're together on the issues, but here we're talking about free trade,' Chilean president Ricardo Lagos said in an interview at the end of the summit. Chile's import tariff stands at 9 per cent and that is due to be trimmed to 6 per cent by 2003, while the Mercosur member nations had an average common external tariff of 14 per cent at the end of 2000, making it difficult for Chile to negotiate tariff reduction with the United States other than on its own, Lagos said. While Chile does have tariffs of 9 per cent on industrial imports, its agriculture duties are as high as 70.5 per cent if the nation's price band system is included in calculations on imports of wheat, flour, vegetable oils and sugar – which are among the most protectionist in the world.[15]

'Our interest in Mercosur remains intact. Macroeconomic and physical integration projects will help all of our people. Our negotiations with the Clinton and Bush administrations will benefit from (Mercosur's) support. We have the same conflicts with the United States as (Mercosur), such as its anti-dumping legislation. This will be complex, lengthy and it won't be easy,' Lagos said.

Brazil is a reluctant partner in FTAA talks because it wants more time to nurture its industrial sector, particularly cars and parts which are in direct competition with the United States, just as in aerospace where Embraer competes head to head with Canada's Bombardier.

Why should the US government and your business care about this region? Mercosur is one of the few commercial blocs in the world with which the United States has a trade surplus and it was the fastest-growing market for US exports between 1992 and 1998. The US Department of Commerce estimates exports to Mercosur almost tripled between 1990 and 1999 and that US investment in the trade bloc over the course of the past decade had reached $40 billion by 1998. The United States, in turn, was the fastest-growing destination of all Mercosur exports between 1995 and 1999, growing at four times the rate of trade within Mercosur. While exports within Mercosur slumped 25 per cent in 1999, exports to the United States grew 11 per cent.[16]

Europe's stake in Mercosur

Everyone has noticed that something significantly different and positive is happening in South America and the nucleus is Mercosur. Brazil's ambassador to the United States, Rubens Barbosa, reckoned US exports to Latin America will be more than what it ships to Japan and the European Union combined as of 2007. The Americans have noticed South America is a youthful, growing and increasingly stable market, and according to South American and European diplomats, that has Europe worried.

'The EU will see what happened to it in Mexico where it lost seven per cent of market share in four years to the US. It will happen again in Brazil and Argentina if it doesn't catch up in free trade talks. There are no legal problems with signing a hemispheric trade deal, it would be legal before the World Trade Organization. The way the Europeans could level the playing field is by signing a free trade agreement with Mercosur,' said Roberto Lavagna, Argentina's ambassador to the EU, WTO and United Nations agencies governing trade and copyright laws.[17]

US exports to Mercosur reached $20.3 billion in 1998 compared with EU shipments of $22.1 billion, according to an EU study. That was the reason European leaders decided to hold an historic summit with their Latin American and Caribbean counterparts in Rio de Janeiro on 28 June 1999. The result was an agreement between the EU and Mercosur, as well as the EU and Chile, to launch reciprocal trade liberalization talks. Both sets of talks have the same basic objectives: to increase economic co-operation, enhance political dialogue, and begin negotiations to reduce tariffs in July 2001. When the EU made a unilateral, comprehensive offer to phase in free trade with Mercosur over the next decade if Mercosur matches the offer, Mercosur and the EU held three rounds of preparatory talks in 2000, starting in Buenos Aires in June, then in Brussels in August and in Brasilia in November.

“Everyone has noticed that something significantly different and positive is happening in South America and the nucleus is Mercosur.”

France, Britain and Ireland have been the most reluctant EU members to pursue free trade with Mercosur since they fear South American food imports would overwhelm their producers. An Organization for Economic Cooperation and Development (OECD) study released in June 2000 found subsidies to EU farmers were equal to 49 per cent of gross farm receipts, boosting output in Europe to the disadvantage of South American producers and exporters. The United States uses its discretionary Export Enhancement Program sporadically and the OECD's report found US subsidies had risen to 24 per cent of gross farm receipts from 14 per cent in 1997, despite deregulation of its farm sector in the mid-1990s. Disagreements over farm trade are likely to be the biggest obstacle to a free trade deal between the EU and Mercosur and Chile for the foreseeable future.

'If trade liberalization in agriculture went through it would triple all the ODA (overseas development assistance) received in developing countries,' said WTO secretary general Mike Moore

Food accounts for about half of annual global economic output. 'One minister in a developing country that imports argued that perhaps the agriculture industry was not as strong because its imports are cheaper because of subsidies. There is still the traditional resistance from Europe, Japan and the Scandinavian countries versus the Cairns Group. There will be no conclusion to a new (WTO trade negotiation) round, given there's a beginning, if there's no substantial movement in agriculture,' Moore added.[18] The full members of Mercosur and Bolivia belong to the the 18-nation Cairns Group, which submitted a proposal to the WTO in November 2000 that said their liberalized economies could not compete in distorted world markets against 'heavily and unfairly subsidized producers in other countries'. Canada and Fiji did not sign the document. Average tariffs on agricultural products were more than eight times higher than those on industrial products, according to the Cairns Group document. Tariffs of more than 300 per cent were not uncommon. Both Pascal Lamy and Chris Patten, the EU's trade and external affairs commissioners, respectively, have admitted agriculture is a thorny issue in talks with Mercosur but have emphasized other sectors where common ground could be developed. Trade officials have said the EU may be prepared to make concessions in agriculture if Mercosur grants it greater access to the burgeoning services sector or to government procurement contracts.

The Europeans have profited handsomely from Argentina's across-the-board privatizations of the 1990s and Brazil is still going through that process during this decade which presents a potentially lucrative opportunity for you. Chapter Four maps out the rules regarding market concentration and foreign investment, and Chapter Five explains how commercial dispute awards are enforced. This South American privatization trend could also leave more room for private sector borrowing in Latin America's largest economy, creating a growing market for your financial services, assuming government borrowing continues to be reduced rather than dominate overall demand for emerging market capital. The US Overseas Private Investment Corporation (*www.opic.gov*) has supplied loans and political risk insurance to projects deemed too hazardous or simply unattractive to traditional banks. But the improvement in Brazil's debt risk profile by major credit rating agencies in late 2000 and early 2001 augurs well for lower sovereign debt servicing costs and the positive spillover effect on borrowing by Brazil-based business. Add to that the fact that Brazil has altered its law on foreign investment to allow domestic companies to take out loans overseas and all of these factors help explain why Brazil was the fourth largest recipient of foreign direct investment in 1999, second only to China among emerging markets, after the US and the UK. This potential new freedom to borrow for Brazilian business could add to the region's growth momentum and would certainly ensure that rolling back state involvement in the economies of this part of the world would be hard to reverse.

What's at stake for your company is access to new, expanding markets. Mercosur's computer, hardware and software market amounted to $9.9 billion in 1999, up from $7 billion in 1997. Car rentals, hotels, fast food restaurants and dry cleaning franchises cashed in annual billings of $20 billion in Mercosur in 1999. Projections for the near term are bullish too, with annual growth rates of 20 per cent forecast for Argentina and 25 per cent in Brazil, the world's third-largest franchising market. But of Brazil's 863 franchises only 73 are foreign-brand networks, suggesting that market may be ripe for mergers and aquisitions. Another area of growth is Mercosur's market for medical equipment where purchses totalled an estimated $5 billion in 2000 between local production and imports. Annual growth in demand for medical equipment is expected to be 8 per cent for the forseeable future. [19]

The imperfect customs union: Mercosur's auto pact

Two major regional industries have yet to be fully liberalized among the nations of the Southern Cone of South America: autos and sugar. Seemingly unrelated, the auto and sugar industries are in fact intimately intertwined. However, this chapter will limit itself to the regional auto accord, while Brazil's 1975 Proalcohol sugar cane fuel alcohol subsidy programme will be described at length in Chapter Six.

The latest auto pact between Mercosur member nations came into effect on 1 January 2001. The Mercosur Automotive Policy Accord schedules a graduated reduction in import tariffs within the trade bloc while ramping up the common external tariffs on imports from outside the region so that both categories of duties converge at their respective target levels by 1 February 2006. Trade in autos and parts accounts for about 30 per cent of all commerce within Mercosur, so the auto pact's system of quotas, vehicle content formulas and rules on fluctuations in trade flows represents an important exception to the ongoing market liberalization process. Industry leaders say the new deal does, however, establish a clear set of rules for the five year period from 2001 to 2006 and while it is less flexible and less liberal than the previous pact, it will usher in free trade at the end of the accord's duration. 'It doesn't make sense to produce the same vehicle in Argentina, Brazil and Mexico, so market liberalization would be a good thing,' said Herbert Demel, president of Volkswagen do Brasil.[20]

The kind of market rationalization likely to take place in South America was presaged by Mexico's example, which became Brazil's top auto export market after the two countries signed a free trade deal, taking in 35,000 units in 1999 from zero in 1997. Goodyear Tire shut down its operations in Argentina and shifted all its regional production to Brazil after the 1999 devaluation. A few other car parts makers followed suit, either moving production entirely or partially to Brazil from Argentina to take advantage of blue-collar wages that are as much as 50 per cent lower, as well as tax incentives offered by some Brazilian states.

Besides, Brazil has enjoyed a technological advantage over Argentina since the 1950s, at least in tyre manufacturing, and the reason is simple. Brazil backed the Allies during the Second World War while Argentina implicitly backed the Axis until it declared war against the Germans in the final days of the conflict. US and Western European manufacturers also chose to dump old technology in Argentine plants and ship state-of-the-art equipment to Brazil in part for this reason, industry insiders say. But the departure of parts makers from Argentina was not limited just to tyre makers. This alarmed those parts makers that remained in Argentina and Uruguay, who lobbied for clearer rules to protect them as they gradually prepare for unfettered competition in 2006.

A Mercosur Automotive Committee was formed and mandated to contract an independent study of the regional industry due no later than 31 December 2002. The accord also states that quality control will be based on both the 1958 United Nations car assembly convention and the US Federal Motor Vehicles Security Standards. Member nations are required to mutually recognize the accreditation and standards of each other's testing agencies by 31 December 2002. So while the car sector is a significant exception to the customs union at the present time, the pact foresees both regulatory and tariff convergence in the near term, with the gradual reduction of internal tariff barriers by 2006.

CASE STUDY:

Volkswagen Argentina

Volkswagen Argentina, like so many other local subsidiaries of other multinationals throughout South America, used to answer directly to regional headquarters in Brazil. Viktor Klima, president of the Argentine unit since October 2000, changed the reporting relationship so that he now answers directly to head office in Germany. The former Austrian chancellor and president of the European Community inherited a division whose production plant in Pacheco faced an uncertain future. Now the automaker plans to invest $250 million in the gear box factory in Cordoba province. The facility is part of the Volkswagen Group's Transax industrial complex that produces 400,000 gear boxes a year on round-the-clock shifts that work 360 days a year. About 80 per cent of output is exported to Europe, Brazil, Mexico and a few other countries.

'This is why it is important for Argentina to continue to sign international trade treaties such as the one it signed recently with Mexico. For VW Argentina at least it means that we can produce an extra 10,000 cars to export to that country,' Klima said.[21].

The Mexican car trade agreement expires in five years and sets import tariffs at 8 per cent, down from 23 per cent. Klima urged the

Argentine government to try to extend the deal and reduce the tariffs to zero. He also said the government should raise tax reimbursements on exports to 16 per cent from the current 12 per cent in order to make its car sector more competitive and help it break into new markets.

Volkswagen's next big investment in Argentina will be the assembly of the Polo Classic exclusively at the Pacheco plant – the company is studying the transfer of all the necessary equipment from Pamplona, Spain. Argentina benefits from Latin America's best educated labour force and has abundant supplies of oil, gas and other raw materials necessary to produce cars and parts, Klima added. 'But interest rates should be lowered, which automatically lowers the country risk rating and people's purchasing power automatically rises,' he added.

Argentina's commercial relationship with Brazil is akin to Austria's trade ties with Germany, with both countries having weathered the effects of the depreciating value of their larger neighbours' currencies. Klima's solution for the smaller trading partner is to improve productivity through close co-operation with everyone involved in the production chain, including unions. Argentina needs to offer more support to its small and medium sized businesses as well, he cautioned. 'It is extremely difficult to invest in Argentina due to the exorbitant interest rates, and even more so for these types of companies that cannot afford new technology or methods of production,' Klima said. However, auto industry consultant Autopolis warned that vehicle sales worldwide may drop by more than 11 per cent by the end of 2002 from 2000. It forecast the biggest decline in 2001, with global sales down 7.1 per cent to 50.6 million vehicles, followed by a 3.8 per cent fall in 2002. Part of the problem is long-term overcapacity, with about a quarter of the world's car and truck plants idle despite record sales in 1999 and 2000.[22] Plant overcapacity in South America is estimated at about 50 per cent.[23]

The car sector is a telling example of Mercosur's gradual and managed approach to trade liberalization. It illustrates how the trade bloc functions and how it is preparing for free trade.

Notes

[1]Jaguaribe, Helio, Universidad de Brasilia, interview in Brasilia, 2 August 2000.

[2]Campbell, Jorge (1999) *Mercosur: Entre la Realidad y la Utopia*, Centro de Economia Internacional y Nuevohacer, Grupo Editor Latinoamericano.

[3]Latin American Trade Partners (*www.aladi.org*) press release, 19 March 2001.

[4]Alegrett, Sebastian, secretary general of the Andean Community of Nations, phone interview from Lima, 8 March 2001.

[5]Stephenson, Sherry (2000) *Services Trade in the Western Hemisphere, Liberalization, Integration and Reform*, Organization of American States/ General Secretariat and The Brookings Institution Press, Washington, D.C., page 186.

[6]Rimoldi de Ladman, Eve, consulting member of the Argentine Council on International Relations, interview, 23 May 2000.

[7]Department of Integration and Regional Programs, 'Integration and Trade in the Americas', Inter-American Development Bank, periodic note, October 1999, page 24.

[8]Department of Integration and Regional Programs, IADB, ibid, page 25.

[9]Rimoldi de Ladman, Eve, consulting member of the Argentine Council on International Relations, interview, 23 May 2000.

[10]ALADI press release, *op.cit*.

[11]Salazar-Xirinachs, Jose Manuel and Robert, Maryse (2001) *Toward Free Trade in the Americas*, Chapter 3: free trade agreements, Organization of American States and Brookings Institution Press.

[12]Alegrett, Sebastian, *op.cit*.

[13]Graca Lima, Jose Alfredo, Brazilian undersecretary of trade and commercial affairs, phone interview to Brasilia, 9 March 2001.

[14]Integracion & Comerico, numero especial, Inter-American Development Bank, 2000, pp. 264–265.

[15]Lavagna, Roberto, Argentine ambassador to the EU, WTO and United Nations agencies governing trade and copyright laws, interview in Buenos Aires, 20 December 2000.

[16]Ashby, Christopher, US Ambassador to Uruguay, speech at 'Doing business between Mercosur & the United States' seminar, Montevideo, 25 September 2000.

[17]Lavagna, *op.cit*.

[18]Moore, Mike, Secretary General of the World Trade Organization, interview in Buenos Aires, 28 November 2000.

[19]PricewaterhouseCoopers, studies prepared for US State Department's 'Doing Business between Mercosur & the United States' seminar in Montevideo, 25 September 2000.

[20]Demel, Herbert, president, Volkswagen Brazil, interview in Rio de Janeiro, 8 May 2000.

[21]Klima, Viktor, president, Volkswagen Argentina, press conference in Buenos Aires 6, March 2001.

[22]Autopolis report, released in London, 14 March 2001.

[23]Demel, Herbert, *op.cit*.

3

Birth of a South American middle class?

From oil-rich Venezuela to power-poor Brazil, debt-crippled Ecuador to investment-grade Chile, South America's investment profile covers the entire gamut. This chapter will cover the demographic profiles of the 10 largest South American republics and their key economic indicators to help you to assess the market's long-term growth potential and financial risks involved.

Remember that much of Latin America was colonized by Spain, and the republics of the new world gained their independence from that European power when imperial, royal Spanish society was in decline and decay. That's in large part why the region inherited oligarchies known as *caudillos* and societies polarized between the wealthy landed gentry and the masses of landless poor. Brazil's colonial history began as a bit of an afterthought of the Portuguese crown, which was much more preoccupied with its Asian spice trade. Nonetheless, the territory ceded to Portugal under the Treaty of Tordesillas yielded valuable dyewood, vast fields of sugar cane were then planted in the northeast, and after that gold and diamonds were discovered in the interior. Like Spain, Portugal's days of glory had passed and after the fall of the Marquis of Pombal it was clear that the colony was much more vigorous than the mother land. But, unlike Spanish Americans, the Brazilians were more given to compromise, so their shift to independence was gradual and peaceful.

The middle-class struggle

With the exception of Argentina, which took in about 3 million Italian immigrants between 1870 and 1920 who fed the ranks of its middle class, no other Latin American country could boast any significantly sized group of middle income earners. What happened during the last century was a mass migration that continues to this day to the mega cities of South America: Sao Paulo, Rio de Janeiro and Buenos Aires, to name the largest. The swelling populations of these and other cities increased demand for goods and services while millions were plunged into poverty worse than that they had known in the countryside where they could at least cultivate their own food and were relatively isolated from disease. The advent of industry in the major urban centres helped pull some South Americans into higher income brackets, but while Argentina, Chile and Uruguay are considered among the 'high human development' countries in the 2000 UN Human Development Report, the remaining South American republics are categorized as 'medium human development' – roughly comparable to Russia, China and South Africa.

Obviously, purchasing power has a lot to do with people's access to quality education, decent health care and basic public services. In the case of Latin America and the Caribbean, this region enjoyed higher growth levels in the 1970s than it had in the previous decade. Then the series of debt crises during the 1980s eroded people's purchasing power, stretching the income and consumption gap between the poorest and the richest members of society. Expectations are that the economies of Latin America and the Caribbean will grow as much as 4 per cent per year this decade, compared with an average 3.3 per cent per year in the 1990s, thanks to successes in reducing inflation and attracting private investment.[1]

> ““The advent of industry in the major urban centres helped pull some South Americans into higher income brackets””

What about the region's emerging middle class? These groups of middle income earners, considered the traditional driving force behind most market economies, have come through the past three decades in various states, according to development experts. The proportion of people earning middle incomes in Venezuela and Argentina has shrunk since the 1970s while their ranks have grown in Brazil and Uruguay. Still, in the case of Brazil which makes up more than half the continent's population, there are significant differences in income distribution between residents of rich, industrial Sao Paulo state and the state of Minas Gerais, for example. 'The data in South America compared to other developing countries is definitely better, but you have quite high levels of inequality that are explained by the differences at either end of the distribution of income levels,' said Enrique Ganuza, chief economist for Latin America and the Caribbean at the United Nations Development Programme.

'There's a clear deterioration in Argentina and an improvement in Brazil, so if you look at the four Mercosur countries, all in all, you have a clear detrioration of the middle class in the 1980s and a stabilization in the 1990s, with the improvement in Brazil since 1994 raising the level for the region[2]

Brazilian economic stabilization measures since 1994 have helped to improve economic conditions in the country, while development experts estimate access to quality health care and education is better there now than a generation ago. Like Spain in recent decades, a number of these countries are starting to see the emergence of a middle class. Table 3.1 details the region's socio-economic indicators.

An estimated 40 per cent of households among the 109 million people residing in the Andean nations (Bolivia, Colombia, Ecuador, Peru and Venezuela) live below the poverty line compared with 20 per cent in Chile, where the middle class appears to be growing faster.[3] Brazilian President Fernando Henrique Cardoso unveiled $30 billion in social programme spending for 2001 alone to help pull the poorest members of his society out of abject poverty. Eighty per cent of those funds is targeted at health and education for the nation's poorest 25 million people. One of the largest programmes earmarks more than

Table 3.1 South American socio-economic indicators

HDI rank	GDP per capita (1995 US$)					1987–1998 share of income		Pct below
	1975	1980	1985	1990	1998	Poorest 20%	Richest 20%	poverty
35. Argentina	$7,317	$7,793	$6,354	$5,782	$8,475	–	–	25.5
38. Chile	$1,842	$2,425	$2,345	$2,987	$4,784	3.5	61.0	20.5
39. Uruguay	$4,092	$4,962	$3,964	$4,611	$6,029	5.4	48.3	–
65. Venezuela	$4,195	$3,995	$3,357	$3,353	$3,499	3.7	53.1	31.3
67. Suriname	$888	$930	$801	$787	–	–	–	–
68. Colombia	$1,612	$1,868	$1,875	$2,119	$2,392	3.0	60.9	17.7
74. Brazil	$3,464	$4,253	$4,039	$4,078	$4,509	2.5	63.8	17.4
80. Peru	$2,835	$2,777	$2,452	$2,012	$2,611	4.4	51.2	49.0
81. Paraguay	$1,297	$1,871	$1,754	$1,816	$1,781	2.3	62.4	21.8
91. Ecuador	$1,301	$1,547	$1,504	$1,475	$1,562	5.4	49.7	35.0
96. Guyana	$873	$819	$626	$554	$825	6.3	46.9	–
114. Bolivia	$1,010	$1,016	$835	$836	$964	5.6	48.2	–
All developing countries	$761	$892	$921	$1,026	$1,308			
Latin America	$3,166	$3,679	$3,407	$3,380	$3,930			

*HDI: human development index

Source: UN Development Programme, Human Development Report 2000, *www.undp.org/hdro*

$2 billion to encourage poor families to send their children to school rather than sending them off to work.[4] Gender inequality is also a problem, especially in rural areas where women are virtually landless despite the fact they are the main producers of food in many parts of Latin America. Countries that provide women with equal access to education, work and other benefits perform better in terms of economic growth and have lower rates of child malnutrition and mortality, according to a World Bank report.[5]

In Argentina, it is estimated that more than half of the nation's 37 million people are part of the country's long-established middle class, but economic turmoil in the 1980s eroded its relative purchasing power. Chile's middle class, in contrast, is believed to have grown in recent decades, and a larger number of Brazilians are now said to count on a regular amount of discretionary income. Improved economic and political stability, growing consumer demand and more efficient markets are why businesses and fund managers like you have been earmarking a growing proportion of their emerging market investment for Latin America in recent years. In fact, Latin America and the Caribbean overtook Asia as the top recipient of foreign direct investment in 1999, receiving $90 billion, according to the United Nations Conference on Trade and Development, as you can see in Table 3.2. Those two regions received the lion's share of foreign direct investment in the 1990s.

'Direct investors seem indifferent to short-term macroeconomic difficulties experienced by several countries in the region with relatively stable institutional and policy frameworks, such as Argentina, Brazil, Bolivia, Chile and Peru. Long-term growth prospects in these countries were not substantially affected by the recent economic slow-down. Inflows to Brazil are expected to maintain high levels,' said Fiorina Mugione, project officer for UNCTAD's division on Investment, Technology and Enterprise Development.[6] 'In contrast, investors are reducing their involvement in countries with unstable institutional frameworks, such as Paraguay, Colombia, Ecuador and Venezuela. However, given the investment potential of these countries, particularly in the oil industry in the case of the Andean countries, inflows should resume rapidly as stability and predictability increase.'

Table 3.2 Foreign direct investment global inflows to developing regions (1998)

South, East and South-East Asia:	$77.3 billion
Latin America and Caribbean:	$71.7 billion
Central and Eastern Europe:	$17.5 billion
Africa:	$8.0 billion
Central and Western Asia:	$7.5 billion

Foreign direct investment in Mercosur (1997–1999)

	1997	1998	1999
Argentina	$8.094 billion	$5.697 billion	$21.000 billion
Brazil	18.745 billion	$28.718 billion	$30.000 billion
Paraguay	$240 million	$195 million	$100 million
Uruguay	$126 million	$164 million	$100 million
Mercosur members:	$27.205 billion	$34.774 billion	$51.200 billion
Bolivia	$731 million	$872 million	$800 million
Chile	$5.417 billion	$4.792 billion	$8.900 billion
Mercosur associates:	$6.148 billion	$5.664 billion	$9.700 billion
Mercosur members + associates:	$33.353 billion	$40.438 billion	$60.900 billion
Total Latin America + Caribbean:	$68.255 billion	$73.767 billion	$90.485 billion

Source: World Investment Report 2000 – United Nations, *www.unctad.org*

'We've had a very high level of foreign direct investment in Argentina and Brazil in the last five years, so does Mercosur help? Yes. Business prefers to see us working together. The US State Department and US Treasury didn't care about Mercosur and the US Trade Representative thought it was a commercial fortress, but in the last three years they realized it's a process of modernization for these four countries,' said Jorge Campbell, a former Argentine commerce undersecretary from 1986 to 1999 and one of the original architects of the trade bloc.[7]

Emerging markets around the world are jockeying for a greater share of foreign direct investment since recovery from the Asian, Russian and Brazilian financial crises between 1997 and 1999. Macroeconomic stability is the single most important reason Mercosur has experienced so much growth in internal and external trade. Now the plan to create a common market by co-ordinating declining debt, deficit and inflation targets between the Southern Cone nations is a further step towards the price stability that both you and the consumers of your services and products need to maintain a sustainable equilibrium between supply and demand. 'I think it's a good thing because it helps business understand what it is about and helps business make decisions which are three, four, five to ten years from now,' said Pascal Lamy, the EU's trade commissioner. 'Everything builds on trade. Economic convergence, regulatory convergence, a common energy or transport policy give better future fine points to business.'[8] Investors interested in setting up shop in this part of the world either from scratch or through strategic alliances, mergers and acquisitions share the same concerns when they go 'country shopping': what is the quality of local management, what is the quality and accessibility to public information, are regulations harmonized? Both the World Economic Forum (WEF) and the International Institute for Management Development (IMD) compile indexes to measure the competitiveness of certain countries (see Table 3.3).

Table 3.3 Country competitiveness indexes

WEF ranking	**1999**	**1998**	**1997**	**1996**
Argentina	42	36	37	37
Brazil	51	46	42	48
Chile	21	18	13	18

Source: www.wef.org

IMD ranking				
Argentina	33	31	28	32
Brazil	35	37	33	37
Chile	25	26	24	13

Source: www.imd.ch

'I think all countries and regions are aware attracting investment is a very competitive business, so transparency, integrity, taxes that encourage entrepreneurs, clear accountancy practices and the rule of law are important. Latin America managed to get its nose ahead of Asia in attracting foreign direct investment (in 1999) and what happens in the future will be determined here. European investors should look at a broader range of investment opportunities, well beyond the traditional sectors,' said Chris Patten, the EU's external affairs commissioner.[9] Chapter Five will delve more deeply into issues such as taxes, labour laws, intellectual property rules and shareholder rights that can influence investment choices.

Everyone admits corruption, principally kickbacks to government from businesses or bribes extorted by unions, are a problem in South America, but in some cases there has been improvement (see Table 3.4). 'Corrruption has always been big, but control and sanctions are more real now in Brazil. The government is no longer paralyzed by its own corruption,' said Christophe Swinarski, a human rights consultant who served as observer of the International Committee of the Red Cross in the Southern Cone of South America from 1987 to 1991. Unlike developed nations, public servants have not been relatively well paid since the financial crash of 1929 which means many government officials seek their postings on the assumption that

"Corruption syphoned off the region's wealth to its upper class and the military dictatorships of the past generation"

Table 3.4 Corruption perceptions index of 90 nations

Country ranking
Finland 1
Sweden 3
Canada 5
Switzerland 11
United States 14
Chile 18
Spain 20
Japan 23
Costa Rica 30
Poland 43
Brazil 49
Argentina 52
Colombia 60
Venezuela 71
Nigeria 90

Source: Transparency International, 2000

their salaries will have to be supplemented by unofficial payments. Corruption syphoned off the region's wealth to its upper class and the military dictatorships of the past generation.[10] The ability to reverse this culture will depend on political will, more equitable income distribution and a better functioning judiciary. In the case of the Andean Community of Nations, political instability and violence on top of corruption have steered many investors away. 'We need to attract foreign direct investment to the Andean region, but investors on the outside see Ecuador, Peru and Colombia as having common problems, but they're really very different,' said Colombia foreign trade minister Marta Lucia Ramirez. 'We've been working on attracting high-technology centres and it's a frustration.'[11]

The re-emerging markets in South America

Looking at Latin America's last few years from a distance you could conclude it weathered the emerging market financial crises relatively well. The region posted 0.4 per cent growth in gross domestic product in 1999 compared with 2.0 per cent in 1998. The International Monetary Fund expected the robust growth of 4.2 per cent in 2000 to be reduced to 2.5 per cent in 2001. The region's fiscal deficit, another measure of the economic rollercoaster Latin America has been riding, rose to its highest level in the last 10 years in 1999 when it reached 3.1 per cent of GDP, although it then receded to 2.4 per cent of GDP in 2000. But for the average Latin American on the street, the struggle to make ends meet is taking longer. Unemployment remained virtually unchanged at 8.6 per cent in 2000 from 8.7 per cent in 1997. Inflation tumbled to 7.8 per cent from 10.2 per cent in the same period and the IMF forecast inflation of 6.1 per cent in 2001, which is a boon to people's purchasing power. Growth throughout Latin America and the Caribbean in 2001 was forecast at 2.5 per cent, while Brazil and Mexico were expected to lead the region in growth.([12]) Credit rating agency Standard & Poor's had a positive outlook for Brazil in 2001.

'Which emerging market in the world has a decent, fairly well-educated workforce and consumer market and in relative terms can progress on the socioeconomic level? I would tend to say that in Brazil, Chile, Argentina and Uruguay those factors are ever improving. As an emerging market it's not too difficult to take a look at (Mercosur) and come away with a conclusion that it's a good place to be. It's certainly not going backwards,' said Tony Santos, a lawyer for US and European telecommunications, high-technology and internet firms[13].

Table 3.5 gives an idea of the quality of life in the South American countries.

Brazil

Brazil had become Latin America's leading economic and political power by the 1970s and hasn't looked back since. Roughly the size of the continental United States, Brazil is a country of contrasts where per-capita income in the northeast is comparable to some of the poorest countries in Africa while in Sao Paulo state, which accounts for about half of the national economy, per-capita income is comparable to that of New York state. Federal revenues secretary Everardo Maciel is largely credited with reducing tax evasion in Brazil, a feat yet to be accomplished in many of the neighbouring countries. Tax receipts equalled about 30 per cent of Brazil's gross domestic product in 1999 and were estimated to be about 32 per cent in 2000. Brazil overcame more than half a century of military intervention in governing the nation when Jose Sarney was democratically elected in 1985. For a long time Brazil called itself the 'country of the future' but now, thanks to a much more stable socio-political and market environment as well as a growing middle class, the world's ninth-largest economy appears poised to fulfil its ambitions. 'With inflation under control, there's been a growing proportion, an ever larger number of middle-income earners, and you see this in food consumption and the growth in consumption of other finished goods, manufactured goods like refrigerators and TVs. Durable goods had not experienced large growth before. There's still a long way to go, but we've come a long way in recent years, and with more liberalization and a reduction in taxes this will continue to improve,' said Jose Alfredo Graça Lima, Brazil's undersecretary for international trade and commerce.[14]

Table 3.5 South American quality of life indicators

HDI rank	Pct of population without access to			Literacy rate		Education spending
	Safe water 1990–98	Health svc 1981–93	Sanitation 1990–98	Adult 15 & up	Youth 15–24	Pct of total govt spending 1995–97
35. Argentina	29	–	32	96.7	98.5	12.6
38. Chile	9	5	–	95.4	98.7	15.5
39. Uruguay	5	0	–	97.6	99.3	15.5
65. Venezuela	21	–	41	92.0	97.7	22.4
67. Suriname	–	9	–	–	–	–
68. Colombia	15	13	15	91.2	96.6	19.0
74. Brazil	24	–	30	84.5	92.0	–
80. Peru	33	–	28	89.2	96.4	19.2
81. Paraguay	40	–	59	92.8	96.8	19.8
91. Ecuador	32	20	24	90.6	96.7	13.0
96. Guyana	9	4	12	98.3	99.8	10.0
114. Bolivia	20	–	35	84.4	95.4	11.1
All developing countries	28	–	56	72.7	84.1	–
Latin America	22	–	29	87.7	93.7	–

*HDI: human development index

Source: U.N. Development Programme, Human Development Report 2000, *www.undp.org/hdro*

President Fernando Henrique Cardoso, re-elected on 4 October 1998 at the head of a four-party, centre-right coalition government, should reap the benefits of the austerity measures implemented during the first half of this mandate. The next elections are due in October 2002. Sao Paulo is a microcosm of Brazilian society, even though the city is derided by other citizens as the least Brazilian of the country's cities. Poet Vinicius de Moraes called Sao Paulo the 'tomb of samba' and there's no doubt the world's third largest city after Mexico and Tokyo is a business city – it is also the cradle of South American industry. Sao Paulo state has more than 75,000 factories which account for 40 per cent of Brazilian imports from Mercosur countries and 54 per cent of exports to the same markets. The city is 27 miles (45 kilometres) from the port of Guaruja and Sao Paulo state has some of the largest ports in Brazil: Santos, Sao Vicente and Cubatao. More than 2 million of the greater metropolitan area's 17 million people regularly use internet services. Only 140 years ago the southern hemisphere's biggest city was a town of only 30,000 people with about 50 streets. By 1940 it was South America's manufacturing capital with 1.5 million residents and 4,000 factories. Now it's not unusual to hear rush-hour alerts of 80 miles (130 kilometres) of traffic jams. The sprawling city has tentacles stretching out in all directions along the railway commuter lines built by the foreign operators in the first half of the last century when that public service was tendered to the private sector under concessions. Most middle-class families have two cars to navigate through Sao Paulo's traffic snarls and the city accounts for half the cars on Brazil's roads. Sao Paulo is violent and polluted, where the rich and the emerging middle class live in buildings under 24-hour security surveillance. Income distribution in Brazil remains highly unequal. A study found buying power in 1998 was heavily concentrated in the hands of the richest 3 per cent of households at $111,348, versus 53 per cent of households which had a purchasing power of $2,106 a year. Only 16 per cent of Brazilian households had $20,611 in annual income and 29 per cent disposed of $8,662 a year. Food and related consumption led 1997 purchases at 23 per cent, followed by housing and transportation at 11 per cent each, then clothing at 10 per cent.[15] Urban reclamation projects are beginning to yield results. Latin America's largest shantytown, on the hillsides overlooking Rio de Janeiro's beaches, has paved roads, electricity, as well as some running water and telephone services.

Brazil is one of only three nations in the world that fronts 10 or more countries and that physical fact has shaped its foreign policy outlook. It fancies itself a 'pivot' nation in the region, much like India's role as a regional linchpin in central Asia, or South Africa in the African continent. Chile and Ecuador are the only South American nations that do not share a common border with the continent's largest country. Brazil's 9,182 miles (14,691km) of sparsely populated borders front Argentina, Bolivia, Colombia, French Guiana (France), Guyana, Paraguay, Peru, Suriname, Uruguay and Venezuela. It has 4,682 miles (7,491km) of coastline and only 5 per cent of its 8.5 million square miles is arable land, 1 per cent dedicated to permanent crops. Natural resources include bauxite, gold, iron ore, manganese, nickel, phosphates, platinum, tin, uranium, petroleum, hydropower and timber. Brazil also has Latin America's largest population estimated in mid-2000 at about 172.9 million people, whose distribution by age and gender is detailed in Table 3.6.

Table 3.6 Brazilian demographic profile (2000 estimate)

Population: 172.9 million
Age distribution
0–14 years: 29 per cent (male 25.6 million; female 24.7 million)
15–64 years: 66 per cent (male 55.8 million; female 57.6 million)
65 years and over: 5 per cent (male 3.7 million; female 5.5 million)
Population growth: 0.94 per cent
Birth rate: 18.84 births/1,000 population
Death rate: 9.37 deaths/1,000 population
Net migration rate: –0.03 migrants/1,000 population
Sex ratio:
At birth: 1.05 male/female
Under 15 years: 1.04 male/female
15–64 years: 0.97 male/female
65 years and over: 0.68 male/female
Total population: 0.97 male/female
Infant mortality rate: 38.04 deaths/1,000 live births
Life expectancy: total population 62.94 years
Male 58.54 years
Female 67.56 years
Total fertility rate: 2.13 children born/woman

Source: Office of the Director of Central Intelligence: *www.odci.gov/cia/publications/factbook*

Fifty per cent of Brazil's economy consists of the services sector, industry makes up 36 per cent and agriculture accounts for the balance at 14 per cent. Forty per cent of the labour force works in services, 27 per cent in industry and 31 per cent in agriculture, where many are landless peasants who have frequently protested for land reforms. Brazil has one of the most industrialized economies of the developing world and its industry produces a wide variety of goods: textiles, footwear, chemicals, cement, lumber, iron ore, tin, steel, cars and parts, farm machinery and equipment as well as aircraft. In fact regional aircraft maker Empresa Brasileira de Aeronautica S.A. (Embraer) is the world's fourth largest jet airplane maker and the nation's leading exporter in dollar terms, earning $2.7 billion from exports in 2000 when orders from abroad rose 60 per cent from 1999. As a consequence of its industrial development and its large population, Brazilian demand for electricity exceeds supply by 16 per cent, where 3,500 megawatts of power will be needed each year for the next decade to bridge the nation's power gap. As of 2000 Brazil buys all output from the binational generation station at Paraguay's Itaipu hydroelectric dam, the world's largest. Brazilian total electricity consumption in 1998 reached 336.2 billion kilowatts per hour versus domestic production of 316.9 billion kilowatts per hour. More than 90 per cent of Brazil's electricity output comes from hydro dams, 5 per cent from fossil fuels, 3 per cent from other sources and about 1 per cent from nuclear plants. Chapters Six and Seven describe the opportunities in Brazil's power sector and the parallels with California's power deficit. Fundamental reforms in the electricity sector will likely attract more investment at a lower cost and reduce the level of public-sector debt through privatization. Bolivia and Argentina are building natural gas pipelines to supply more energy to Sao Paulo state and Figure 3.1 shows the extent of the network. Those two countries have proven natural gas reserves totalling 28.3 billion cubic feet versus Brazil's 8 billion cubic feet.[16] A natural gas pipeline loop linking Argentina, Bolivia and Chile to Brazil's industrial south is being completed.

“As a consequence of its industrial development and its large population, Brazilian demand for electricity exceeds supply by 16 per cent”

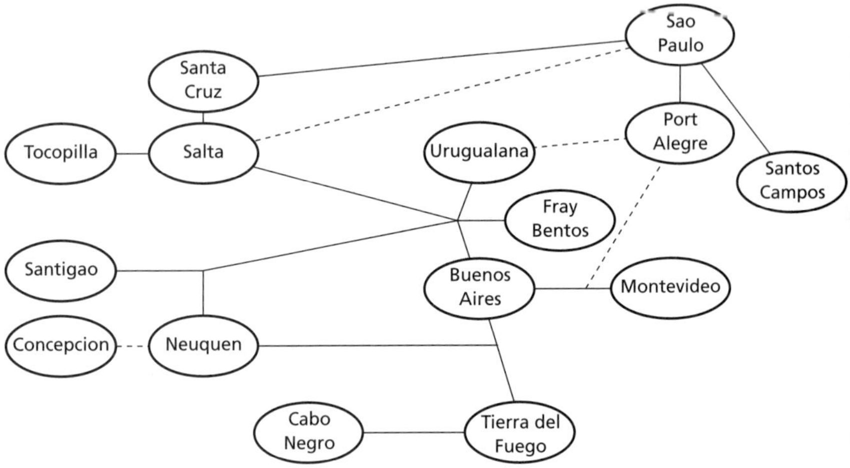

Figure 3.1 Energy in the region

Source: Cambridge Energy Research Associates

Brazil ended 2000 with a current account deficit of $25.3 billion, and widened to 4.88 per cent of GDP in the 12 months to July 2001. Its 2000 trade deficit of $691 million was largely the result of a 49 per cent run-up in oil prices compared with 1999. Otherwise Brazil would have posted a trade surplus thanks to a record $55.086 billion in exports of goods and services in 2000, up 14.7 per cent from 1999, but imports including oil also rose 13.2 per cent to $55.777 billion. Domestic industry is having trouble meeting local demand so many manufacturers are cutting back on exports to feed the national market in 2001. What that means is the trade deficit may grow further, which forces the Central Bank of Brazil to keep interest rates high to cap inflation as cheap imports enter the economy. Consequently, Brazil cannot allow its economy to grow more than 4–5 per cent per year without risking a surge in inflation. If the economy were to grow faster the trade and current account deficits could hammer the currency, rattle foreign investors and spur inflation. But capping growth at between 4 and 5 per cent means it could take decades to pull millions of Brazil's poorest citizens out of poverty.

Brazil's three fastest growing export markets in 2000 were the United States, up 35 per cent to $1.24 billion, followed by Argentina, which imported 18 per cent more Brazilian goods and services for a total of $560 million, and then Asia, up 29 per cent at $527 million.[17] The total amount of public and private foreign debt coming due in 2001 should reach $27.7 billion, slightly down from $27.8 billion in 2000, but interest payments on the debt were expected to rise to $18.7 billion in 2001 from $18 billion in 2000.[18] The total external debt was equal to about 37.4 per cent of Brazil's economic output in 2000. Its current account deficit was about 4.2 per cent of GDP in 2000 which, while still high, was comfortably financed by $30.65 billion in foreign direct investment in the same period. Unemployment at the end of 2000 fell to nearly a three-year low of 6.8 per cent. For further macroeconomic data, please see the following websites: *www.ibge.gov.br*; *www.ipea.gov.br*; *www.dieese.org.br*

Argentina

Argentina enjoys Latin America's highest level of per capita income and the standard of living in capital city Buenos Aires is akin to that of western European cities. But chronic tax evasion and government corruption has meant that what was an economy twice the size of Brazil in 1930 has been in a prolonged state of decay and is now less than half the size of Brazil's market.[19] Although it is not fair to blame the nation's turn of fate entirely on Juan Domingo Peron, an example of the populist leader's stubborn adherence to his preset economic programme was the way in which he spent billions of dollars in central bank reserves on questionable projects, such as buying back public concessions when the private operators had only a few years remaining in their contracts. Peron did introduce some overdue and progressive labour reforms that helped pull Argentina out of the era of rich *estancieros* and into the modern urban industrial age with social security. But the generous and comprehensive public health, housing and social benefits in his 1946–1951 five-year plan proved to be too rich for the nation's finances. So Argentina turned to international capital markets to finance its new welfare state just as large numbers of citizens were moving to the main urban industrial centres, driving up demand for imported consumer goods and diverting significant amounts of agricultural exports to the domestic market.

Peron had served as military attache in the Argentine embassy in Italy during Benito Mussolini's dictatorship, which profoundly inspired his populist movement, and a number of historians suspect him and his wife, Evita Duarte, of harbouring pro-fascist sentiments and of being anti-semitic. Some people in Argentine industry believe their country paid dearly in terms of lack of technology transfers after the Second World War, in contrast to Brazil, precisely because of Argentina's decision to declare war against the Axis only in the final days of the conflict. One thing certainly had a profound effect on Argentina's terms of trade: the United States' decision in 1948 that Marshall Plan dollars could not be used to buy Argentine goods. Peron was also behind the exponential growth in the size of the nation's public sector as an employer. Ultimately, it was Peron's unwillingness to alter his reform programme in the face of changing world economic conditions that set the nation on its snowballing path of deficits and rising debt. Peronist President Carlos Menem, whose 1989–1999 tenure was acclaimed for privatizations but marred by corruption scandals, set deficit spending on an accelerated trajectory which exacerbated the gap between the rich and the poor.

Buenos Aires is now a city of stark contrasts, consumers can find the latest in European fashion at the upscale shops in Recoleta, while illegal immigrants cram into tin-roofed huts with mud floors in the southwestern suburbs. Argentina is South America's second-largest economy and the administration of president Fernando de la Rua, an indecisive leader, is trying to come to grips both with tax dodgers and bureaucrats who skim off the public purse, and the liquidity crisis of late 2000 that escalated well into 2001. Tax receipts of about $46 billion in 2000 were equal to about 15 per cent of GDP. Some economists estimate that Argentina collects as little as 50 per cent of what it should in taxes. That is why the nation's value added tax is 21 per cent and is the largest revenue earner for the federal government, garnering about half of state income but also eroding the purchasing power of its population. Tax revenues did rise 3.1 per cent in 2000 but this was due mainly to an extension of the consumption tax to new items and a hike in income tax plus an amnesty on tax evaders. Democracy is nearing its third decade as Argentina is due to hold its next federal elections in 2003.

Like Brazil, the bulk of Argentina's 37 million people are concentrated along the south Atlantic coast. Table 3.7 breaks down Argentina's demographic profile. About a third of its citizens live in the Greater Buenos Aires region and half the country lives in the federal capital and surrounding Buenos Aires province, a territory the size of France. That also means Argentina shares a mostly empty frontier with its five neighbours: Bolivia, Brazil, Chile, Paraguay and Uruguay. Natural resources include lead, zinc, tin, copper, iron ore, manganese, petroleum, natural gas, uranium and heavy water as well as the fertile plains of the pampas.

Table 3.7 Argentine demographic profile (2000 estimate)

Population: 37 million
Age distribution 0–14 years: 27 per cent (male 5.06 million; female 4.83 million) 15–64 years: 63 per cent (male 11.63 million; female 11.61 million) 65 years and over: 10 per cent (male 1.58 million; female 2.24 million)
Population growth: 1.16 per cent Birth rate: 18.59 births/1,000 population Death rate: 7.59 deaths/1,000 population Net migration rate: 0.65 migrants/1,000 population
Sex ratio: At birth: 1.05 male/female Under 15 years: 1.05 male/female 15–64 years: 1 male/female 65 years and over: 0.71 male/female Total population: 0.98 male/female
Infant mortality rate: 18.31 deaths/1,000 live births Life expectancy: total population 75.05 years Male 71.67 years Female 78.61 years Total fertility rate: 2.47 children born/woman

Source: Office of the Director of Central Intelligence: *www.odci.gov/cia/publications/factbook*

Despite the tougher times its middle class has faced in recent decades, Argentina still enjoys one of the most equitable income distributions in South America. In 1998 2 per cent of households earned $196,652 versus 54 per cent of households with $15,063 in annual income. Eight per cent of households earned $60,433 and another 36 per cent had $18,662.[20] The economy is dominated by the services sector which accounts for almost two-thirds or 64 per cent of gross domestic product, followed by industry at 29 per cent and agriculture at 7 per cent. Industry consists of food processors, car and parts makers, manufacturers of consumer durables, textiles, chemicals and petrochemicals, printing, metallurgy and steel. Argentina imported 5.85 billion kilowatts per hour of electricity in 1998 as demand of 75.57 billion kilowatts per hour exceeded domestic production of 75.237 billion kilowatts per hour. Electricity exports in 1998 totalled 250 million kilowatts per hour. Hydro dams were the main source of electricity, accounting for half of domestic output, followed by fossil fuels at 43 per cent and nuclear energy at 9 per cent.

Argentina ended 2000 with a deficit of $6.59 billion and a federal debt of $128 billion. The total external debt was more than 50 per cent of GDP, higher than any of the six other major South American economies. Argentina's unemployment rate in October 2000 was 14.7 per cent and underemployment was 9.5 per cent. Interest rates are high, with banks charging around 28 per cent for personal loans and 11.5 per cent on mortgages by the end of 2000. Argentina's cost of living fell 0.7 per cent in 2000, the second consecutive year after consumer prices dropped 1.8 per cent in 1999 following a slight rise of 0.7 per cent in 1998.

“Despite the tougher times its middle class has faced in recent decades, Argentina still enjoys one of the most equitable income distributions in South America”

Venezuela

Venezuela was ruled by generally benevolent strongmen for most of the first half of the 20th Century. Democratically elected governments have been in power since 1959. President Hugo Chavez, who staged a failed but bloody coup attempt in 1992, was first elected in 1998 and then re-elected in 2000 under a new constitution. The world's third-largest oil producer borders Brazil, Colombia and Guyana, which is a key source of bauxite for Venezuela's aluminium industry. It has South America's second-longest river after the Amazon and barges ferry cargo up and down the shallow Orinoco River most of the year. More than 23.5 million people live in Venezuela (see Table 3.8), which has the largest reserves of crude oil outside of the Middle East.

Table 3.8 Venezuelan demographic profile (2000 estimate)

Population: 23.5 million
Age distribution
0–14 years: 33 per cent (male 3.97 million; female 3.72 million)
15–64 years: 63 per cent (male 7.41 million; female 7.36 million)
65 years and over: 4 per cent (male 500,000; female 592,000)
Population growth: 1.6 per cent
Birth rate: 21.09 births/1,000 population
Death rate: 4.94 deaths/1,000 population
Net migration rate: –0.19 migrants/1,000 population
Sex ratio:
At birth: 1.08 male/female
Under 15 years: 1.07 male/female
15–64 years: 1.01 male/female
65 years and over: 0.84 male/female
Total population: 1.02 male/female
Infant mortality rate: 26.17 deaths/1,000 live births
Life expectancy: total population 73.07 years
Male 70.05 years
Female 76.31 years
Total fertility rate: 2.51 children born/woman

Source: Office of the Director of Central Intelligence: *www.odci.gov/cia/publications/factbook*

The highest 10 per cent of income earners in Venezuela account for 35.6 per cent of household purchases while the lowest 10 per cent buy 1.5 per cent of goods and services. The economy is dominated by industry, primarily the oil patch, which generates 63 per cent of gross domestic product and a significant proportion of government revenues. The services sector accounts for about a third of Venezuela's economy and agriculture makes up only 4 per cent of GDP. The labour force, however, is concentrated in services (64 per cent) followed by industry (23 per cent) and agriculture (13 per cent). Chavez wants to diversify his nation's economy away from its overwhelming dependence on petroleum and has the good fortune to lead a country that has abundant sources of other forms of energy, such as hydro and natural gas. Venezuela's industry also produces iron ore, construction materials, steel, aluminum, textiles, food and car engines and could be a more important mining centre given the right conditions. These development issues are addressed in Chapters Six and Seven.

Venezuela more than met its electricity needs in 1998, producing 70.39 billion kilowatts per hour mainly from hydro stations (75 per cent) and fossil fuel plants (25 per cent). Consumption was 65.46 billion kilowatts per hour in 1998. Venezuela ended 2000 with a deficit equal to about 1.8 per cent of its $109 billion economy. The nation's total external debt was equal to 28.8 per cent of its GDP in 2000. Venezuela's unemployment rate in May 2000 was 13.5 per cent and estimated underemployment was 52 per cent. Interest on personal and mortgage loans were 40 per cent and 36 per cent, respectively.

Colombia

Colombia's challenge is more basic than confronting government corruption and tax evasion. The country has been in a state of civil war for four decades, and the conflict has intensified in the past 10 years, with 35,000 civilians being killed. It has the dubious honour of being the world kidnapping capital and rebel sabotage of oil pipelines is a regular occurrence. The nation's second-largest crude oil export pipeline operated by Occidental Petroleum Corp., which pumps 220,000 barrels per day through remote areas of Colombia along the northeastern border with Venezuela, was bombed almost 100 times in 2000. President Andres Pastrana unveiled Plan Colombia in 2000 to put a definitive end to the clash, but many fear the leftist FARC guerillas and rightist paramilitary groups which control large areas of the country will spill over into neighbouring regions of Brazil, Ecuador, Panama, Peru and Venezuela. The conflict is largely funded by the harvesting, processing and trafficking of cocaine and heroine, so the United States has stepped in with funding and military support to quash the supply of narcotics. If this fundamental matter of national security can be resolved, Colombia will be in great need of investment to overhaul its aging infrastructure. The next presidential elections are scheduled for May 2002. 'Obviously, all these political problems like you see in Colombia impedes investment there and in its neighbours.

People need to understand the different challenges each country is facing. I'm optimistic about democracy in Peru and things are looking good in Bolivia,' said Sebastian Alegrett, secretary general of the Andean Community of Nations.[21]

Colombia is also lobbying for the renewal of the 1991 Andean Trade Preferences Act with the United States. 'There have been expressions of good will to expand and extend this agreement,' Alegrett added. The deal gives Colombia, Ecuador, Peru and Bolivia reduced US tariffs on their exports. The preferential agreement is due to expire on 4 December 2001. Colombia, a nation of more than 40 million people (see Table 3.9), has about 2,000 miles (3,200km) of coastline almost evenly divided between the Caribbean Sea and the Pacific. Split between tropical coastal areas and mountain highlands that exceed 15,000ft (5,000m), Colombia covers 1.14 million square miles.

Table 3.9 Colombian demographic profile (2000 estimate)

Population: 40 million
Age distribution
0–14 years: 32 per cent (male 6.46 million; female 6.31 million)
15–64 years: 63 per cent (male 12.21 million; female 12.85 million)
65 years and over: 5 per cent (male 833,000; female 1.02 million)
Population growth: 1.68 per cent
Birth rate: 22.85 births/1,000 population
Death rate: 5.73 deaths/1,000 population
Net migration rate: –0.33 migrants/1,000 population
Sex ratio:
At birth: 1.03 male/female
Under 15 years: 1.02 male/female
15–64 years: 0.95 male/female
65 years and over: 0.82 male/female
Total population: 0.97 male/female
Infant mortality rate: 24.7 deaths/1,000 live births
Life expectancy: total population 70.28 years
Male 66.43 years
Female 74.27 years
Total fertility rate: 2.69 children born/woman

Source: Office of the Director of Central Intelligence: *www.odci.gov/cia/publications/factbook*

Its highest 10 per cent income earners account for almost half, or 47 per cent, of household consumption, while the lowest 10 per cent consume 1 per cent of goods and services. As of 1 January 2001 Colombia set a new minimum wage of $136 per month and the value added tax on consumption was fixed at 16 per cent. The service sector accounts for 55 per cent of Colombia's GDP, followed by industry at 26 per cent and agriculture at 19 per cent. The nation's labour force is concentrated in services (46 per cent) and agriculture (30 per cent), with the remainder (24 per cent) working in industry. Manufactured goods include textiles, processed food, oil, footwear, beverages, chemicals, cement, coal, gold and emeralds. Colombia imported 94 million kilowatts per hour of electricity in 1998. Electricity production reached 45.02 billion kilowatts per hour and consumption was 41.963 billion kilowatts per hour. Almost 70 per cent of the nation's electricity is generated by hydroelectric dams, with fossil fuel plants making up the difference.

Colombia's deficit was 3.6 per cent of its $82 billion GDP in 2000 and under a $2.7 billion IMF economic adjustment package signed during the 1999 recession, the deficit should not exceed 2.8 per cent of GDP in 2001 and 1.5 per cent in 2002. A weak peso and high oil prices helped the country register at $2.25 billion trade surplus in 2000, up from $1.58 billion in 1999. About half of its $13.04 billion in exports went to the United States in 2000. The nation's total external debt was equal to 40.7 per cent of its GDP in 2000. Colombia's unemployment rate in October 2000 was 20.5 per cent and estimated underemployment was 18 per cent. Interest on personal loans averaged at 36.8 per cent.

Chile

Chile was ruled by General Augusto Pinochet from 1973 to 1990. During that time leftist opposition was eliminated and an estimated 10,000 people were killed or vanished, freeing the way for Pinochet to impose sweeping market and labour reforms that were the basis for its present investment-grade status. Flanked by Argentina to the east and Bolivia and Peru to the north along the Atacama desert, Chile's top export partners are the United States, the European Union and Japan. Socialist

> “Chile is the world's leading producer of copper, which is the nation's top foreign revenue earner”

President Ricardo Lagos was elected on 12 December 1999 and the next elections are due to be held in December 2005.

Five per cent of the country's 756,950 square kilometres is arable land and while it is known for its wine and salmon exports, Chile is the world's leading producer of copper, which is the nation's top foreign revenue earner. Other natural resources produced by the nation of 15 million people (see Table 3.10) include timber, iron ore, nitrates, precious metals, molybdenum and hydropower.

Table 3.10 Chilean demographic profile (2000 estimate)

Population: 15 million
Age distribution
0–14 years: 28 per cent (male 2.14 million; female 2.04 million)
15–64 years: 65 per cent (male 4.92 million; female 4.96 million)
65 years and over: 7 per cent (male 453,000; female 641,000 million)
Population growth: 1.17 per cent
Birth rate: 17.19 births/1,000 population
Death rate: 5.52 deaths/1,000 population
Net migration rate: 0 migrants/1,000 population
Sex ratio:
At birth: 1.05 male/female
Under 15 years: 1.05 male/female
15–64 years: 0.99 male/female
65 years and over: 0.71 male/female
Total population: 0.98 male/female
Infant mortality rate: 9.6 deaths/1,000 live births
Life expectancy: total population 75.74 years
Male 72.43 years
Female 79.22 years
Total fertility rate: 2.2 children born/woman

Source: Office of the Director of Central Intelligence: *www.odci.gov/cia/publications/factbook*

Chile's highest 10 per cent of income earners accounted for 41.3 per cent of household purchases and its lowest 10 per cent bought 1 per cent of goods and services. The services sector dominates Chile's economy, accounting for 61 per cent of gross domestic product in 2000 followed by industry at 33 per cent and agriculture at 6 per cent. The service sector was the largest employer, accounting for 59 per cent of the labour force, while industry employed 27 per cent of workers, and 14 per cent of labourers were dedicated to agriculture. Industries include mineral extraction, fish and food processing, iron and steel, wood and wood products as well as cement, transportation equipment and textiles. Chile was self-sufficient in its use of electricity in 1998, consuming 26.67 billion kilowatts per hour from a roughly equal supply from both fossil fuel and hydro generation plants.

Total external debt in 2000 was equal to about 51.1 per cent of GDP, second only to Argentina of the six largest South American economies. Chile's economy grew 5.4 per cent in 2000, up from the 1.1 per cent contraction in 1999. The current account deficit was 1.6 per cent of GDP and Chile's unemployment rate was 9.4 per cent in the September-November 2000 period. Interest on personal loans and mortgages was 7.2 per cent and 7.7 per cent, respectively. The consumer price index rose to 4.5 per cent in 2000 after touching its lowest level since 1938 the year before at 2.3 per cent. Inflation in 1998 was 4.7 per cent.

Peru

Peru was ruled throughout the 1990s by strongman Alberto Fujimori who won his third re-election in 2000 under highly questionable conditions before resigning over a bribery scandal involving his spy chief Vladimiro Montesinos. His legacy includes ridding the nation of most of the Maoist Shining Path and Tupac Amaru guerrillas and instituting market-friendly reforms.

Peru is about the size of Alaska and has a population of 27 million people (see Table 3.11) dispersed from the arid western coastal plains to the high Andes and the eastern lowlands of the Amazon jungle. It covers 1.29 million square kilometres and borders Bolivia, Brazil, Chile, Colombia and Ecuador. Since the time of the Spanish conquest, Peru has continued to be a significant supplier of copper, silver and gold. It is also rich in phosphates, potash, iron ore, coal and hydropower. But the Andean nation is also prone to earthquakes, tsunamis, landslides and flooding, not to mention the adverse effects of the El Nino weather phenomenon.

Table 3.11 Peruvian demographic profile (2000 estimate)

Population: 27 million
Age distribution
0–14 years: 35 per cent (male 4.78 million; female 4.63 million)
15–64 years: 61 per cent (male 8.22 million; female 8.12 million)
65 years and over: 4 per cent (male 580,000; female 684,000)
Population growth: 1.75 per cent
Birth rate: 24.48 births/1,000 population
Death rate: 5.84 deaths/1,000 population
Net migration rate: –1.1 migrants/1,000 population
Sex ratio:
At birth: 1.05 male/female
Under 15 years: 1.03 male/female
15–64 years: 1.01 male/female
65 years and over: 0.85 male/female
Total population: 1.01 male/female
Infant mortality rate: 40.6 deaths/1,000 live births
Life expectancy: total population 70.01 years
Male 67.63 years
Female 72.5 years
Total fertility rate: 3.04 children born/woman

Source: Office of the Director of Central Intelligence: *www.odci.gov/cia/publications/factbook*

Development experts have said it is difficult to assess the evolution of Peru's middle class in the past few decades, but one thing is certain: the rich control a huge amount of the Andean nation's wealth. The highest paid 10 per cent of Peru's population account for more than a third of household purchases while the lowest 10 per cent buy 2 per cent of goods and services. Agriculture accounts for 13 per cent of GDP with the balance about evenly split between the service sector and industry. Mining, petroleum exploration and exploitation, car assembly, steelmaking, shipbuilding, metal fabrication as well as fishing, food processing and textiles are the foundation of the manufacturing sector. 'Peru probably has the most developed legal system of all the Andean nations, except Chile. It has good minority shareholder rights and it's consistent in enforcing its laws,' said Frank Gill, Andean region specialist at New York economic consultancy IDEA Global.com.[22]

Peru was a net importer of electricity in 1998 when it drew 2 million kilowatts per hour. About three-quarters of the electricity it produces domestically comes from hydro stations, with the remainder coming from fossil fuel plants. Overall, Peru produced 18.28 billion kilowatts per hour and consumed 17 billion kilowatts per hour. Peru's total external debt was equal to about 50.8 per cent of its $54 billion economy in 2000 and its current account deficit was 2.9 per cent of GDP, down from 3.5 per cent in 1999. The nation's estimated unemployment rate for 2000 was 9 per cent and estimated underemployment was 51.4 per cent. Interest charged on personal and mortgage loans was 20 per cent and 14 per cent, respectively.

Ecuador

Ecuador settled its border war with Peru in 1999 but continues to be plagued with internal problems, from the collapse of its banking system, its currency devaluation and subsequent debt default in October 1999 to a 'proto-coup' in January 2000 that deposed Harvard-educated Jamil Mahuad over plans to adopt the US dollar as the national currency. The coup plotters installed his vice president, Gustavo Noboa, as president to end out Majuad's term which was scheduled to end in 2002 and he pushed the dollarization programme through. Video tapes aired by Peruvian television in March 2001 showed Fujimori and Mahuad allegedly discussing ways to secure enough votes from Ecuadorean legislators to back the peace deal. One video tape reportedly made by Montesinos but not aired allegedly shows the two leaders planning to bribe 20 Ecuadorean Congressmen with a total of $20 million to support the peace deal. While the allegations certainly tainted the image of the peace process, they were unlikely to reignite hostilities between the two nations.

After oil, Ecuador's second biggest source of income in 2000 was money sent home to families from relatives living and working abroad, according to Central Bank manager Leopoldo Baez. That amount has tripled since 1995. 'Ecuador is still living in the '70s in terms of regulations while the rest of Latin America has moved on. Contract enforcement is extremely erratic and you have a very untransparent legal system,' said IDEA Global.com's Gill. 'But Ecuador is dollarized and that's a big help because foreign exchange hedging is a big concern for multinationals,' he added.

Ecuador is about the size of Italy and despite being located along the equator, it mostly has a temperate climate since much of the country is at high elevations. It is prone to frequent earthquakes, landslides and volcanic activity as well as periodic droughts. It covers 283,560 square kilometres and borders Colombia and Peru. Six per cent of its land is arable and 5 per cent is dedicated to permanent crops of which bananas are a significant harvest, making Ecuador the world's largest exporter of the tropical fruit. See Table 3.12 for Ecuador's demographic profile.

Table 3.12 Ecuadorean demographic profile (2000 estimate)

Population: 12.9 million
Age distribution
0–14 years: 36 per cent (male 2.38 million; female 2.30 million)
15–64 years: 59 per cent (male 3.79 million; female 3.88 million)
65 years and over: 4 per cent (male 263,000; female 301,000)
Population growth: 2.04 per cent
Birth rate: 26.51 births/1,000 population
Death rate: 5.52 deaths/1,000 population
Net migration rate: –0.56 migrants/1,000 population
Sex ratio:
At birth: 1.05 male/female
Under 15 years: 1.03 male/female
15–64 years: 0.98 male/female
65 years and over: 0.87 male/female
Total population: 0.99 male/female
Infant mortality rate: 35.13 deaths/1,000 live births
Life expectancy: total population 71.06 years
Male 68.26 years
Female 73.99 years
Total fertility rate: 3.18 children born/woman

Source: Office of the Director of Central Intelligence: *www.odci.gov/cia/publications/factbook*

Income distribution is concentrated in the hands of the top 10th percentile of the population which accounts for 37.6 per cent of household income versus that of the bottom 10th percentile which takes in 2.3 per cent. Services account for 50 per cent of GDP followed by industry at 36 per cent and agriculture at 14 per cent. About 45 per cent of the labour force works in the service sector, 30 per cent are farm labourers and 25 per cent work in manufacturing. More than 70 per cent of Ecuador's electricity is produced by hydro stations and the rest from fossil fuel plants. Electrical output in 1998 was 9.66 billion kilowatts per hour versus consumption of 8.98 billion kilowatts per hour. Ecuador neither imported nor exported electricity. The Andean nation is Latin America's fourth largest exporter of oil and sixth largest producer of petroleum. It has a large aquaculture industry that exports shrimp and fish and it also manufactures chemicals, plastics and wood products.

> **"Like Mexico and Chile, Uruguay enjoys investment-grade status and has one of South America's highest standards of living"**

Ecuador balanced its 2000 budget as part of a strict IMF agreement to pull it from the brink of financial disaster. The unemployment rate in October 2000 was 13.2 per cent and estimated underemployment was 62.2 per cent. Average interest on personal loans was 16.15 per cent.

Uruguay

Uruguay gained its independence from Brazil in 1825 as a peace deal with Argentina to act as a buffer between the two nations in the 19th century. Like Mexico and Chile, Uruguay enjoys investment-grade status and has one of South America's highest standards of living. A military junta ruled from 1973 to 1985. Current president Jorge Batlle was sworn in on 1 March 2000 and the next elections are to be held in 2004. Covering 176,220 square miles (456,410 square kilometres), Uruguay is roughly the size of the state of North Dakota and relies heavily on exports for its economic growth. In contrast to the remainder of the South American republics which are relatively young, Uruguay's population is older and growing at a slower rate (see Table 3.13).

Uruguay's economy is dominated by its services sector (62 per cent), followed by industry (28 per cent) and agriculture (10 per cent). The manufacturing sector includes food processors, makers of transportation equipment, petroleum products, chemicals, mineral extraction, beverages and electrical machinery. Almost all of Uruguay's electrical output is generated by hydro stations. Production was 9.47 billion kilowatts per hour in 1998 versus consumption of 6.53 billion kilowatts per hour. Exports that year totalled 2.36 billion kilowatts per hour and imports were 78 million kilowatts per hour.

Table 3.13 Uruguayan demographic profile (2000 estimate)

Population: 3.33 million
Age distribution
0–14 years: 24 per cent (male 417,000; female 397,000)
15–64 years: 63 per cent (male 1.03 million; female 1.06 million)
65 years and over: 13 per cent (male 178,000; female 253,000)
Population growth: 0.77 per cent
Birth rate: 17.42 births/1,000 population
Death rate: 9.06 deaths/1,000 population
Net migration rate: –0.63 migrants/1,000 population
Sex ratio:
At birth: 1.06 male/female
Under 15 years: 1.05 male/female
15–64 years: 0.97 male/female
65 years and over: 0.70 male/female
Total population: 0.95 male/female
Infant mortality rate: 15.14 deaths/1,000 live births
Life expectancy: total population 75.24 years
Male 71.9 years
Female 78.75 years
Total fertility rate: 2.37 children born/woman

Source: Office of the Director of Central Intelligence: *www.odci.gov/cia/publications/factbook*

Uruguay's unemployment rate was 14.6 per cent in the August to September quarter of 2000, with underemployment estimated at 6.6 per cent. Interest on personal loans denominated in pesos was 49.4 per cent in November 2000 and 10–12 per cent for dollar-denominated mortgage loans. Inflation reached 5.05 per cent in 2000, up from 4.17 per cent in 1999, according to Uruguay's government data collection agency, the National Statistics Institute.

Bolivia

Bolivia is one of the poorest nations in the western hemisphere despite its great natural wealth. About two-thirds of its 8 million people (see Table 3.14) live below the poverty line. Sometimes called a beggar on a golden chair, Bolivia also finds itself at the heart of South America and sits on a territory that links the Mercosur member nations to those belonging to the Andean Community of Nations. The landlocked country covers more than 1 million square kilometres and enjoys free access to Chile's Pacific ports. Diplomatic relations between the two countries have just begun to thaw after Bolivia lost a considerable part of its Pacific coast territory in the 1878–1885 'Nitrate War' with Chile over that land and its valuable fertilizer ingredient. Then President Hugo Banzer officially met with Chile's Lagos for the first time at the Ibero-American Summit in Panama in 2000 in what was considered a rapprochement of the two neighbouring nations, when they discussed economic and infrastructure development in the Atacama desert region. Banzer ruled Bolivia as a military dictator in the 1970s but was democratically elected in 1997. Democracy returned to Bolivia in the 1980s and the next elections. Banzer stood down on 6 August 2001 at the age of 75 – a full year before the end of his mandate – after being diagnosed with cancer. He handed over power to his 41-year-old vicepresident Jorge Quiroga. The Texas trained engineer and former IBM employee is due to serve out Banzer's term through to 6 August 2002 and has been a proponent of closer business ties to the United States.

Table 3.14 Bolivian demographic profile (2000 estimate)

Population: 8.15 million
Age distribution
0–14 years: 39 per cent (male 1.62 million; female 1.56 million)
15–64 years: 56 per cent (male 2.25 million; female 2.35 million)
65 years and over: 4.5 per cent (male 164,000; female 200,000)
Population growth: 1.83 per cent
Birth rate: 28.15 births/1,000 population
Death rate: 8.36 deaths/1,000 population
Net migration rate: –1.47 migrants/1,000 population
Sex ratio:
At birth: 1.05 male/female
Under 15 years: 1.04 male/female
15–64 years: 0.96 male/female
65 years and over: 0.82 male/female
Total population: 0.98 male/female
Infant mortality rate: 60.44 deaths/1,000 live births
Life expectancy: total population 63.7 years
Male 61.19 years
Female 66.34 years
Total fertility rate: 3.66 children born/woman

Source: Office of the Director of Central Intelligence: *www.odci.gov/cia/publications/factbook*

The richest 10 per cent of Bolivians consume 31.7 per cent of GDP while the poorest 10 per cent bought 2.3 per cent of the nation's goods and services. The economy is divided between services (47.9 per cent), industry (35.5 per cent) and agriculture (16.6 per cent). Industry is made up mainly of mining and smelting, petroleum and natural gas exploration and exploitation, tobacco, textiles and food and beverages. Petrolera Andina, Bolivia's largest gas company and an important producer of oil, pumped 219 million cubic feet of natural gas per day and 9,400 barrels of oil per day in 2000. Bolivian electricity output in 1998 was 2.58 billion kilowatts per hour while consumption was 2.41 billion kilowatts per hour. It imported 20 million kilowatts per hour in 1998 and exported 4 million kilowatts per hour. Bolivia has wrestled inflation under control since it skyrocketed to 23,500 per cent in 1985. Consumer prices reached 3.41 per cent in 2000 from 3.13 per cent in 1999, according to government figures.

Paraguay

Paraguay is also a landlocked nation, slightly smaller than California, with an underground economy that may be equal to its formal gross domestic product. The 35-year military dictatorship of Alfredo Stroessner was overthrown in 1989 and the strongman has since enjoyed asylum in Brazil, where his residential status is under review by the Brazilian Supreme Court. Relatively free and regular presidential elections have been held since, interspersed by coup attempts linked to former cavalry chief Lino Oviedo, who is under arrest in Brazil. The first such uprising instigated by Oviedo led Paraguay's three other Mercosur partners to ratify the 1998 Ushuaia Protocol which declares democracy to be a fundamental principle of Mercosur membership. In order to comply with the trade bloc's principle of non-intervention except through international bodies to safeguard human rights, the Ushuaia Protocol sets trade sanctions as the maximum penalty for violating a nation's democratic institutions.[23] The second coup attempt occurred in March 1999 when gunmen assassinated vice president and Oviedo opponent Luis Maria Argana in Asuncion, leading to the impeachment of Oviedo supporter president Raul Cubas. The head of the Senate, Luis Gonzalez Macchi, took over the presidency and elections are slated for May 2003. A third uprising in 2000 was staged by a cavalry regiment loyal to Oviedo and took place in Asuncion but was quickly put down. The unit was split up and redeployed throughout the hinterland. 'Landless peasants could be a factor in future political instability. If they find a political leader, it could become a volatile situtation,' said human rights consultant Christophe Swinarski.[24]

Six per cent of Paraguay's 406,750 square kilometres is arable land which is cultivated by a large and disenfranchized landless peasant class (see Table 3.15). Much of its exports and imports are moved either by truck or on river barges that ply the Parana and Paraguay river systems which separate it from its neighbours Argentina, Bolivia and Brazil.

Table 3.15 Paraguayan demographic profile (2000 estimate)

Population: 5.59 million
Age distribution
0–14 years: 39 per cent (male 1.11 million; female 1.07 million)
15–64 years: 56 per cent (male 1.57 million; female 1.56 million)
65 years and over: 5 per cent (male 121,000; female 142,000)
Population growth: 2.64 per cent
Birth rate: 31.27 births/1,000 population
Death rate: 4.81 deaths/1,000 population
Net migration rate: –0.09 migrants/1,000 population
Sex ratio:
At birth: 1.05 male/female
Under 15 years: 1.03 male/female
15–64 years: 1.01 male/female
65 years and over: 0.85 male/female
Total population: 1.01 male/female
Infant mortality rate: 30.81 deaths/1,000 live births
Life expectancy: total population 73.68 years
Male 71.22 years
Female 76.27 years
Total fertility rate: 4.16 children born/woman

Source: Office of the Director of Central Intelligence: *www.odci.gov/cia/publications/factbook*

Paraguay is a prime example of inequality in income distribution, with the richest 10 per cent consuming 46.6 per cent of the nation's

GDP while its poorest 10 per cent can afford only 0.7 per cent. Since smuggling, counterfeiting and bartering are such significant activities in Paraguay it is difficult to assess its economic profile, but the service sector appears to account for about half of the formal GDP while agriculture and industry seem to share the balance about equally. In fact, Paraguay is so notorious for its black-market trade in stolen cars, for example, that when Gonzalez Macchi illegally imported a 1999 BMW 528i into the country, prosecutors stepped in to investigate whether the luxury car was stolen. Police estimate 400,000 of the 600,000 cars in the country were bought on the black market, most of them having been stolen from Argentina, Brazil or Uruguay.

Almost half of Paraguay's labourers work on farms, in many cases for subsistence wages. The sugar, cement, textile, lumber and beverage industries are also important employers. Paraguay's economy benefits from the fact that it has two of the largest hydro dams in the world that are situated near southern Brazil's industrial base. Electricity output totalled 50.324 billion kilowatts per hour in 1998 versus domestic consumption of only 1.494 billion kilowatts per hour. Paraguay exported 45.307 billion kilowatts per hour of electricity in 1998.

Consumer market forecasts

Five specific areas of growth in the coming years in the Mercosur nations are:

1 franchise operations;

2 demand for computer hardware, software and peripherals;

3 demand for medical equipment;

4 demand for electricity generation equipment;

5 energy and mining equipment.

After the United States and Canada, Brazil is the world's third-largest franchising market with 863 brands and 48,000 locations, of which only 73 are foreign brands. Argentina has 168 franchise brands, Uruguay has 138 and Chile has 74, most of which are US restaurant, hotel, car rental, fast-food and dry-cleaning networks. Annual billings in the Mercosur nations are estimated at $20 billion and yearly market growth in Brazil and Argentina is 25 per cent and 20 per cent, respectively. Franchising in the United States, for example, generates more than 50 per cent of total annual retail sales in that market.[25] Based on these forecasts it seems your business may be able to capitalize on greater growth potential in franchise retailing in the Southern Cone of South America, especially in the region's 'golden crescent': the Sao Paulo–Buenos Aires–Santiago corridor where per capita purchasing power is significantly higher than the rest of the continent. Brazil's retail sector is going through an intense period of competition due largely to the impact of the internet. There has been a rise in promotions, discounts and marketing costs as a result.

> **“your business may be able to capitalize on greater growth potential in franchise retailing in the Southern Cone of South America, especially in the region's 'golden crescent”**

Once again, the market for computers and related equipment also looks promising for your business in the Southern Cone. Mercosur's computer sales market was estimated to be 4.5 million units in 2000. Brazil's market alone for hardware, software and peripherals was worth $6 billion in 1998. The total regional market in 1999 was worth $9.9 billion, up 41 per cent from $7 billion in 1997. Multinational manufacturers are increasingly using Mercosur-based production plants as an export launching pad to the rest of South America. Moderate growth is expected in the region's demand for your health care equipment. Both the public and private health care systems in Mercosur countries purchased an estimated $5 billion in medical equipment in 2000, mainly in Brazil which is modernizing and decentralizing its health care delivery system. Capital investments are forecast to grow at a rate of 8 per cent per year for the foreseeable future. Trade in electrical machinery, components, appliances, systems, parts and accessories used in the generation of electrical power between the US and Mercosur surpassed $4.7 billion in 1998 but fell to $4.4 billion during the region's economic slowdown in 1999. Demand in 2000 grew an estimated 4 per cent. Given Brazil's electric power deficit and its neighbours' plans to increase supply, you can already see attractive projects under way, some of which are described in Chapters Six and Seven.

Another promising area of investment for you is in the metals and mining sector. Latin America's share of world mining investment is forecast to be 41 per cent in the 1998–2007 period, followed by North America at 11 per cent. Growth in the Southern Cone's mining sector alone is expected to range between 5 and 10 per cent in the coming years and a mining treaty ratified between Argentina and Chile at the end of 2000 is expected to attract $4 billion in investments to Argentina alone in the five following years. Chile's annual earnings of $9 billion through its mining sector could grow even further.[26]

CASE STUDY:

Brazilian brewer AmBev

No matter where you go in the world, with the exception of the Islamic republics, people who analyze commodities, equities and consumer markets will all tell you the same thing: consumption of meat and beer per capita rises as discretionary income rises. Brazil's Companhia de Bebidas das Americas (AmBev) is well aware of that truism. 'We expect economic growth in Brazil in the coming years. AmBev will certainly benefit from this growth. Historically the brewing industry grows at one-and-a-half times the rate of growth in Brazil's gross domestic product. In other words, if GDP grows 4 per cent then the consumption of beer will grow 6 per cent. With respect to South America, the same relative growth possibilities exist through growth in income and per capita consumption,' said Victorio De Marchi, co-president of the world's fourth-largest brewer.[27]

Born of the union of Brazilian beverage companies Brahma and Antarctica approved in March 2000, AmBev has since had its sights set on continental expansion. The brewer's predecessors entered the Argentine and Venezuelan markets in 1994 where they held a 15 and 10 per cent share of those respective markets by the end of 2000. Once merged into AmBev, the company acquired two local brewers in Uruguay in 2000 where it now holds a 50 per cent share of the market. 'AmBev also expects to continue growing in Brazil where per capita beer consumption now is fluctuating near levels comparable to other Latin American countries. Brazil's annual per capita beer consumption is 50 litres compared to Venezuela, for example, where annual consumption is 70 litres per capita. That difference represents an important growth opportunity for AmBev in Brazil,' De Marchi added.

Investment bank Salomon Smith Barney started its coverage of AmBev in January 2001 after the company listed its shares on the New York Stock Exchange in September 2000 and gave it an 'outperform' rating, forecasting its shares would rise to $30 each from $25 at the time. Salomon said it expected AmBev's earnings before interest, taxes, depreciation and amortization (EBITDA) in 2001 to reach $895 million, up 25 per cent from 2000, and that its EBITDA would touch $1.06 billion in 2002. Part of the reason for this forecast is growth potential in the key 20 to 35 years age bracket. 'Industry experts are forecasting a 26 per cent increase in per capita beer consumption in the young adults category, the 20 to 35 year olds, in Brazil between now and 2005,' said John Paul MacDonald, a spokesman for Canada's oldest brewer, Molson Inc.[28]

One condition Brazil's antitrust agency (CADE) imposed on the AmBev merger was that the brewer shed five breweries and its Bavaria brand, which Molson acquired in November 2000, gaining a 3.3 per cent toehold in the Brazilian beer market – the world's fourth largest. 'In our international operations we're targeting countries with high growth potential. Between now and 2010 Brazil will surpass Germany to become the world's third largest beer consumer by volume...we plan to spend three or four years developing the Bavaria brand before we want to bring Molson into that market,' MacDonald said, adding that the fact that his company's chief executive worked for four years in Brazil and four years in Venezuela prior to joining Molson was an advantage in the company's decision to enter the South American market. 'CADE's decision was to compel AmBev to cede some facilities in order to introduce a fourth player in the Brazilian brewing market in order to counterbalance the (market) concentration resulting from the merger. Molson entered the Brazilian market as an absolutely independent player and there are no intentions to form any kind of partnership, not even as an entry strategy for AmBev into the North American market,' De Marchi said. But AmBev is also the fifth-largest soft-drinks maker in the world and it plans to take on the world with its highly popular jungle berry drink Guarana Antarctica. That brand sold about 800 million litres in 1999 and the company plans to double that sales volume. 'Under the deal signed between Pepsi Co. and AmBev, Pepsi Co. grants AmBev the use of its international network for the sale of Guarana Antarctica. This way AmBev now has access to a worldwide distribution network for the sale of its soft drinks. Currently AmBev is doing a detailed study to identify the markets in which Guarana would gain the greatest penetration. We believe AmBev can easily gain a 1 per cent share of the world soft drink market with Guarana,' De Marchi concluded.

As you have seen in the last few pages, when you are investing in South America you are essentially dealing with a 'middle income' region of the world. Argentina, Chile and Uruguay rank as 'high human development' countries in the 2000 UN Human Development Report and the remaining South American republics rank as 'medium human development'. There are varying degrees of political instability, ranging from coups, attempted coups and civil war in Ecuador, Paraguay and Colombia to social protests by those people lacking in even the most basic of public services in countries like Argentina, Bolivia and Brazil. If you consider the bigger picture, beyond the past decade, the region as a whole seems to have recovered some economic stability, democratic institutions in general are maturing, and many countries are successfully replacing one elected government with another in relatively free and fair elections. These countries have young populations and a growing proportion of these people have brighter hopes for access to quality education, decent health care and improved public services, which augurs well for quality of life here and a better business climate for your business.

Notes

[1]Ocampo, Jose, executive secretary of the United Nation's Economic Commission for Latin America and the Caribbean, press briefing in Bogota, 19 February 2001.

[2]Ganuza, Enrique, chief economist for Latin America and the Caribbean at the United Nations Development Programme, phone interview to New York, 27 February 2001.

[3]Alegrett, Sebastian, secretary general, Andean Community of Nations, phone interview to Lima, 8 March 2001.

[4]Cardoso, Fernando Henrique, press conference in Brasilia, 8 March 2001.

[5]King, Elizabeth and Mason, Andrew (2001) World Bank report 'EnGendering Development Through Gender Equality in Rights, Resources and Voice', released 7 March 2001. *www.worldbank.org*

[6]Mugione, Fiorina, project officer at the United Nations Conference on Trade and Development's division on Investment, Technology and Enterprise Development, interview from Geneva, Switzerland, 12 March 2001.

[7]Campbell, Jorge (2000), former Argentine commerce undersecretary from 1986 to 1999 and one of the original architects of Mercosur, interview in Buenos Aires, 27 September 2000.

[8]Lamy, Pascal (2000) European Union trade commissioner, interview in Buenos Aires, 29 September 2000.

[9]Patten, Chris (2000) European Union external affairs commissioner, interview in Buenos Aires, 8 November 2000.

[10]Swinarski, Christophe (2000) human rights consultant and former human rights observer of the International Committee of the Red Cross to Argentina, Brazil, Uruguay and Paraguay (1987 to 1991) as well as Bolivia and Chile (1989 to 1991), interview in Buenos Aires, 18 December 2000.

[11]Ramirez, Marta Lucia, Colombian foreign trade minister, interview in Rio de Janeiro, 7 May 2000.

[12]United Nations Economic Commission for Latin America and the Caribbean, preliminary 2000 regional economic overview, 20 December 2000. International Monetary Fund, revised 2001 regional economic outlook, 10 August 2001.

[13]Santos, Tony, lawyer for US and European telecommunications, high-technology and internet firms, phone interview to Miami, 18 July 2000.

[14]Graça Lima, Jose Alfredo, undersecretary for international trade and commerce for Brazil, phone interview to Brasilia, 9 March 2001.

[15]Silvagni, Ricardo, PricewaterhouseCoopers Argentina, presentation at 'Doing business between Mercosur and the United States' seminar in Montevideo, 26 September 2000.

[16]Andean Development Corporation (2000), Vias para la integracion, Accion de la CAF en la infraestructura sostenible de Suramerica, page 72.

[17]Spindola, Lytha, Brazilian foreign trade secretary, press briefing in Brasilia, 2 January 2001.

[18]Goldfajn, Ilan, Brazil Central Bank economic policy director, and Gleizer, Daniel, Brazil Central Bank director of international affairs, press briefing in Brasilia, 27 December 2000.

[19]Conosa, Eduardo, professor of economics at Universidad de Buenos Aires, speech to the World Economic Forum conference on Mercosur in Rio de Janeiro, 8 May 2000.

[20]Silvagni, *op.cit.*

[21]Alegrett, Sebastian, *op.cit.*

[22]Gill, Frank, Andean region specialist at IDEA Global.com, interview in New York, 10 January 2001.

[23]Rimoldi de Ladman, Eve, consulting member of the Argentine Council on International Relations, interview in Buenos Aires, 23 May 2000.

[24]Swinarski, *op.cit.*

[25]O'Brien, Joe, International Franchise Association, presentation at 'Doing business between Mercosur and the United States' seminar in Montevideo, 26 September 2000.

[26]PricewaterhouseCoopers, briefing paper for the 'Doing business between Mercosur and the United States' seminar in Montevideo, 25–26 September 2000.

[27]De Marchi, Victorio, co-president of AmBev, interview from Sao Paulo, 14 March 2001.

[28]MacDonald, John Paul, spokesman for Molson Inc., phone interview to Montreal, 14 March 2001.

4

Rules of the investment game

That fact Latin America has made great strides in stabilizing its macroeconomic conditions since the mid-1990s and that democracy appears to be taking firm root in its largest republics are welcome changes to old problems that have long plagued the New World. Investors and economists also recognize that the region weathered the emerging market crises of the late 1990s better than Asia and Russia because Latin America had developed a sounder financial services system, in part thanks to its significant 'home-grown safe haven' component, or foreign bank presence. Argentina is the most open to foreign banks of the major Latin American economies, followed by Mexico which is beginning to open up. Brazil has been more reluctant, although it has recently opened its financial services market to outside players who held a 15.3 per cent stake in the sector in 1998, up from 7.3 per cent in 1993. Foreign banks held a 40 per cent share of the Argentine market by 1999 and 15 per cent of the Mexican banking sector in the same year.[1] One example of a foreign bank with a long-term expansion strategy in the region is illustrated at the end of Chapter One in the case study of Banco Santander Central Hispano.

Now another series of fundamental reforms lie ahead which, if implemented, could consolidate and sustain these macroeconomic reforms. The task before South America's republics is to create transparent, predictable and accountable legal and regulatory laws and agencies. 'The Mercosur countries aren't offering a better Mercosur. That's Argentina's responsibility, but even more it's Brazil's responsibility. We don't have legal harmonization and Brazil, as the biggest country, sets the pace of Mercosur's development,' said Argentine congressman Carlos Raimundi (Argentine ruling alliance coalition – Buenos Aires province), president of the Argentine section of the joint Mercosur parliamentary commission.[2] Frameworks that deal with price fixing, bid rigging and abuse of market dominance are either lacking or badly in need of review in this part of the world. Foreign investment rules and intellectual property legislation are also either archaic or insufficient in assuring foreign investors that they are playing on a level field. But there are signs of improvement. 'Brazil's capital markets laws are stricter than many other nations and its corporate governance laws are well developed and being followed by other emerging market countries,' said Hugo Rossi, of the commercial law enforcement division of Argentina's Justice Ministry.[3] These are the kinds of reforms that could give this region a much more competitive edge in attracting foreign direct investment from the United States and the European Union.

You are not going to find a uniform body of law that covers all of South America. Laws here draw more from continental European thinking than Anglo Saxon-based law, which is why European companies have an easier time in coming to grips with the rules of the game here compared with their US-based counterparts. What this chapter describes is the relative level of similarity in the areas of business law that are most relevant to you and your business. In the Mercosur group of nations there are three bodies of law which have either basic points in common or that have been harmonized.

“Foreign investment rules and intellectual property legislation are also either archaic or insufficient in assuring foreign investors that they are playing on a level field”

- One area regards *competition policy*. The Common Market Council approved the 'Basic Elements of the Defense of Competition in Mercosur' on 14 December 1994. The 'Basic Elements' document was intended to harmonize member nations' federal competition or anti-trust laws and to create a co-ordinated capacity to prevent anti-competitive practices. Five months later the Commerce Commission approved a draft Protocol for the Defense of Competition within Mercosur (24 May 1995) which prohibits all concerted business practices whose purpose is to restrict or distort competition or the free access to the market. The draft protocol also forbids the abuse of a dominant position. But this protocol is only an addition, not a substitute, to the federal competition laws of the Mercosur member states.

- The second body of law deals with *foreign investment regulations*. Mercosur has passed two harmonization measures in this area: the Colonia Protocol for the Promotion and Reciprocal Protection of Investment in Mercosur ('Colonia Protocol') and the Protocol Regarding Promotion and Protection of Investments from Countries not Part of Mercosur ('Third Party Countries Protocol').
- The third area of legal convergence is on *intellectual property*. Mercosur passed a protocol in 1995 to harmonize trademark and indications of origin legislation. All Mercosur member nations have signed the WTO's Trade-Related Aspects of Intellectual Property Rights (TRIPS) agreement as well as the Paris, Berne and Geneva treaties. Prior to the creation of Mercosur, Argentina and Brazil signed a taxation agreement which stipulates that income on investments made in one country by an investor resident or headquartered in the other country will be taxed in the country where the investment was made and will be exempt from taxes in the home country. The bilateral Double Taxation Treaty went into effect on 7 November 1982 and was one of the earliest efforts at economic co-operation between the future Mercosur nations.

As you will see later in this chapter there is some common ground in these areas. International trade lawyers will tell US companies that laws in this part of the world are not as flexible as those in the United States but that in some cases they are more flexible than those European firms are accustomed to. But even if Brazil and Argentina, or the continent's six major economies, manage to harmonize their laws, there's a more basic issue that has to be resolved first. 'There is a lack of transparency and effectiveness in the legal systems. Namely, the ability to resolve disputes by using existing institutions within these countries.

They are not, at least in the view of US and western Europeans, necessarily up to the job,' said Tony Santos, a lawyer for US and European telecommunications, high-technology and internet firms.[4]

Trade referees

Chilean president Ricardo Lagos said at a meeting with Brazil's Fernando Henrique Cardoso in July 2000 that a precondition for his country's full entry into Mercosur would be the establishment of a permanent trade dispute resolution mechanism. Five months later Brazilian Congressman Julio Redecker (Brazilian Progressive Party – Rio Grande do Sul state) presented a draft proposal to create a permanent trade conflict resolution body to Mercosur's Common Market Council when it met in Florianopolis, Brazil.[5] Up until then Mercosur nations had only twice used ad hoc trade dispute panels foreseen under the 1994 Ouro Preto Protocol in solving commercial rows. The first time was in early 1999 when the three-member panel ruled in favour of Argentine dairy and hog exports to Brazil. Permanent commerce tribunals are seen as the trade bloc's only way of counterbalancing Brazil's overwhelming domination of the customs union and depoliticizing commercial conflicts. Argentine president Fernando de la Rua has joked that he enjoys calling his Mercosur counterparts but presidents shouldn't be spending their time solving disagreements over such things as the export price of powdered milk.

Under the 1991 Treaty of Asuncion, the Protocol of Brasilia and 1994 Protocol of Ouro Preto, you have to solve your disputes within Mercosur by going through a three-step process: consultation, filing of claims and arbitration. Government officials handle each of these stages which, once again, politicizes the disputes and raises fears of arbitrary or less predictable outcomes. Fortunately, legislators in both Brazil and Argentina appear to understand that this must change for local and foreign business to have more faith in the system. 'We need to give Mercosur more legal, judicial security to show business that rulings will be enforced. Chambers of commerce should go to these panels without a government bureaucrat accompanying them,' said Carlos Raimundi, president of the Argentine section of the joint

Mercosur parliamentary commission.[6] Up to now, the most frequent sources of conflict have been differences in import tariffs and anti-dumping rulings. Here's how the system worked up to 2000. The first consultative stage would begin with Mercosur's Commerce Commission. If the Commission could not resolve the dispute on its own, it would refer it to the Common Market Group. If the CMG could not reach a unanimous decision on how to solve the dispute, it would refer the issue to the Common Market Council. Finally, if the Council could not reach consensus on how to solve the conflict, a trade dispute resolution panel would be called to consider the claim by the plaintiff nation. That was not necessarily a sequential process. In the 1999 dairy and hog ruling affecting Argentina and Brazil, the Argentine Foreign Ministry began the process by filing its claim while a later dispute on textiles went directly to arbitration.

The selection of an arbitration panel is similar to how it is done in the North American Free Trade Agreement. All Mercosur member nations have a permanent list of commercial judges from which each of the opposing countries selects one panelist. Once those two panelists are chosen they are then responsible for picking a third judge who is not from either of the two countries involved in the dispute and that person chairs the arbitration meetings. The panel must report back within 60 days but can ask for a one-time 30-day extension. Alternatively, the panel can seek a suspension of the hearing in order to mandate a fact-finding mission before reconvening to consider the issue. In the Argentine-Brazilian hog dispute the panel used a six-month suspension for that purpose. The arbitration panels meet either in a neutral country or at Mercosur's administrative headquarters, which shares a former seaside luxury hotel with a casino in downtown Montevideo, Uruguay. Like the games of chance that take place on the other side of the wall at Mercosur headquarters, the arbitration panel results cannot be appealed, but nations may seek clarifications.[7]

The current system looked good on paper but in practice it is flawed. The likely reason no one has bothered with what appears to be the least contentious stage, consultation, is that Articles 2 and 3 of the Protocol of Brasilia give the Common Market Group only 15 days to negotiate a unanimous settlement. Article 7.1 of the Protocol of Ouro

Preto extended that deadline to 30 days and Article 7.2 set the 60-day deadline for the arbitration panel to return with a finding. The system was always intended as a temporary and first measure and some of the more dubious ideas originally proposed for the eventual creation of a permanent trade dispute resolution body have been abandoned. One example was the idea of basing the agency in Asuncion, Paraguay, a city that has seen more political violence and coup attempts than most South American capitals in recent years. Even if Asuncion was a more stable place to do business and practice law, the reality is that there are few regularly scheduled flights going there and the city lacks the infrastructure necessary to support an efficient and swift supranational agency entrusted with such a vital role in the supervision of commerce. Common sense prevailed and, until the first physical meeting of panelists took place on 28 April 1999, arbitration was conducted by telephone. The rulings are made by secret ballot based on majority findings and no abstentions are allowed. 'If we had permanent trade dispute panels we'd need three full-time judges and 50 full-time staff,' said Guillermo Mitchelson Irusta, the Argentine judge who sat on Mercosur's first arbitration panel. 'I'd suggest making ad hoc trade dispute panels a bit more permanent as a first step towards permanent conflict resolution. You build a common market one step at a time.'[8]

Mercosur member nations have always intended to create a permanent trade dispute resolution agency (see Annex III of the Treaty of Asuncion; Chapter 6, art. 34 of the Protocol of Brasilia; and Chapter 6, art. 44 of the Protocol of Ouro Preto). 'Undoubtedly, a permanent conflict resolution system creates more bureaucracy and delays, but it also builds up a body of jurisprudence. This would move conflict resolution into the realm of jurisprudence from the political arena with the naming of independent judges,' said trade lawyer Liliana Bertoni.[9]

“If we had permanent trade dispute panels we'd need three full-time judges and 50 full-time staff”

Nafta trade disputes have been resolved by ad hoc panels similar to those used by Mercosur up to now. Under Chapter 11, part B of Nafta, the United States, Canada and Mexico have agreed that their panels will follow one of three sets of rules in reaching their findings. Panels can refer to the World Bank's International Center for Settlement of Investment Disputes (ICSID) rules, the 1958 United Nations Convention on Enforcement Panel Arbitration Awards (UNCEPA) rules or the ICC rules of the United Nations Conference on Trade and Development. This could conceivably serve as a building bloc between Nafta and Mercosur towards the realization of a hemispheric free trade zone.

Policing competition

'Cross-border mergers and acquisitions, including the purchase by foreign investors of privatized state-owned enterprises, are driving foreign investment volumes to new records,' said Rubens Ricupero, secretary general of the United Nations Conference on Trade and Development. Worldwide, merger and acquisition activity has grown at an annual rate of 42 per cent during the past two decades. Privatizations have been the most important draw on foreign direct investment in Latin America in recent years and this explains in large part why the region attracted the largest share of FDI of any developing region in the world in 1999 at $90 billion. Global flows of foreign direct investment topped $1.1 trillion in 2000, double the amount just three years before that and more than five times the $200 billion invested only a decade ago.[10] This has been a boon to regional economies and governments understand that they need to update the rules they impose on mergers and acquisitions. That is why you hear analysts criticize the lack of integration between South American nations. What they mean is that efforts to harmonize laws and regulations among the Andean Community and Mercosur member nations have been stalled. At present, circumstances are such that anti-trust laws in South America can range from being similar to very different from country to country. Peru and Venezuela overhauled their anti-trust laws followed by Colombia later in the 1990s, building momentum towards passing a new protocol on competition policy at the Andean Community level when the five member nations met in late 1998. But trade experts said the General Secretariat has been blocking passage of the new competition rules by making amendments since then so that the Andean countries have given up trying to pass the legislation at a regional level. Andean Community secretary general Sebastian Alegrett said the trade bloc was due to start reviewing its competition policy in May 2001 in order to modernize Decision 285 which deals with anti-trust issues.[11]

Given the variety of economic and political profiles of South America's 12 republics, many multinationals have opted to set up shop in Brazil as their regional base of operations, although a significant number have offices and regional headquarters in Argentina and a few other countries too.

Brazil passed a new competition law in 1994 (Federal Law 8,884) which reorganized the Administrative Council for Economic Defense (CADE) as an independent agency tied administratively to the Ministry of Justice. Under Brazil's original competition law dating back to 1962 the CADE was a direct dependency of the presidency of the Council of Ministers. Since 1994, the CADE is authorized to 'pierce the corporate veil' in probing market dominance, bankruptcy, insolvency or cessation of activities cases and take action against executives and companies. CADE can impose fines of up to 30 per cent of the offending party's gross annual sales and no less than the benefit garnered from the market misconduct. According to Brazilian law firm Tozzini, Freire, Teixeira e Silva (*www.tozzini.com.br*) the statute defines 'dominant position' as 20 per cent of the domestic market or if any of the parties to the transaction has a worldwide turnover in excess of $200 million. The present statute allows companies to choose between pre-merger or post-merger clearance through CADE. The anti-trust authority is supposed to reply within about 120 days, which is why post-merger is the preferred alternative of the vast majority of companies. Notification is required within 15 business days as of the first binding document executed between companies. The government agency also has the discretionary power to order divestitures if the merger or acquisition results in a market concentration deemed detrimental to competition or consumers.[12]

But in practice the system does not always run as smoothly as it sounds on paper. The merger of Brazilian brewers Antarctica and Brahma first proposed in July 1999 was finally approved by CADE 273 days later on 30 March 2000. Brazilian government officials said the complexity of the merger was behind the longer than expected delay in approving the deal. Once cleared, the two beverage manufacturers joined forces to create Companhia de Bebidas das Americas (AmBev), which is now the world's fourth largest brewer and fifth largest soft drinks company and held a 42 per cent share of the South American market in 2000. CADE approved the merger on the condition that the new company shed its Bavaria-brand breweries. AmBev sold Bavaria to South American newcomer Molson Inc. in November of the same year, giving Canada's oldest brewer a niche brand and a 3.3 per cent stake in the Brazilian market. You can read more about AmBev's merger and its divestiture of Bavaria to Molson at the end of Chapter Three.

Until recently, anti-trust law had always lagged far behind economic reality in Argentina. Then the Argentine Congress passed a new competition policy (Law No. 25,156 of 28 September 1999) a few months after Spain's Repsol bought more than 97 per cent of outstanding shares in YPF, Argentina's largest company by market capitalization and a former state energy firm, for $15 billion in 1999. As a result, Repsol-YPF had to divest itself of service stations and a refinery in order to reduce its dominance of the Argentine market. It agreed to a $1 billion asset swap with state-owned Petroleo Brasileiro S.A. (Petrobras) where it would take 30 per cent of the Brazilian company's REFAP refinery with a capacity of 188,000 barrels per day (bpd), a 10 per cent stake in the Albacora Leste oil field, and gained the right to sell fuel products at 250 service stations in south and central Brazil. That would give Repsol-YPF about 2.5 per cent of the Brazilian market, which the oil and natural gas company hopes to raise to 7–10 per cent. In exchange, Repsol-YPF agreed to sell Petrobras its EG3 refinery with a 30,500-bpd capacity and 700 EG3 service stations in Argentina, which accounted for about 12 per cent of market share. That would bring Repsol-YPF's stake in the Argentine market down to 45 per cent and introduced Petrobras as a new competitor in a marketplace that includes Shell and ExxonMobil unit Esso. It would also fulfil Petrobras' ambitions to expand into fresh markets in Latin America and Africa.

Under the new law, any merger, acquisition or joint venture involving companies with after-tax sales of more than $200 million or $2.5 billion worldwide must be notified to the National Tribunal for the

Defense of Competition. Deals involving non-Argentine companies merging abroad may also have to be notified to Argentine anti-trust authorities if those companies have local subsidiaries or export significant amounts into this marketplace. For example, if a US company with offices in Argentina merged with a European company that exports only into Argentina, local authorities would need to be notified of the transaction if those exports were significant and the companies' consolidated after-tax sales in the domestic market exceeded the $200 million threshold.

According to Argentine law firm Alfaro-Abogados, the new anti-trust law was fine-tuned under presidential decree 89/2001 issued in January 2001. That amendment speeds along the approval mechanism in Chapter III of Law 25,156 regarding mergers and acquisitions by facilitating approval in circumstances where companies involved in a transaction do not hold dominant positions in their respective markets or business volumes above the threshold set in the law. In addition, the decree set up a new consultation procedure with a view to eliminating unnecessary filings before Argentina's National Tribunal for the Defense of Competition. It also spells out how a competition probe panel is selected. The Argentine president chooses seven members of a tribunal from a list of candidates put together by the jury foreseen in section 19 of Law 25,156. The tribunal is then mandated to begin its work no more than 60 days after the members have been named. The decree defines the concept of confidential filings as stated in Law 25,156. Whenever a petition is filed with the National Tribunal for the Defense of Competition you, the petitioner, can ask that the information be treated as confidential. If your request is denied, you can ask for your documents back and the government will treat your company as though your filing had never been made. But if the competition office does grant confidentiality to your petition, or parts of a petition, government employees who may have access to your information are required to preserve the confidentiality, as required

“Whenever a petition is filed with the National Tribunal for the Defense of Competition you, the petitioner, can ask that the information be treated as confidential”

under Confidentiality Law 24,766. If they disclose the information or use it for purposes other than what is covered by the new competition law, they are liable under civil or criminal law for the damages that may cause.[13]

Freer flowing funds

Argentina, Uruguay and Paraguay allow the free flow of foreign capital in and out of their economies without restrictions, but Brazil is still lagging behind in this area, despite recent changes that have reduced restrictions on capital flows there.([14]) Still, given the sheer size of Brazil's economy it attracted the fourth-largest amount of foreign investment in the world in 1999 at $31.4 billion, second only to China among emerging markets, and following the United States and the United Kingdom. Foreign investment in Brazilian business could add to the region's growth momentum and would certainly ensure that receding state involvement in the economies of this part of the world would be hard to reverse. Foreign direct investment in Brazil totalled $29.8 billion in 2000.[15]

Lawyers at Tozzini, Freire, Teixeira e Silva explain that Brazilian law requires foreign capital to be registered with the Central Bank if your company wants to remit profits or any capital invested or invest again after repatriating the original profit in Brazil abroad at the commercial exchange rate. Your company must register foreign capital, currency or goods remitted to Brazil as direct investments or loans as well as capital and profit repatriations, profit investments and changes in the monetary value of your company. The registration has to be made in the currency actually remitted as well as in local currency for investments made in Brazilian reals. You have to register with the Central Bank within 30 days of the settlement of your foreign exchange contract. Currently, as provided by the Brazilian Central Bank's circular of 15 August 2000 (Circular 2,997), you can register on the internet via the Central Bank's online system (SISBACEN) into the RDE-IED module. The electronic registration before the Central Bank authorizes capital and profit repatriations at the commercial exchange rate. Generally speaking, remitting dividends is not subject to withholding tax. Profit repatriations are also exempt from withholding tax. The repatriation of capital investments and reinvestments, up to the amount recorded in the Central Bank's investment registration certificates, is tax exempt. But any remittances over and above the registered amount face a 15 per cent withholding tax. Royalty and technical assistance fees payments are also subject to a 15 per cent withholding tax, in the absence of any lower rate established by a double taxation treaty. However, repayment of interest and royalties to an individual or legal entity from a country with a tax rate of less than 20 per cent is subject to a 25 per cent withholding tax. You should be aware that there is some uncertainty as to whether this exception applies to dividend distributions owing to the lack of case law in this area.[16]

Privatization in South America's two largest economies would not have attracted as many bidders and reaped as much revenue for government coffers had it not been for a relaxing of controls on foreign capital flows. Argentina put the privatization ball in motion when it sold the controlling stake in air carrier Aerolineas Argentinas to Spain's Iberia in 1991. After that, it split the nation's state-controlled telecommunications sector into a duopoly between Telecom, a joint venture between French and Italian telecommunications companies, and Spain's Telefonica. Then it followed up with utilities such as potable water services which were conceded to companies like US-based Azurix and France's Suez-Lyonnaise des Eaux (Aguas Argentinas). Argentina has fully deregulated its telecommunications sector in November 2000, unleashing strong competition in long-distance rates with the subsequent fall in prices, much as was the case when Chile deregulated its telecoms sector a few years earlier. The net result is that Argentina has privatized all of its state assets, including the post office, and more Argentines have telephones and running water after waiting for years to gain access to those services when they were under the control of government agencies.

'I believe we had to suffer considerably for the last 15 years to understand that omnipotent government does not lead to greater competitiveness. It is essential you create good systems of accountability and transparency in government and corporations,' said Brazilian Central Bank president Arminio Fraga.[17]

Brazil had to overhaul its legal environment before it could follow Argentina's example in privatizing state assets. In 1995 constitutional and legislative amendments opened up lucrative public service concessions and other activities previously reserved to federally owned and controlled firms in Brazil. In 1997 the federal government divested itself of its most profitable state-owned company: aluminium, iron ore and pulp and paper conglomerate Compania Vale do Rio Doce (CVRD) which became one of the largest private corporations in Brazil and one of the five largest Latin multinationals with foreign assets valued at $1.9 billion and foreign sales of $3 billion in 1998. The newly privatized conglomerate attributed its financial success to the fact that it cut operating costs by 25 per cent.[18] In 1998, Brazil privatized its energy-generating companies and then state phone company Sistema Telebras. Next on the agenda was the privatization in 1999 of energy-distribution companies and then in 2000 began the process of calling for tenders to operate water utilities which immediately became bogged down in a court dispute over the first privatization of potable water services in the Amazon city of Manaus.

Mergers and acquisitions in Brazil have gained momentum over the course of the past decade (see Tables 4.1 and 4.2), with at least 3,286 transactions publicly disclosed in the media, to 496 in 1999 from 186 in 1990. The number of deals involving foreign companies over the same period grew more than fourfold to 244 in 1999 from 56 in 1990.[19] All of this activity occurred in the context of inflation being reigned in and fewer controls on foreign capital flows.

'European Union foreign direct investment in Mercosur is higher than to the United States. My company has invested heavily in water, energy and waste services here. We have €4 billion in revenues from Mercosur and we have accelerated our investment in utilities here, especially in energy,' said Yves-Thibault de Silguy, a former European Union monetary policy commissioner and advisor to the president of the executive board of French-based conglomerate Suez-Lyonnaise des Eaux, the world's fifth largest independent electricity producer.[20]

Brazil allows some technology to be imported as capital goods meaning it is taxed at a lower rate, while Argentina treats technological imports as an investment, making them costlier to bring in.[21]

Argentina also repealed in December 1999 a decree (No. 343) which had granted tax-free import of used capital goods.[22]

Table 4.1 Brazilian merger and acquisition profile 1990–1999

	Number of deals	Per cent of total
Chemical and petrochemical sector	413	13 per cent
Food sector	298	9 per cent
Banks and financial services sector	278	8 per cent
Computer programming and publishing	221	7 per cent
Transport material	220	7 per cent
Services sector	199	6 per cent
Metallurgical sector	174	5 per cent
Comercio Varejista	152	5 per cent
Public services	143	4 per cent
Machinery	138	4 per cent
Telecommunications	128	4 per cent
Transportation	94	3 per cent
Electronics	90	3 per cent
Mining sector	79	2 per cent
Beverages (and tobacco)	74	2 per cent
Other	585	18 per cent
Total:	**3,286**	**100 per cent**

Note: only includes publicly disclosed transactions reported by the media
Source: PricewaterhouseCoopers Brazil (*www.pwcglobal.com*)

Table 4.2 Brazilian merger and acquisition activity 1990–1999

Year	Total	Foreign capital	Percentage of total
1990	186	54	30 per cent
1991	184	33	18 per cent
1992	252	48	19 per cent
1993	260	58	22 per cent
1994	249	60	24 per cent
1995	322	79	25 per cent
1996	395	120	30 per cent
1997	460	178	39 per cent
1998	482	238	49 per cent
1999	496	244	49 per cent
Total:	**3,286**	**1,112**	**34 per cent**

Note: only includes publicly disclosed transactions reported by the media
Source: PricewaterhouseCoopers Brazil (*www.pwcglobal.com*)

Another source of foreign direct investment in the region comes from the US government agency Overseas Private Investment Corporation (*www.opic.gov*), which provides political risk insurance, loan guarantees and financing through direct loans to US businesses of all sizes that invest in emerging markets. As of the end of 2000 all 12 South American republics and French Guyana were eligible for Opic project funding. Opic can offer up to $400 million in total project support for any one project: up to $200 million in project finance and up to $200 million in political risk insurance. The funds are earmarked for projects to which conventional institutions are unable or unwilling to lend. The agency will not lend to projects that can secure adequate financing from commercial sources. Repayments are based on cash flows generated by the project rather than on government or sponsor guarantees. At the end of 1999, there were 27 Opic-sponsored funds with a combined investment capital of $3.3 billion for projects worldwide. 'A free trade agreement can bring the type of certainty to long-term foreign direct investments in Latin America that will help bring the benefits sought by these countries,' Opic president and chief executive George Munoz told 150 business leaders in Houston.[23] Opic also provides political risk insurance to investors pursuing opportunities in emerging markets, where the rules of the investment game can change drastically and suddenly.

There are three types of coverage:

- *currency inconvertibility*, or the inability to convert profits, debt service and other returns from local currency into US dollars and transfer those dollars out of the host country;
- *expropriation*, or the loss of an investment due to expropriation, nationalization or confiscation by a foreign government;
- *political violence*, or the loss of assets or income due to war, revolution, insurrection or politically motivated civil strife, terrorism or sabotage.

As a final note of interest to investors like you, Brazilian private companies and financial institutions can now seek foreign loans without prior approval from the Central Bank since the passage in mid-2000 of Brazil's National Monetary Council Resolution number 2,770.

Foreign loans still need to be registered with the Central Bank and the commercial bank closing the foreign exchange agreement is responsible for doing so within 10 business days after the funds enter Brazil. The idea is to make it easier to secure foreign loans as well as give local companies and banks access to better interest rates (Brazil's benchmark Selic rate was more than 15 per cent at the beginning of 2001) as well as lowering the notoriously high 'Brazil cost' of doing business. Since mid-year 2000, foreign companies or individuals are also allowed to move capital between positions on securities and fixed-income funds when investing in the Brazilian financial and capital market.[24]

“Repayments are based on cash flows generated by the project rather than on government or sponsor guarantees”

Cover your patents

All but one (Bahamas) of the 34 FTAA negotiating countries are members of the World Trade Organization and adhere to the Agreement on Trade-Related Aspects of Intellectual Property Rights (TRIPS). In the past decade the Americas have seen a series of deals that have improved the guarantees of intellectual property in those countries. The TRIPS deal gave developing countries a five-year transition period in which to comply with their commitments, and trade experts expect the United States and Canada to take a hard line in negotiating intellectual property rights guarantees in the hemispheric free trade talks. In the case of the Andean Community there are four Community Decisions that cover intellectual property. Decision 486, the most recently adopted, establishes a common regime on industrial property, in other words patents, industrial designs, trademarks, appellations of origin and layout designs of integrated circuits, among others. The decision also includes enforcement guidelines. 'Decision 486 is in line with WTO's TRIPS agreement. I believe we have something new and modern, although there's been no reaction from the United States yet,' said Andean Community secretary general Sebastian Alegrett.[25] Decision 351 covers copyrights and Decision 391 addresses genetic resources, while Decision 345 protects plant breeder's rights.[26]

In the case of Mercosur, member nations in August 1995 signed the Protocol for the Harmonization of Intellectual Property Rules with Respect to Trademarks and Geographical Indications. Basically, the protocol guarantees the protection of trademarks and geographical indications of origin and is a first step towards harmonizing regional rules in those areas. But the protocol has yet to be ratified by the four member nations so there is no binding agreement in force at the regional level. 'In terms of intellectual property, Argentina is probably the major sore point in the region. There are significant problems in Brazil as well but the biggest problem is enforcement. It has a very good law,' said Mark Smith, of the Latin America and Caribbean section of the US Chamber of Commerce.[27] (See Tables 4.3, 4.4 and 4.5.)

Both Brazil and Uruguay require that patented medicines be produced in their territories for them to uphold the patent protection and some Argentine legislators have argued Argentina should include a clause to that effect in its patents legislation and form a 'Mercosur front' on this issue. The United States filed a complaint with the World Trade Organization against Brazil on this matter to which Brazilian authorities responded by threatening to cancel patents it has granted for AIDS drugs produced by two multinationals if they don't lower their prices. That was the tack South Africa took which succeeded in forcing multinationals to lower prices on those medicines in that country, which has an estimated 203,000 AIDS cases. 'We have a different opinion regarding the interpretation of article 68 of our patents law and article 27 of WTO TRIPS because there's no case law. So, what you're seeing is legal interpretations of these two pieces of legislation. Now that the TRIPS agreement five-year transition period is over, I think the United States has decided to take this opportunity to test the law,' said Brazilian undersecretary for trade and commercial affairs Jose Alfredo Graça Lima.[28] UK-based relief agency Oxfam has squarely sided with developing countries on this issue, accusing pharmaceutical companies and developed nations of 'conducting an undeclared war against the world's poorest countries'. Oxfam has asked the WTO to change its patent rules to allow developing countries to produce low-cost versions of drugs that treat AIDS, respiratory tract infections and childhood diarrhoea. The agency suggested creating a $5 billion international fund to assist in disease

Table 4.3 Scope and coverage of free trade and integration arrangements with intellectual property provisions

Agreement Issues covered	TRIPS	Nafta	Andean Community	Bolivia–Mexico	Costa Rica–Mexico	Chile–Mexico FTA	Group of Three	Mexico–Nicaragua
Copyright and related rights	√	√	√	√	√	√	√	√
Trademarks	√	√	√	√	√	√	√	√
Geographical indications	√	√	√	√	√	√	√	√
Patents	√	√	√	√				
Industrial designs	√	√	√	√			√	
Utility models			√	√				
Plant varieties	√	√	√	√			√	√
Layout designs of integrated circuits	√	√	√					
Undisclosed information	√	√	√	√	√		√	√
Satellite signals		√		√	√	√	√	√
Control of anti-competitive practices in contractual licences	√	√		√	√	√	√	√
Enforcement	√	√	√	√	√	√	√	√

Source: Organization of American States (*www.oas.org*) and (*Brookings Institution www.brookings.edu*).

Table 4.4 General provisions and basic principles

Agreement	**Protection of intellectual property**	**More extensive protection**	**NT**	**MFN**	**Intellectual property conventions**	**Co-operation and technical assistance**	**Control of anti-competitive practices**	**Transfer of technology**
Andean Community			√	√				
Nafta	√	√	√		√	√	√	
Group of Three	√	√	√	√	√		√	√
Bolivia–Mexico	√	√	√	√	√	√	√	√
Costa Rica–Mexico	√	√	√	√	√	√	√	
Chile–Mexico	√	√	√	√	√	√	√	
Nicaragua–Mexico	√	√	√	√	√	√	√	
Mexico–Northern Triangle	√	√	√	√	√	√	√	
TRIPS		Art.1	Art. 3	Art.4	Incorporated by reference; multiple articles	Arts. 67 & 69	Art. 40	Art. 7

Source: Organization of American States (*www.oas.org*) and Brookings Institution (*www.brookings.edu*).

research and subsidize drug distribution in poor countries in compensation. Some pharmaceutical companies have reduced prices on HIV-related drugs but the debate remains polarized and a definitive solution seems to be far off.

Table 4.5 Intellectual property conventions incorporated in free trade agreements

Convention	Nafta	Bolivia–Mexico	Costa Rica–Mexico	Chile–Mexico	Nicaragua–Mexico	Mexico–Northern Triangle
Paris	√	√	√	√	√	√
Berne	√	√	√	√	√	√
Rome		√	√	√	√	√
Geneva	√	√	√	√	√	√
UPOV	√					
Brussels		√			√	
Lisbon		√	√			
UCC						

Rome Convention: International Convention for the Protection of Performers, Producers of Phonograms and Broadcasting Organizations, October 26, 1961.
Geneva Convention: Convention for the Protection of Producers of Phonograms Against Unauthorized Duplication of their Phonograms, Geneva, October 29, 1971.
Brussels Convention: Convention Relating to the Distribution of Programme-Carrying Signals Transmitted by Satellite, Brussels, May 21, 1974.
Lisbon Agreement: Agreement for the Protection of Appellations of Origin and their International Registration, 31 October 1958, revised at Stockholm on 14 July 1967 and amended 1979.
UCC: Universal Copyright Convention, adopted at Geneva (1952), revised at Paris (1971).

Source: Organization of American States (*www.oas.org*) and Brookings Institution (*www.brookings.edu*).

All but the four smallest economies of South America (Bolivia, Paraguay, Guyana and Suriname) are members of the International Chamber of Commerce where many of these issues are aired among business leaders. In comparison with other developing regions of the world, Latin America has been slow in signing bilateral investment treaties, having begun to do so only since the late 1980s. These agreements are a way of guaranteeing high standards of legal protection for foreign investments in the host country. The first deals signed were largely between developed and developing countries, but it is becoming increasingly common for developing countries to sign deals among themselves. There are at least 300 bilateral investment treaties that have been signed by Latin American countries either among themselves or with developed countries, most often the European Union, the United States or Canada.[29] An expert in the area of bilateral agreements, trade lawyer Carlos Alfaro, recommends that US-based companies should find out whether the countries in which they plan to operate have signed a bilateral investment treaty with the United States. 'The US bilateral investment treaty (BIT) programme supports several key US government economic policy objectives, from protection of US interests overseas to promotion of market-oriented policies in other countries to promotion of US exports,' said Alfaro.

> **"In comparison with other developing regions of the world, Latin America has been slow in signing bilateral investment treaties"**

The idea behind the BIT programme is to protect US investments in foreign counties where investments are not yet protected by existing treaties. The program tries to encourage foreign countries to adopt market-oriented domestic policies that treat private investment fairly. With respect to Latin America, BITs serve as a complement to US regional initiatives on investment liberalization in the Free Trade Area of the Americas. The programme provides US investors with six benefits:

- The BIT ensures US companies 'most favoured nation' (MFN) treatment.
- The programme sets clear limits on the expropriation of investments according to international law standards and entitles US investors to fair compensation.
- The BIT also ensures the right to transfer investment-related funds in and out of the host country.
- It limits the ability of host governments to require US investors to adopt inefficient and trade-distorting practices.
- The programme also entitles the US investor to submit an investment dispute with the host government to international arbitration.
- It also grants US investors the right to hire the top managerial staff of their choice, regardless of nationality.

Argentina is the only Mercosur country to have signed a US bilateral investment treaty and only Bolivia and Ecuador among the Andean Community member nations had done so as of the end of 2000, according to the US Office of Investment Affairs (IFD/OIA) (see Table 4.6).

Table 4.6 Countries which have signed a bilateral investment treaty with the US

Country	Date of signature	Date entered into force
Argentina	November 14, 1991	October 20, 1994
Bolivia	April 17, 1998	(See note 2)
Ecuador	August 27, 1993	May 11, 1997
El Salvador	March 10, 1999	(See note 1)
Haiti	December 13, 1983	(See note 1)
Honduras	July 1, 1995	(See note 2)
Jamaica	February 4, 1994	March 7, 1997
Nicaragua	July 1, 1995	(See note 2)
Panama	October 27, 1982	May 30, 1991
Panama–Amendment	June 1, 2000	(See note 1)
Trinidad & Tobago	September 26, 1994	December 26, 1996

Source: www.state.gov/www/issues/economic/bit_treaty.html

Notes:

1 Entry into force pending ratification by both parties and exchange of instruments of ratification.

2 Entry into force pending US ratification and exchange of instruments of ratification.

Argentina signed three finance and investment treaties with the United States that should be of particular interest to US-based business. A treaty on reciprocal protection of investment came into force in 1994. Another treaty was signed in 1971 with the Export-Import Bank of New York related to a co-operation programme to finance the purchase of US goods. There is also an agreement relating to investment guarantees that has been in force since 1961. Brazil signed two agreements that US companies should be aware of. One relates to investment guarantees which has been in force since 1965 and the other deals with trade, investment and financial matters that has been in effect since 1976.[30]

What you see in this chapter is evidence of an improving legal environment in South America's key markets. Anti-trust laws are more up to date, restrictions on capital flows have either been removed or, in the case of Brazil, are showing some signs of easing, and changes in intellectual property laws are coming closer in line with WTO regulations. Despite this, many of your companies will find the legal atmosphere in the region quite foreign to what you are accustomed to and less flexible than in the United States but, in some respects, more flexible than in Europe.

As you have seen in the previous chapters, there are tangible improvements taking place in South America, from nurturing a low-inflation environment to improvements in the regulations controlling your investments there. In the next chapter we will look at the evolution in the region's labour market and what the business climate is like.

Notes

[1]Peek, Joe, Gatton Chair in International Banking and Financial Economics, and Rosengren, Eric S., vice president and economist, Federal Reserve Bank of Boston, 'The role of foreign banks in Latin America', presented to Jornadas Bancarias y Monetarias Banco Central de la Republica Argentina, 4 August 2000.

[2]Raimundi, Carlos, Argentine congressman and president of the Argentine section of the joint Mercosur parliamentary commission, interview in Buenos Aires, 1 March 2001.

[3]Rossi, Hugo, commercial law enforcement division of Argentina's Justice Ministry, interview, 2 August 2000.

[4]Santos, Tony, lawyer for US and European telecommunications, high-technology and internet firms, interview, 18 July 2000.

[5]Tizado, Javier, Argentine Industry Secretary, interview, 18 December 2000.

[6]Raimundi, Carlos, *op cit*.

[7]Baneo Villegas, Eduardo, lecture on Mercosur conflict resolution at Universidad del Salvador, 11 October 2000.

[8]Mitchelson Irusta, Guillermo, Argentine judge on the first ad hoc Mercosur trade arbitration board, panel discussion on Mercosur conflict resolution at Escuela Posgrado de la Ciudad Argentina (EPOCA), 18 October 2000.

[9]Bertoni, Liliana, trade lawyer, panel discussion on Mercosur conflict resolution at EPOCA, 18 October 2000.

[10]Ricupero, Rubens, secretary general of the United Nations Conference on Trade and Development, press statement dated 3 October 2000, *www.unctad.org*.

[11]Alegrett, Sebastian, secretary general of the Andean Community of Nations, phone interview to Lima, 8 March 2001.

[12]Tozzini, Freire, Teixeira e Silva, *www.tozzini.com.br*, briefing note, 15 February 2001.

[13]Alfaro, Carlos, *cealfaro@alfarolaw.com*, founder of Alfaro-Abogados Law Firm and partner in Mercosur Alliance of Law Firms: Alfaro Navarro-Tozzini, Freire, Teixeira e Silva, *www.tozzini.com.br*, brief issued from New York, 6 February 2001.

[14]Rossi, *op. cit.*, interview, 2 August 2000.

[15]Goldfajn, Ilan, Brazil Central Bank economic policy director, and Gleizer, Daniel, Brazil Central Bank director of international affairs, press briefing, 27 December 2000.

[16]Tozzini, Freire, Teixeira e Silva, *www.tozzini.com.br*, *op cit.*

[17]Fraga, Arminio, Brazil Central Bank president, speech to the World Economic Forum conference on Mercosur, 8 May 2000, *www.wef.org*

[18]Dauster, Iorio, chairman, Compania Vale do Rio Doce, panel discussion at the World Economic Forum conference on Mercosur, 8 May 2000.

[19]Beer, Raul, PricewaterhouseCoopers Brazil, presentation to 'Doing business between Mercosur and the United States' seminar, 26 September 2000.

[20]De Silguy, Yves-Thibault, advisor to the president of the executive board of French conglomerate Suez-Lyonnaise des Eaux, interview, 7 May 2000.

[21]Rossi, *op.cit.*, interview, 2 August 2000.

[22]Loewenthal, Paloma, institutional relations manager, American Commercial Barge Line Company, Hidrovias S.A., interview, 19 December 2000.

[23]Munoz, George, president and chief executive of the US Overseas Private Investment Corporation, speech to Greater Houston Partnership on 11 January 2001, viewed on website *www.opic.gov* 20 February 2001.

[24]Tozzini, Freire, Teixeira e Silva, *www.tozzini.com.br*, brief issued from New York, 15 February 2001.

[25]Alegrett, *op.cit.*, interview, 8 March 2001.

[26]Organization of American States and Brookings Institution, Towards Free Trade in the Americas, Chapter 9.

[27]Smith, Mark, US Chamber of Commerce, Latin America and Caribbean section, interview in Washington, D.C., 12 January 2001.

[28]Graca Lima, Jose Alfredo, undersecretary of trade and commercial affairs for Brazil, phone interview to Brasilia, Brazil, 9 March 2001.

[29]United Nations Conference on Trade and Development, 'Bilateral investment treaties quintupled during the 1990s', press statement released 15 December 2000.

[30]Alfaro, Carlos, *cealfaro@alfarolaw.com*, founder of the Alfaro-Abogados law firm and partner in the Mercosur Alliance of Law Firms: Alfaro Navarro-Tozzini, Freire, Teixeira e Silva, *www.tozzini.com.br*, briefing note, 15 February 2001.

5

The Latin labour and business climate

As far as multinationals are concerned, the business climate in South America is far from being ideal, but they acknowledge that conditions in this part of the world are improving in terms of increased macroeconomic and political stability and changes for the better in the legal environment. Here you will find an overview of labour market flexibility in the region and the specifics of labour conditions in the Mercosur countries. Later in this chapter there is a description of other factors that you and your company are likely to need to know when you go 'country shopping', such as taxes, shareholder rights and the macroeconomic effects of certain development policies under way in countries like Bolivia. But first we look at how the US business community views Brazil and a multinational miner's activities throughout South America.

An improving business horizon

'Overall, Brazil is the most attractive market because of the number of consumers and overall economy, but it's the most difficult because of the laws on tax and labour. A lot of people, when they go to South America, try Chile first because it's easier to understand and Argentina too, but Brazil is where the bucks are. There's a lot of frustration as well, so you've got to have good local people helping you out. They haven't resolved freeing up the auto and sugar industries and they've delayed eliminating the tariff on the list of most sensitive products that was supposed to end this year (2001). They've done better than expected in keeping Mercosur together, but there are a lot of questions left to be solved,' said Mark Smith, of the Latin America and Caribbean section of the US Chamber of Commerce.[1]

An opinion poll taken of members of the US Chamber of Commerce, which includes 65 of the largest US-based multinationals active in Brazil such as Coca-Cola, Bank Boston and Caterpillar, found most respondents bullish on the country's short to medium-term prospects despite the legal embroglios it often presents. Some 51.6 per cent of respondents told the Chamber in January 2001 they expected real annual growth of 4–6 per cent in Brazil during 2001 and even more, 67.7 per cent, forecast a similar range for 2002 and 2003. (See Table 5.1.)

Table 5.1 Brazil-US Business Council 2001 – Brazil outlook and membership services survey

How do you perceive Brazil's overall GDP growth prospects for the next 12 months?	
• Strong growth (real annual growth of 4–6 per cent)	51.6%
• Moderate growth (real annual growth of 2–4 per cent)	48.4%
In the medium term (next 24–36 months)?	
• Strong growth (real annual growth of 4–6 per cent)	67.7%
• Moderate growth (real annual growth of 2–4 per cent)	29.0%
• Moderate downturn (up to –2 per cent)	3.3%
How much growth, if any, do you expect for your company next year in Brazil?	
• Extremely strong growth (6 per cent or higher)	58.6%
• Moderate growth (real annual growth of 2–4 per cent)	27.6%
• Strong growth (real annual growth of 4–6 per cent)	10.3%
• Little or no growth (less than 2 per cent)	3.5%
What level of inflation do you expect next year in Brazil?	
4–5 per cent	35.5%
5–8 per cent	32.2%
3–4 per cent	22.6%
More than 8 per cent	6.5%
1–3 per cent	3.2%
How would you characterize your investment plans in Brazil for 2001 compared with your investments in 2000?	
• Significantly increased	35.5%
• Slightly increased	29.0%

- Not changed 25.8%
- Slightly reduced 9.7%

How has your confidence in Brazil's commitment to free market reforms changed since last year?

- No change 51.6%
- More confident 38.7%
- Less confident 6.5%
- Significantly less confident 3.2%

Please rank the following Brazilian government agenda items in terms of their priority for the business community (1–5, with 1 representing most important).

- Tax reform 1.63 (weighted average)
- Public sector spending reforms 2.36
- Implementation of social security reforms 2.55
- Corporation law reform 3.46

How would you rate the following infrastructure areas in Brazil in terms of impact on your business? (1 significantly positive; 2 moderately positive; 3 neutral; 4 moderately negative; 5 significantly negative)

- Telecommunications 2.4 (weighted average)
- Airports 2.52
- International ports 3.25
- Roads 3.48
- Inter-coastal waterways 3.58
- Rail 3.72

Please rank the following issues in order of difficulty presented to your business in Brazil (1 represents biggest challenge; 6 represents least challenge).

- High taxes 1.9
- Excessive bureaucratic red tape 2.67
- Interest rates 3.5
- Labour costs 3.61
- Lack of infrastructure 3.77
- Exchange rate 4.68

What impact do you think the negotiation of a US-Chile free trade agreement will have on the FTAA process?

- Positive 29%
- Slightly positive 22.6%
- Not changed 22.6%
- Negative 22.6%
- Significantly negative 3.2%

What impact do you think the new Bush administration will have on the hemispheric trade agenda compared with the Clinton administration?

- Positive 64.5%
- Not changed 22.6%
- Significantly positive 12.9%

Source: US Chamber of Commerce survey issued 12 January 2001

CASE STUDY

Barrick Gold

Founded in 1983, Barrick Gold Corp. has quickly become one of the world's largest gold producers, with high-quality gold reserves exceeding 51 million ounces. Barrick has the capability of producing 3 million ounces of gold every year for the next 10 years at well under $200 per ounce thanks in part to its large forward price hedging programme. Its major properties are located in the United States (Nevada), Chile and Canada but it is also active in Africa and throughout South America. 'We have great hopes for South America in the near term. There's more infrastructure than in remote Africa. We're involved in a project in Tanzania right now where it's nothing but flat land, nothing like working in the Andes, but we have to bring in power sources from a long way away,' said Barrick executive vice president of development Alan Hill shortly before boarding a flight for Tanzania.([2]) 'The infrastructure's more advanced in South America and they've been open to free enterprise for a longer time so the industry's more advanced there. The work skills are excellent and there's a long history of mining in South America. In fact, Peru has one of the longest histories of mining in the world and Peru has an excellent workforce,' he added.

In South America, Barrick has the Pierina project in Peru and the Pascua-Lama project on the Chile-Argentina border that, once in production, should add close to 1 million ounces to Barrick's output. Alongside Pascua-Lama is the Veladero mine, a joint venture between Barrick and mining company Homestake a company with which it announced a merger in June 2001. 'Let's face it, South America has only opened up in the last 10 years while North America's been run several times over, so there's not as much to find,' Hill said. Barrick also owns significant land positions in Bolivia and Brazil and like other miners, the company admits Venezuela is one of the exceptions to the promising mining outlook for this continent. 'My experience has been that there has been a lot of government interference and participation in Venezuela. They typically want a 5–10–15 per cent government interest in the stake, which really cuts into your profitability. If they change that, then people could be interested in mining there,' Hill said.

Elsewhere on the continent, Barrick has found building and upgrading infrastructure to be the most 'debilitating' aspect of its mining projects, but Hill commended most South American governments for doing as much as they can to share the costs and make it as attractive as possible for miners to dig there. 'The Argentina-Chile mining treaty makes it easy to transport from Chilean ports into Argentina. Chile's only 100 miles wide so despite the remoteness and altitude which add to your capital costs, the site is accessible,' Hill explained.

The advantage to South Americans is that the economic spin offs of many mining projects here are greater than in North America where the creation of indirect jobs for every mining job is five to one – it can be as high as eight to one in the southern hemisphere. 'Peru is a jewel and so's Brazil. Argentina only started to get its act together and the treaty with Chile is a big help,' Hill concluded.

Changes in the Latin labour scene

The Latin American labour market has long been characterized by greater job security compared with North America, so workers there have been more accustomed to wider variations in their wage levels. In other words, the labour market has adjusted to recession through reductions in wages, not reductions in head count. It is a system that bears some resemblance to the labour market in Japan or to a lesser extent western Europe. What this means for your business is that you can hire and fire more easily now, but once you've fixed an employee's wage or salary you will not be able to alter it very easily. A 1999 World Bank study of labour market flexibility in 13 Latin American countries between the 1960s and 1995 found that as nations moved to stabilize consumer prices, employee wages lost their elasticity, so unemployment has increasingly become the alternate economic 'pressure valve' during contractions. While the report found that five of the six countries that had instituted price stabilization programmes (Argentina, Bolivia, Chile, Costa Rica, Mexico and Peru) saw less growth in employment during periods of post-reform growth, those workers who retained their jobs were more productive and enjoyed a greater share of income.

Brazil did not institute its Plan Real price stabilization programme until 1994, so it and Venezuela, a country with rising inflation, were included as counter examples. The study was based on a formula devised in 1962 by economist Arthur Okun which essentially studies the effect of a 1 per cent deviation from economic growth trends on unemployment, employment and wages.[3] Of the 13 countries studied, seven posted high levels of inflation around the time of their last successful implementation of price stabilization programmes (see Table 5.2): Argentina adopted its currency board monetary system in 1991 after hyperinflation reached almost 5,000 per cent in 1989, Bolivia instituted counter-inflationary policies in 1985 and 1986 after hyperinflation touched 23,500 per cent in 1985, Brazil launched its Plan Real in 1994, Chile implemented stabilization policies in 1974 and 1982 as did Costa Rica in 1983/84 and Mexico in 1988, followed by Peru in 1992.

“the labour market has adjusted to recession through reductions in wages, not reductions in head count”

Table 5.2 Cyclical labour market effects

Country	Wage flexibility	Employment flexibility	Unemployment flexibility
Null hypothesis	fell	increase	increase
Argentina	fell	slight increase	slight increase
Bolivia	fell	increase	slight increase
Chile	fell	increase	increase
Costa Rica	slight fall	increase	increase
Mexico	increase	slight increase	slight fall
Peru	fell	slight increase	slight increase
Counter examples			
Null hypothesis	increase	fell	fell
Brazil	increase	fell	steady
Venezuela	increase	fell	fell
Rest of sample			
Colombia	unsteady	fell	increase
Guatemala	unsteady	fell	increase
Panama	steady	increase	increase
Uruguay	increase	fell	fell

Source: World Bank (*www.worldbank.org*)

While it may be easier now to hire and fire employees in many Latin American countries than in the past, an employer's labour costs and commitments can be substantial – see Table 5.3.

Table 5.3 Social security contributions in Mercosur member nations

Country	Argentina (pct)	Brazil (pct)	Paraguay (pct)	Uruguay (pct)
Employer contribution	33	34.8 to 36	16.5	18.625
Employee contribution	17	8 to 11	10	19.125 to 24.125

Source: PricewaterhouseCoopers *www.pwcglobal.com*

The Southern Cone countries have differing labour laws but they plan to eventually harmonize their legislation. You can read the relevant legislation, statistics and other information about labour rules in Argentina, Bolivia, Brazil, Chile, Paraguay and Uruguay on a common website: *www.observatorio.net*.

Argentina

In Argentina the labour day by law lasts eight hours and totals 48 hours per week, with the exception of farm and domestic workers. There is no general rule regarding night work but overnight shifts between the hours of 9 p.m. and 6 a.m. cannot exceed seven hours. Overtime is defined as preparatory or supplementary work that can only be done outside of normal working hours, although some exceptions are allowed. The weekly resting period is defined as running from Saturday 1 p.m. until Sunday midnight, with some exceptions. Workers with up to five years of service are entitled to 14 consecutive calendar days' annual holiday with pay but are not allowed to take cash in lieu of time off. Pregnant employees are forbidden to work in the 45 days prior to their due date and 45 days following childbirth. The employee has the right to reduce the pre-birth period to 30 days with an equivalent increase in post-birth leave.

Employers are justified in terminating an employee's contract if they fail to observe their obligations to the point of causing a serious offence that precludes them from continuing their employment. That determination must be made by a judge. The employee is entitled to 15 days notice' if they have worked less than three months and one month's notice if they have more than 33 months but less than five years' seniority. Compensation for dismissal without justified cause is the equivalent of one-twelfth of the employee's monthly salary multiplied by each month of service or fraction exceeding 10 days.

Brazil

In Brazil the working day is a maximum eight hours. A worker on night shift is entitled to a minimum premium of 20 per cent on the daytime hourly pay and overnight shifts are defined as taking place between 10 p.m. and 5 a.m. Overtime is limited to two hours per day and the employer must obtain authorization from the Ministry of Labour. The weekly resting period is defined as 24 consecutive hours which must entirely or in part fall within the Sunday. Workers with at least one year of service are entitled to 30 calendar days' annual holiday with pay if they have had fewer than five days of absence from work. Employees may ask for cash in lieu of time off for up to a third of their vacation entitlement. Pregnant employees are not allowed to work for a month prior to their due date and two months afterwards.

Brazilian law lists a series of circumstances under which an employer is justified in terminating a worker's contract. In the case of dismissal without justified cause an employee must be given eight days' notice when payroll payments are weekly or 30 days' notice in cases of longer payment frequencies. The lack of notice entitles the employee to compensation. Severance pay is one month for each year of service or fraction of a year exceeding six months.

Paraguay

Paraguay's labour day by law lasts a maximum of eight hours and totals 48 hours per week. Night work cannot exceed seven hours a day and 42 hours per week and is defined as running between 8 p.m. and 6 a.m. Overnight shifts carry a 30 per cent premium on daytime wages. Overtime cannot exceed three hours a day, three times a week, and no prior government authorization is required. There is one resting day per week, normally on Sunday. Employer and employee may agree to distribute Saturday's working hours by adding those hours to the other days of the working week. Employees with up to five years' service are entitled to 12 consecutive days of annual vacation with pay but they are not allowed to take cash in lieu of holidays.

Employers have the right to suspend the labour contract of pregnant employees six weeks before childbirth and those labourers are not allowed to return to work during the six weeks following childbirth.

Paraguayan statutes enumerate a series of acts that justify dismissal. Dismissal without just cause requires 30 days' notice if the employee has worked up to one year and 45 days if the length of service is between one and five years. Severance is 15 days' pay for each three years of service.

Uruguay

A work day in Uruguay is eight hours with a maximum of 48 hours per week in the manufacturing sector and 44 hours per week in the commerce and services sectors. Night shift premiums are determined in collective labour agreements and overnight shifts occur between the hours of 9 p.m. and 6 a.m. Overtime is capped at eight hours per week and no government authorization is required unless the additional hours will exceed the eight hour weekly limit. In the manufacturing sector the weekly resting period is one 24-hour period after every six days of work, while in the commerce and services sectors is the weekly resting period one-and-a-half days. Workers with up to five years of service are entitled to 20 days' annual vacation with pay but are not allowed to take cash in lieu of time off. Pregnant employees have the right to six weeks off work before and six weeks off after childbirth but the pre-birth leave can be accumulated and added to the post-birth period.

Dismissal without just cause is up to the employer but compensation is payable unless the there has been notorious misconduct by the employee, which is determined by a judge. There is no obligation for delivery of notice of termination. When the dismissal is not due to notorious misconduct, the severance pay is one month for each year of service.([4])

Building a better business climate

Brazil would do itself a great favour if it overhauled its byzantine tax system and made it more similar to those of its neighbours. It has taxes on production and transport that add to the final bill of goods and services whether they are delivered inside its domestic market or in other countries, making it less competitive on the world market. Any government serious about being competitive in a liberalized trade environment must eventually come around to taxing goods and services at the point of sale so that it does not harm its own industry's competitiveness. 'The tax structure here is very onerous and tax reform is certainly a priority for us. Although there's a need to generate a fiscal surplus, there's also a need to inject more investment to make our economy more dynamic, so all of these things have to be addressed. The tax structure will have to be reformed,' said Brazilian undersecretary of trade and commercial affairs Jose Alfredo Graça Lima .[5]

'If we want to be more competitive, we have to impose taxes in a way that's less of a burden on business...Market liberalization, tax reform and reducing the cost of capital, lowering interest rates, that's the equation for our success,' said Graça Lima.

Brazil's three other partners in the Mercosur trade bloc have more or less that kind of system in place. Tax collection in Argentina, Paraguay and Uruguay is structured in a similar way so that, although there is no harmonization of a regional tax regime, there is a relative level of consistency in the spirit of their tax policy. All three countries have a federal value added tax (VAT) that is applied uniformally nationwide. While Argentina and Uruguay's VAT levels are comparable – 21 per cent and 23 per cent respectively – the Paraguayan consumption tax is considerably lower at 10 per cent. In contrast, Brazil has a complex system of state, municipal and federal district taxes which vary between 18 and 21.95 per cent. To level the playing field in a free trade zone or common market, the ideal tax policy would be to impose the VAT on consumption of goods and services at the point of purchase and make exports from the point of production relatively free of taxation so that their price on external markets would reflect only the cost of production.

“Brazil would do itself a great favour if it overhauled its byzantine tax system and made it more similar to those of its neighbours”

While that is not currently the case in Mercosur, the similarity in tax policy between Argentina, Paraguay and Uruguay is a step in that direction. Argentina has a tax on gross revenues (IIB) which is not refunded on exported goods and services and therefore incorporated in their costs. That tax is 1 per cent for agriculture and mining primary products, 1.5 per cent for construction and industrial products, 2.5 per cent on wholesale commerce and 3.5 per cent on retail goods and services. The VAT is by far the largest source of government revenue in Argentina, Paraguay and Uruguay, accounting for between 50 and 55 per cent of federal income.[6]

Argentine economy minister Domingo Cavallo, the architect of the nation's Convertibility Law, proposed a Competitiveness Law in early 2001 to pull the nation out of a recession that lasted more than three years. Taking advantage of Mercosur's gradually converging external tariff principle, Cavallo asked Congress to approve a plan where tariffs on imports of capital goods for local companies would be eliminated while import taxes on some final consumer goods would be increased. To finance any gap this might create in government revenues, the threshold for a 0.6 per cent charge on bank transactions was lowered to $1,000 from $10,000 until December 2002. 'We are convinced that with these means we will produce an immediate recovery in competitiveness and cut costs in the productive sector by an average 20 per cent,' said Cavallo.[7] He was sworn in to replace Ricardo Lopez Murphy and Jose Luis Machinea who had quit as economy ministers within weeks of each other in March 2001 because of their failure to pull Argentina out of recession. For his part, Brazilian foreign minister Celso Lafer said that 'a strong Argentina is a priority for all members' and that his government did not oppose the temporary measures.

Economists and analysts in both countries as well as legislators agreed Brazil would do itself more harm by denying Argentina the flexibility of temporarily altering its tariff scheme. Tax experts, however, warned that copying Brazil's Contribucion Provisoria al Movimiento Financiero (CPMF) was a mistake that had cost Brazil some of its competitiveness on world export markets since it was adopted in 1993. They argued Argentina's cascading 0.6 per cent tax on transactions of $1,000 or more would be levied multiple times as the investment makes its way through the economy.

Brazil's VAT accounts for barely one-third of government revenues. That partly reflects Brazil's success in clamping down on income tax evasion in recent years. Now income tax is becoming a growing proportion of government revenue. Brazil's 26 states collect a tax on industrial products (IPI). The states and federal district also tax the movement of goods and services (ICMS). Those services covered by the ICMS are interstate transport, communications and electricity. The ICMS varies from state to state but is about 25 per cent for transport, communication and electricity and about 13 per cent for unfinished goods. Some goods are exempted from the ICMS, which could be deemed discriminatory against certain imports. Then, Brazil's more than 5,000 municipalities recoup a tax on all other services (ISS). That tax also varies from municipality to municipality, with the highest rates imposed by Sao Paulo and Rio de Janeiro at about 5 per cent each. There have been plans to reform the tax collection system to merge these three taxes into one federal VAT on consumption but this has not yet materialized.[8]

Externally, Brazil has entered into double taxation treaties with a number of countries, including Argentina, Austria, Belgium, Canada, China, the Czech Republic, the Slovakian Republic and the Slavic Republic, Denmark, Ecuador, Finland, France, Germany, Hungary, India, Italy, Japan, Korea, Luxembourg, the Netherlands, Norway, the Philippines, Portugal, Spain and Switzerland. An amendment in 2000 to the legislation governing the US Internal Revenue Department allows US companies to deduct taxes paid in Brazil on revenue and income earned in Brazil. Also, tax paid in the US may be offset against federal taxes paid in Brazil but not state and municipal taxes. Argentina signed a double taxation agreement with the United States in 1950 on earnings derived from the operations of ships and aircraft.[9] For a comparison of Mercosur tax levels, see Table 5.4.

Generally, Mercosur's withholding taxes are higher than those of other Latin American countries (see Table 5.5).

Table 5.4 Comparison of Mercosur tax levels

	Argentina	**Brazil**	**Paraguay**	**Uruguay**
Personal income tax	world rate: 9 to 35 pct	world rate: 0 to 37.5 pct	N/A	N/A
Corporate income tax	world rate: 35 pct	world rate: 15 pct 10 pct surtax 9 pct social contribution on net income	30 pct	30 pct
Minimum national income tax	1 pct	N/A	N/A	1.5 pct
Tax on payments to foreign beneficiaries				
Dividends:	35 pct in some cases	N/A	5 pct	30 pct in some cases
Interest:	15.05 pct	15 pct	17.5–35 pct	N/A
Royalties:	21–28 pct	25 pct	17.5–35 pct	30 pct
Technical assit:	21 pct	25 pct	17.5–35 pct	30 pct
VAT:	21 pct	18–21.95 pct	10 pct	23 pct
Other:	Max: 4.9 pct Provincial tax	Max: 5 pct Municipal tax	N/A	N/A

Source: PricewaterhouseCoopers *www.pwcglobal.com*

Table 5.5 Withholding tax rates on payments to US multinational corporations

	Dividends	**Interest**	**Fees/royalties**
Argentina	0–35 pct	15.05–35 pct	21–28–31.5 pct
Bolivia	12.5 pct	12.5 pct	12.5 pct
Brazil	0	15–25 pct	15–25 pct
Chile	20 pct	4–35 pct	20–30 pct
Paraguay	5 pct	17.5 pct	17.5 pct
Uruguay	30 pct*	0	30 pct*
Mexico	5–10 pct	4.9–15 pct	10 pct
Venezuela	0–5–15 pct	4.95–10 pct	5–10 pct

*soak-up tax

Source: PricewaterhouseCoopers *www.pwcglobal.com*

Rights and wrongs

It is in every nation's interests that shareholders have guaranteed rights in order to attract investment. Brazil's proposed new corporations bill would grant minority shareholders more powers and guarantee more transparency in communications between management and shareholders. The Brazilian Bank for Economic Development (BNDES) is lobbying for this reform and offers a financing programme for new corporations that use the proposed standards.[10] So it seems at least some segments of South America's business and political community understand the importance of clear rules on corporate governance that ensure good management and guarantee that dispute settlement awards are respected in order to create a friendlier climate to attract your investments. Each of the four Mercosur member nations' legal codes call for loyal, responsible managers of good conscience. (Argentine Law 19,550 articles 59 and 274; Brazilian Law 6404 article 158, subsection 1; Paraguayan Civil Code article 1111; and Uruguayan Civil Code article 391)

In instances where shareholders disagree with the board of directors, each country sets out specific steps they can take. In Brazil and Argentina, shareholders owning at least 5 per cent of outstanding shares who oppose a board decision can move to have the directors removed (Brazilian Law 6404 article 159; Argentine Law 19,550 article 275). Paraguay and Uruguay do not specify a minimum requirement for a shareholder vote to remove directors (Paraguayan Civil Code article 1114; Uruguayan Law 16,060 article 394). Laws governing mergers and acquisitions in Brazil require that the offer be equal for minority as well as majority shareholders and that the stock market commission (CNVI) may postpone a shareholders' meeting for 30 days to give stock owners time to consider the terms of the acquisition.

If your company is interested in taking part in a consortium it is important to be aware of shareholder guarantees like these. Some economists believe that Brazil's growing demand for energy which you will read about in the next chapter could lead to a proliferation of joint ventures operating on two or more national territories. Guillermo Ondarts, an expert in the area of duty-free zones, said he expects power generators to start investigating the possibilities of setting up plants in the tax-free industrial parks that dot the Argentine frontier along the Brazilian border to take advantage of the absence of import taxes to bring in the equipment necessary to transform natural gas or other sources of energy into cheaper power for Brazilian industry.[11] Brazil and Argentina signed an agreement on binational companies in July 1990 that allowed the creation of joint ventures with 80 per cent of their capital based in those two countries and a maximum of 20 per cent from third countries. Funds invested in the venture from either of the two nations cannot be less than 30 per cent capital participation of the total company. The firm can operate in any sector except those which are restricted constitutionally by Brazil to national companies or where a domestic controlling stake is required or where government procurement rules apply.

“Some rules remain in place in Brazil that are a source of frustration for some foreign companies and investors”

Some rules remain in place in Brazil that are a source of frustration for some foreign companies and investors, such as a section in Law 7078 that requires foreign companies to employ a Brazilian national as administrator. In Brazil, only partners can be administrators of a company, unlike Argentina or Uruguay where a third party can be named. Brazil has exempted Argentina from this requirement and is considering waiving the $100,000 domestic investment requirement it imposes on foreign firms setting up within its borders. All four Mercosur countries have comparable limited liability laws, although Brazil's statute has some cost advantages and less paperwork. If you are an executive based in Brazil you will not be held responsible for illegal acts by other board members but you are required by law to expressly state your dissenting opinion at the board meeting or at the next shareholders' meeting. In Argentina, it is not enough to vote against a motion or abstain because it isn't enough to indicate your opposition. You must explicitly state your opinion otherwise it will be assumed your silence was a tacit form of approval. This is because laws in Argentina, as well as Uruguay, contain the notion of solidarity of the executive team whereas Brazilian law does not.[12]

In recent years South American companies have increasingly issued American depository receipts (ADRs) on US equities markets to attract more foreign investors. ADRs are derivatives of shares already issued on the bourses of Sao Paulo, Buenos Aires, Santiago and other major markets. Argentina and Uruguay grant complete freedom to capital inflows and outflows while Paraguay's Civil Code does not explicitly recognize foreign capital. Only in extreme cases of difficulties in the balance of payments does Argentine and Uruguayan law permit temporary controls on capital flows. Brazil, however, requires foreign currencies to be registered and a proportion to be held by the Central Bank which uses the funds to help pay the public debt.[13]

Only Brazil's constitution allows a domestic company to benefit from temporary tax breaks in 'strategic' sectors or in the interests of national development. Since this principle is enshrined in the constitution it applies as much to the federal government as it does to state governments which have used this to their advantage to convince foreign manufacturers to choose Brazil rather than other South American countries. One example of this is Ford Motor Company's Brazilian unit which was offered $390 million in annual tax concessions from the northeastern state of Bahia in 1999 to set up an assembly plant there. Generally speaking, there are enough similarities in rules governing shareholder rights and the incorporation of a limited liability company that the Mercosur countries have managed to get away without a harmonized regional policy. However, lawyers warn that one fundamental difference between Brazil and its other Mercosur partners is that its constitution states domestic laws take precedence over foreign treaties while the other countries require their laws to conform with international commitments. This at times creates conflict between Brazil and its other partners which complain it changes their regional agreements after signing them, to which the Brazilians respond they are simply following the rules of the 1988 constitution.[14]

Once a final judgment is made in a commercial dispute, how can your business ensure that its award is in fact enforced? Enforcement depends on whether the country in which your company operates has ratified the United Nations Convention of New York of 1958 on the enforcement of arbitration awards. Brazil has not ratified the New York Convention but it has passed the Geneva Protocol of 1923 on arbitration clauses. According to Brazilian law firm Tozzini, Freire, Teixeira e Silva, that means that under the Brazilian system, the courts will conduct a limited review of a final decision of either a civil, commercial or penal suit but without re-examining the dispute's merits. The foreign court's ruling comes into effect in the Brazilian jurisdiction once it has been confirmed by the Federal Supreme Court. To ensure its award is enforced in Brazil, your business must have the ruling translated by a sworn-in translator into Portuguese and bring the final judgment to the Brazilian consulate nearest to the court handing down the judgment to have it authenticated. The foreign judgment, however, will not be enforced if it is contrary to Brazilian national sovereignty or public policy. These are the only aspects concerning the substance of the foreign judgment which Brazil's Federal Supreme Court looks into. If the foreign judgement is confirmed then the plaintiff has to file an action to ensure the ruling is enforced. Payment of a debt in foreign currency out of a confirmed foreign judgment must be made in Brazilian currency at the official exchange rate quoted on the date payment is made.

Brazil's Congress is discussing the adoption of international accounting standards in its new corporate law to help foreign investors better understand the local companies' financial statements. Several Brazil-based companies have already been considering adopting international accounting standards either because they've been acquired by foreign firms or they want to attract foreign funds.[15]

According to Argentine trade lawyer Carlos Alfaro, courts in Argentina will enforce foreign judgments without reviewing the merits of the case on four conditions. First, the decision had to be issued by a competent court, in other words one that had legitimate jurisdiction over the matter, and its ruling is final. Second, if those involved were served summons and given the opportunity to defend themselves. Third, if the ruling is valid in the jurisdiction where it was issued. And finally, if the decision is not contrary to a prior or simultaneous ruling by an Argentine court.[16]

Development policies

Brazil maintains a series of industrial development policies that assist in the financing of purchases, tax credits and accelerated depreciation. It provides financial support to the production of capital goods such as computer hardware and software, telecommunications equipment and public sector procurement, while other countries, such as Argentina, have virtually eliminated all of these incentives. Perhaps one of the biggest differences between Brazil and most of its neighbours is the subsidies and tax breaks some Brazilian state governments continue to offer in order to attract industry, particularly to car makers. The duty-free industrial zone in Manaus in Brazil's northern Amazon offers more incentives to manufacturers than the tax-free production area in the Argentine province of Tierra del Fuego at the tip of South America.[17]

Brazil is not alone in its state-driven model of economic development. Venezuela also advocates this path to foster greater industrial diversification but it is further behind Brazil and could prove to be a worthwhile investment opportunity for your company in the coming years, bearing in mind its current market and political particularities. 'We need to diversify the economy through indigenous industries that are open to the global economy and that are humane and sustainable as well as competitive,' said Venezuelan president Hugo Chavez. His government has targeted five sectors for development, some through public-private joint ventures, but Chavez said investors should not expect a wave of privatizations in his country.[18] The fact is that private sector investment in Venezuela has dropped off sharply in the past decade while public sector investment has grown to as much as 7 per cent of GDP in the high oil price years, from 1 per cent a decade ago. Consequently, lower overall investment in the economy has led to stagnation. More recently, Chavez has used tax breaks to encourage private sector investment in the economy.

Venezuela's problem is also its strength: oil. Crude accounts for 80 per cent of Venezuelan exports and represents 20–25 per cent of its real GDP, so you have an important sector of the economy that sets an artificially low exchange rate. Because of the disequilibrium between the oil and non-oil economy, Venezuela has maintained a high tariff barrier and at times has talked about setting up a macroeconomic stabilization fund to try to sterilize the massive inflow of foreign currencies. That is why, for example, a Toyota Camry costs $34,000 in Venezuela but the same car costs only $22,000 across the Caribbean Sea in the United States. The result is foreign investors have either chosen to enter in Venezuela's service sector or set up manufacturing plants under high tariffs. Venezuela was one of the last countries in South America to adopt import substitution policies in the 1970s, just as most of its neighbours were realizing that tack didn't work. So now it's one of the last to try to diversify its market by opening up its economy to the outside world but it isn't likely to go much further than selling 51 per cent stakes in public companies to foreign investors.

"The government passed its first natural gas law in 1999 to exploit Venezuela's huge reserves"

Chavez's five-point diversification plan starts with the energy sector. He wants to wean Venezuela off its oil dependence and shift to natural gas, hydroelectric power and alternative energies such wind power. The government passed its first natural gas law in 1999 to exploit Venezuela's huge reserves. Another area that offers development and investment potential is the mining sector, if Venezuela can provide sufficient guarantees on property rights. If it does, it has huge amounts of bauxite as well as nickel, gold and iron ore (Chapter Six goes into greater detail on South American reserves of commodities). To develop the energy and mining sectors means a more extensive infrastructure network, especially after the enormous damage wreaked on the country during the flash floods of December 1999. Venezuela's highways are generally in good shape but there are not enough roads. Plans are afoot to add to the country's transportation network and they are described in more detail in Chapter Seven. The underdevelopment of Venezuela's natural resources and the regions where they are concentrated explains part of the political turmoil the country has seen in recent decades, although there is no denying Chavez's assertions that 40 years of government corruption have squandered many opportunities as well. The other two sectors Chavez wants to nurture have a large service component: tourism, and small to mid-sized business development following Bolivia's pioneering work in microfinance.

Microcredit is a two-decades-old financing system first developed by the Grameen Bank in Bengladesh. The idea is to make very small loans, of between \$100 and \$500 and up to \$1,000, to borrowers who have no collateral or credit to offer as security. A group of borrowers vouch for each other for an initial loan which could be as little as \$50 (or \$1 in the case of the original Bengladeshi villagers who benefited from the programme) on a promise to repay. If one member of the group doesn't repay, then all the others assume the debt.

Development workers in La Paz, Bolivia have said the delinquency rate on microloans in Bolivia has been less than 3 per cent compared with 5 per cent at most retail banks in the developed world.[19] Microcredit has spread throughout South America from countries with some of the lowest per capita incomes like Bolivia to those with the highest like Argentina. What the proliferation of microfinance means for the poorest of the region's people is access to an alternative form of leveraged financing. 'Microfinance isn't the solution to poverty but it's an effective tool in the fight against poverty. We've had people come from all over the world to look at the Bolivian experience,' a US diplomat said.

Bolivia is one of the western hemisphere's poorest nations with an average annual per capita income of \$1,000 and an infant mortality rate of 69 per thousand live births, almost double the average of Latin America and the Caribbean. While microfinance is not a driver behind growth in South America's middle class, it is lifting the poverty floor in one of the continent's poorest nations. For the Aymara Indian 'cholas', or peasant women, lining up at Banco Sol (*www.bancosol.com.bo*) in central La Paz, these \$50 loans represent a significant source of investment capital either to build up inventories for their street shops or to buy new machinery. 'No doubt Bolivia has one of the best microfinance systems in the world. It's not perfect, but it's very good and it's run by banks and NGOs (non-governmental organizations). Many people in rural areas are participating in microfinance to purchase working capital like a $50 sewing machine, which may not seem like much but it's a key investment for people on the Altiplano making textiles,' said the International Monetary Fund's representative in Bolivia, Eliahu Kreis, who estimated that 30 per cent of Bolivia's 8 million people earn less than $200 a year.[20] Eventually some of these borrowers will graduate to the traditional financial system which means an expansion of the economy, a potential new customer for your retail bank or consumer for your goods and services as well as an improvement in the standard of living of some of these countries' poorest people. Microfinance is one reason why Bolivian bank deposits are among the highest in South America, equal to about 50 per cent of the nation's annual gross domestic product. Deposits had grown to $4 billion in 2000 from $900 million in 1990, according to the then Bolivian finance minister Ronald MacLean.[21] Considering one in three of South America's 346 million people earn $2 or less each day, microcredit could be a boon to nurturing greater income for the lowest wage earners in the region.

What you have seen in this chapter is how development policies under way in the largest, mid-sized and smaller regional economies could affect the marketplaces in which you are operating, creating future investment and/or business opportunities for you. Changes in recent years in most South American nations' labour laws have brought their labour market conditions closer to North America's from what was more comparable to Western Europe or Japan. Now tax reform appears to be the highest priority for multinationals doing business in the region. The substance of recent legal reforms has contributed to making South America a more attractive environment for foreign direct investment in the form of mergers and acquisitions (see Table 5.6).

Table 5.6 Cross-border M&A sales and purchases, by region, 1990–1999 (in billions of dollars)

	Sales					Purchases				
Economy	**1990**	**1995**	**1997**	**1998**	**1999**	**1990**	**1995**	**1997**	**1998**	**1999**
Developed										
E.U.	62.1	75.1	114.6	187.9	344.5	86.5	81.4	142.1	284.4	497.7
US	54.7	53.2	81.7	209.5	233.0	27.6	57.3	80.9	137.4	112.4
Japan	0.1	0.5	3.1	4.0	15.9	14	3.9	2.7	1.3	9.8
Developing										
Latin America	11.5	8.6	41.1	63.9	37.2	1.6	4.0	10.7	12.6	24.9
Asia	4.1	6.9	21.3	16.1	25.3	5.4	8.8	21.7	6.4	15.9
Cen/East Europe	0.3	6.0	5.8	5.1	10.3	–	0.1	0.3	1.0	1.6
Africa	0.5	0.2	1.7	0.7	0.6	–	0.1	–	0.2	0.4
Unspecified	4.0	0.1	–	0.7	1.8	0.3	–	0.1	–	–
World	150.6	186.6	304.8	531.6	720.1	150.6	186.6	304.8	531.6	720.1

Source: UNCTAD, World Investment Report 2000 *www.unctad.org*

Notes

[1]Smith, Mark, US Chamber of Commerce, Latin America and Caribbean section, interview in Washington, D.C., 12 January 2001.

[2]Hill, Alan, executive vice president of development, Barrick Gold Corp., *www.barrick.com,* phone interview to Toronto, 16 March 2001.

[3]Gonzalez Anaya, Jose Antonio, 'Labour market flexibility in thirteen Latin American countries and the United States – revisiting and expanding Okun coefficients,' World Bank, Latin American and Caribbean Studies, 1999.

[4]Porcaro, Daniel and Rosenbaum, Jorge, PricewaterhouseCoopers Uruguay, presentation to the 'Doing business between Mercosur and the United States' seminar in Montevideo, 26 September 2000.

[5]Graca Lima, Jose Alfredo, undersecretary of trade and commercial affairs for Brazil, phone interview to Brasilia, 9 March 2001.

[6]Porcaro, Daniel, *op. cit.*

[7]Cavallo, Domingo, economy minister of Argentina, press briefing in Buenos Aires, 21 March 2001.

[8]Brazilian law firm Tozzini, Freire, Teixeira e Silva, *www.tozzini.com.br,* briefing note, 15 February 2001.

[9]Alfaro, Carlos, *cealfaro@alfarolaw.com*, founder of the Alfaro-Abogados law firm and partner in the Mercosur Alliance of Law Firms: Alfaro Navarro-Tozzini, Freire, Teixeira e Silva, *www.tozzini.com.br*, briefing note, 15 February 2001.

[10]Tozzini, Freire, Teixeira e Silva, *op. cit.*

[11]Ondarts, Guillermo, economist and duty-free zone specialist, interview in Buenos Aires, 27 March 2001.

[12]Rossi, Hugo, commercial law enforcement division of Argentina's Justice Ministry, interview in Buenos Aires, Argentina, 2 August 2000.

[13]Fundacion Capital (1999), Convergencia Macroeconomica en el Mercosur: 'Un camino critico,' page 129.

[14]Alfaro, Carlos, *op. cit.*

[15]Tozzini, Freire, Teixeira e Silva, *op. cit.*

[16]Alfaro, Carlos, *cealfaro@alfarolaw.com*, founder of Alfaro-Abogados law firm and partner in the Mercosur Alliance of Law Firms: Alfaro Navarro-Tozzini, Freire, Teixeira e Silva, *www.tozzini.com.br*, briefing note, 15 February 2001.

[17]Fundacion Capital (1999), Convergencia Macroeconomica en el Mercosur: 'Un camino critico', pp. 175–180.

[18]Chavez, Hugo, interview in Puerto Ordaz, 20 January 2001.

[19]US Agency for International Development, interview in La Paz, 10 October 2000.

[20]Kreis, Eliahu, International Monetary Fund representative in Bolivia, interview in La Paz, 9 October 2000.

[21]MacLean, Ronald, Bolivian finance minister, interview in La Paz, 6 October 2000.

6

A commodity cornucopia

A quarter of the planet's cattle herd feeds off the grasslands of Brazil, Argentina, Paraguay and Uruguay. Venezuela has the largest reserves of oil outside the Middle East and is the third-largest producer in the world. Chile is the largest producer of copper on the planet and Bolivia has vast reserves of natural gas. South America's wealth in raw commodities is staggering. But, as grain traders often like to say, grain is 90 per cent politics and 10 per cent agriculture. Food alone accounts for about half of annual global economic output and the South Americans are major suppliers of soybeans, corn, beef, sugar, coffee, bananas, cocoa and citrus fruits, to name a few.

'If trade liberalization in agriculture went through it would triple all the ODA (overseas development assistance) received in developing countries. One minister in a developing country that imports argued that perhaps the agriculture industry was not as strong because its imports are cheaper because of subsidies. There is still the traditional resistance from Europe, Japan and the Scandinavian countries versus the Cairns Group. There will be no conclusion to a new (WTO Millenium) Round, given there's a beginning, if there's no substantial movement in agriculture,' said World Trade Organization secretary general Mike Moore.[1]

Brazil, Argentina, Uruguay, Paraguay and Bolivia are all members of the 18-nation Cairns Group which submitted a proposal to the WTO in November 2000 explaining that their liberalized agriculture sectors cannot compete in distorted world markets against 'heavily and unfairly subsidized producers in other countries'. An OECD study in June 2000 found European Union subsidies to farmers were equal to 49 per cent of gross farm receipts while the US Export Enhancement Program accounted for 24 per cent of gross farm receipts, up from 14 per cent in 1997 despite US moves to deregulate its farm sector in the mid-1990s. Whether these governments are negotiating their trade position within the Free Trade Area of the Americas or a free trade zone with the European Union, you can be certain demands for concessions in agriculture will be high on their list of priorities. The developed world has put off substantial farm reforms for a long time and the number of bargaining chips it can offer in its stead are dwindling, so it seems likely that sooner rather than later you will be eating food that came from South America. This chapter isn't just about food but about the raw materials that are produced here for consumption worldwide, from energy and farm products to metals and minerals. Your company is likely to use at least one of these commodities in the goods and services it provides and this chapter tries to predict the trends in those sectors.

South America's power paradox

There is no doubt that South America has huge reserves of crude oil, natural gas and some of the largest hydroelectric dams in the world, but power outages are still common on this continent. The reason is that there are few cross-country power grid connections. Brazil is especially aware of this problem as its power supply is not able to keep up with domestic demand and this was one of the main drivers behind the first summit of South American presidents in Brasilia at the end of August 2000. The leaders met to consider studies prepared by the Inter-American Development Bank (IADB – *www.iadb.org*), the Andean Development Corporation (CAF – *www.caf.com*) and Fondo Financiero para el Desarrollo de la Cuenca del Plata (Financial Fund for the Development of the River Plate Basin, Fonplata – *www.fonplata.org*) on the construction of infrastructure projects, energy transport grids and telecommunications connections on a continental scale. Chapter Seven will look at the planned projects in greater detail. Venezuela, the largest supplier of oil to the United States, has gone from being a quota buster to an Opec (Organization of Petroleum Exporting Countries) enthusiast under the presidency of Hugo Chavez. 'For now, at this time, we believe $25 a barrel is a fair price for the world market. At a price of $30 today, speaking in terms of today's prices, that's equivalent to $7 in 1980 according to Opec figures. We have to explore for new reserves and a price of $10 a barrel doesn't allow us to do that exploration,' said Chavez.[2] After kicking out foreign petroleum companies 20 years ago, South American governments are trying to woo those operators back to the region in order to import their advanced technologies and technical know-how. These governments want to develop the use of natural gas domestically in order to continue exporting oil, a key earner of foreign reserves and a major factor in the balance of payments for countries like Venezuela, Colombia and Ecuador. Venezuela has succeeded in bringing in Conoco and BP Amoco to develop its heavy crude reserves in the past 10 years and Brazil is beginning to follow in its footsteps to develop what might be large off-shore oil reserves.

South America could be divided into three power regions: the north, which has huge amounts of energy, the south, which is more or less able to meet its own needs and in some cases export some energy, and Brazil, a power market equal to that of all the other South American markets combined but where domestic demand is outpacing supply.

In the north, Venezuela is the major producer and exporter of crude oil to a world market that consumed about 76 million barrels per day in 2000. Colombia is a significant producer as well after the discovery of a huge field about a decade ago. You will hear analysts talk about Colombia and its state-owned exploitation firm, Ecopetrol, as a shining example of bringing in foreign oil companies to develop the resource. But everyone agrees that the ongoing, four-decades-old civil war is a major impediment to increasing production, with existing pipelines being blown up by rebel forces on a regular basis. Ecuador also exports a significant amount of oil and should double that quantity once its second export pipeline, with a capacity of 450,000 barrels per day, comes on stream. Natural gas output, however, has not yet been as significant a factor in this region. Trinidad is a significant exporter of natural gas while Venezuela could be, but it has long opted to develop its oil reserves because that has been easier to do. Energy analysts believe the reserves of natural gas in Venezuela's Cristobal Colombo patch near Trinidad may be huge and that the country's total reserves could be as much as 142.5 trillion cubic feet[3], but there are differences in opinion on the economic viability at this time of extracting the energy source from Cristobal Colombo.

The former Dutch colony now known as Suriname, sandwiched between Venezuela and Brazil, planned to hold its first ever auction of seven oil exploration licences in November 2001. State oil company Staatsolie plans to offer six near-shore licences and one onshore licence that will remain open until May 2002. There has also been talk of building a liquified natural gas (LNG) pipeline linking northern and southern South America, but some analysts believe crossing the massive and dense Amazon means that project is not realistic. Trinidad is one of the world's biggest exporters of natural gas, with Repsol-YPF, Cabot, British Gas, and BP Amoco acting as the main operators. The use of LNG makes transport economically viable because in liquid form natural gas takes up one six-hundredth of the space that it does as a gas. Some industry experts say we are more likely to see an LNG pipeline between Venezuela and the state of Florida because the Caribbean Sea is very shallow and it would be a much easier infrastructure project to execute than a southbound pipeline through Brazil. As far as the oil sector is concerned, Venezuela, Colombia and Ecuador have traditionally been more tied to the United States market than to those of their southern neighbours. (Map 6.1.)

“After kicking out foreign petroleum companies 20 years ago, South American governments are trying to woo those operators back to the region in order to import their advanced technologies and technical know-how”

Venezuela also operates 'El Guri', the second-largest hydroelectric dam in the world, along the Necuima Canyon, which has an installed capacity of 10,000 megawatts and supplies about three-quarters of the nation's electricity needs as well as exporting power to the Brazilian

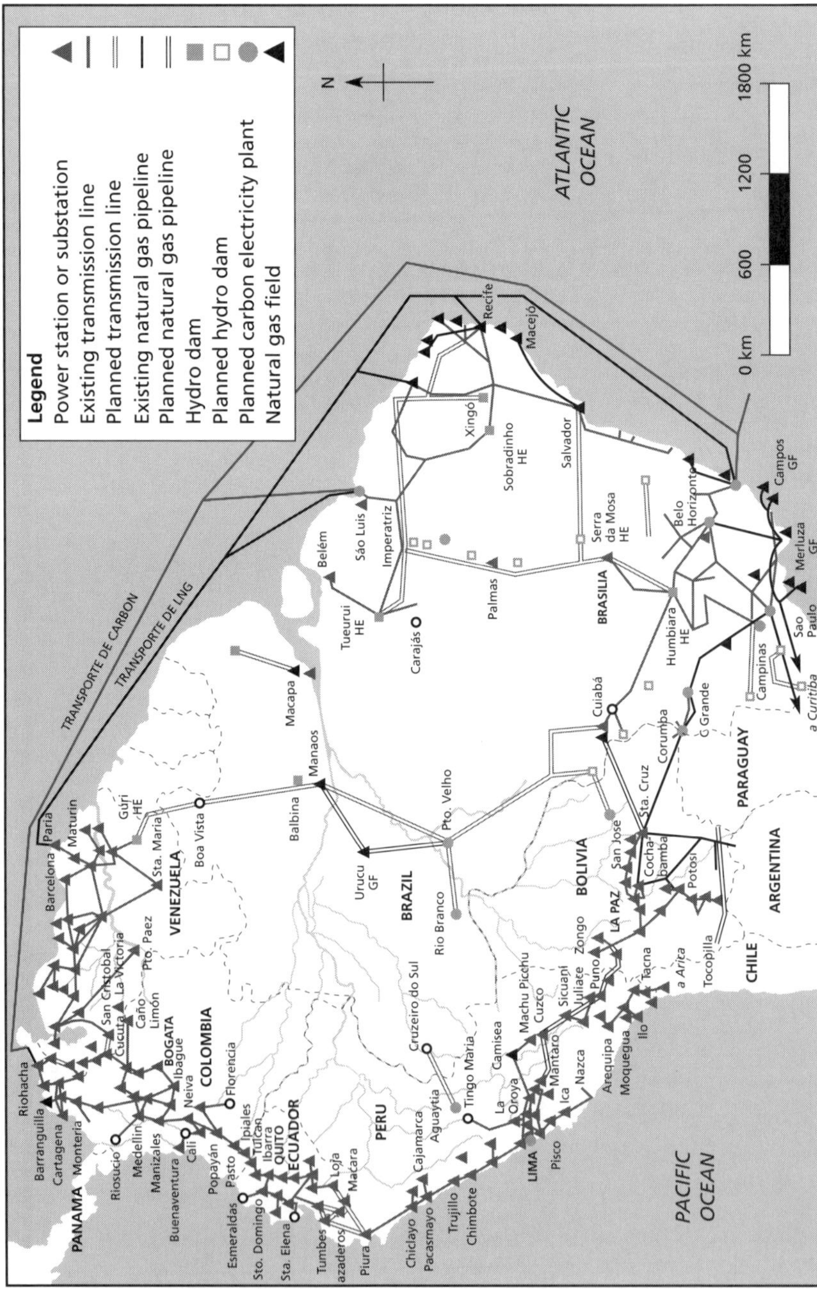

Map 6.1 Energy Integration Projects between Andean Nations and Brazil

Source: Andean Development Corporation

city of Boa Vista in the northwest. The only other dam on the planet that has a larger installed capacity is Itaipu along the Brazil-Paraguay border, at 12,600 megawatts (see Table 6.1). As you can see, South America has the power it needs, but it does not necessarily have the grids to carry it from the point of generation to the point of consumption. That is a major concern for governments and industry – Chapter Seven describes the plans to remedy the problem. Originally, the Itaipu binational power generator was mandated to supply electricity to both Brazil and Paraguay but it now transmits entirely to power-hungry Brazil. Analysts believe Venezuela could build eight more hydroelectric dams of comparable sizes to El Guri so that between oil, water and gas this nation would be a significant player in power markets for the foreseeable future. (Map 6.2)

Table 6.1 The world's top 10 hydroelectric dams

	Country(ies)	**Installed capacity (MW)**
1. Itaipu	Brazil/Paraguay	12,600
2. El Guri (Raul Leoni)	Venezuela	10,000
3. Sayano-Shushensk	CIS	6,400
4. Grand Coulee	USA	6,180
5. Krasnoyarsk	CIS	6,000
6. Churchill Falls	Canada	5,428
7. La Grande 2	Canada	5,328
8. Bratsk	CIS	4,500
9. Ust-Ilim	CIS	4,300
10. Tucuri	Brazil (under construction)	3,960

Source: CVG Edelca (Venezuela)

The south of the continent is composed of net importers and net exporters of energy. Among the major net importers are Brazil, Uruguay and Chile while the net exporters consist of Argentina and Bolivia. The bulk of Brazilian power import demand is concentrated in the south where most of its industrial base is concentrated, especially in Sao Paulo state. Since Argentina is only a relatively small net exporter of oil, the focus of increased energy output in this region is natural gas. In fact, the natural gas pipeline linking Santa Cruz de la Sierra, Bolivia to Sao Paulo, Brazil is the biggest energy project in Latin American history and the third-largest natural gas pipline in the

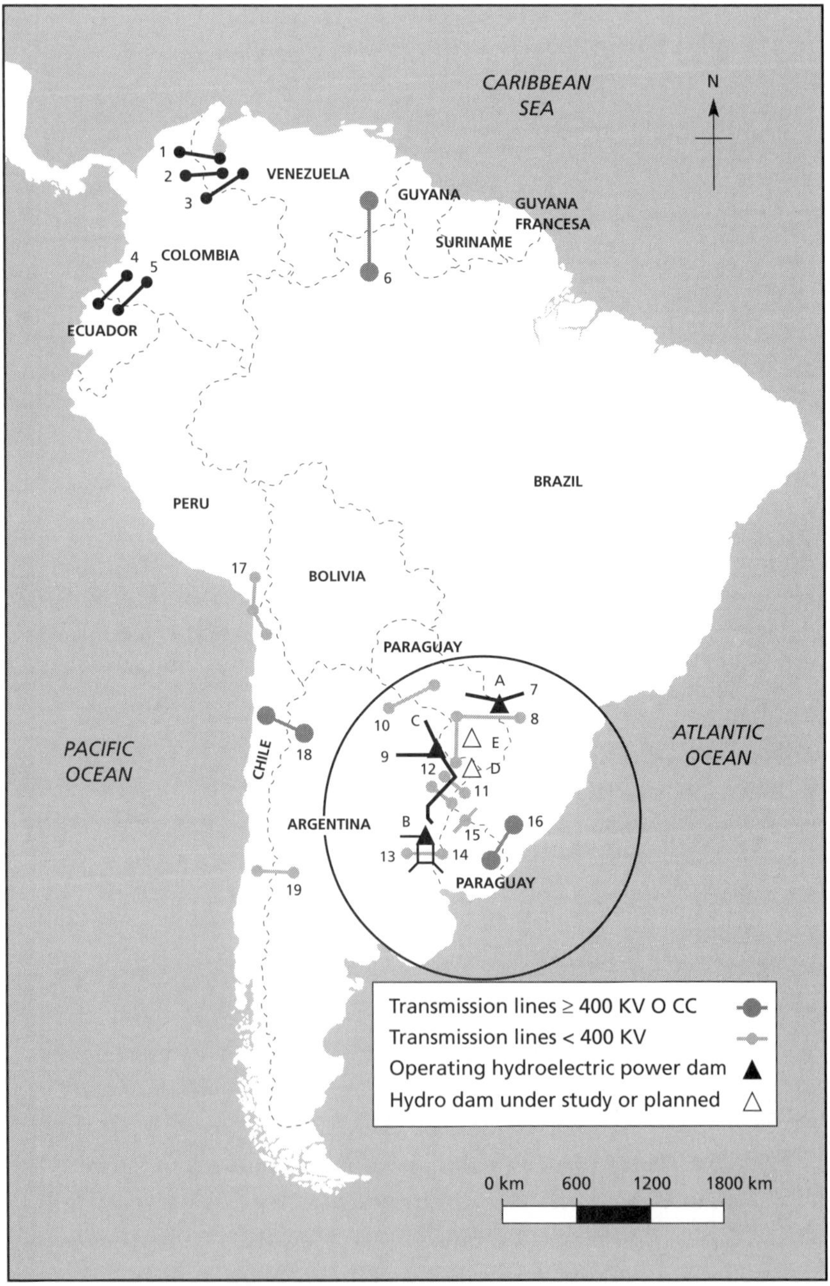

Map 6.2 Main Power Generation Stations and Interconnections

Source: Andean Development Corporation

world. But as Table 6.2 shows, Argentina's Neuquen basin is the key to regional natural gas output. Known as the 'West Texas' of Argentina for its rich oil and gas reserves, Neuquen province is deep in southern Patagonia along the Andes which separate this country from Chile. The natural gas loop links Argentina's main petrochemical centre, Bahia Blanca, to the Chilean capital, Santiago, on to the Bolivian high plains around La Paz, then over to Brasilia and back down to Buenos Aires through Uruguay, which is positioning itself as the regional storage centre of natural gas for both Buenos Aires and southern Brazil. Construction of a key section of the loop, the $170 million Cruz del Sur natural gas pipeline running underneath the Rio de la Plata to link Argentina to Uruguay, began in March 2001.

"There has been intermittent talk of connecting Peru's Camisea natural gas field to the Bolivian leg of the loop but development of the remote patch has been a non-starter for years"

Table 6.2 South American natural gas reserves, demand and production estimates in 1998 (trillions of cubic feet)

	Reserves	Demand	Production
Argentina	24.1	1.08	1.05
Bolivia	4.3	0.04	0.11
Brazil	8.0	0.20	0.20
Colombia	6.9	0.25	0.25
Chile	3.5	0.11	0.07
Ecuador	3.7	0.004	0.05
Peru	7.1	0.02	0.02
Venezuela	142.5	0.99	0.99
Total:	200.1	2.694	2.74

Source: Andean Development Corporation report on integration routes, August 2000

There has been intermittent talk of connecting Peru's Camisea natural gas field to the Bolivian leg of the loop but development of the remote patch has been a non-starter for years. There are other resource alternatives that are more easily accessible and cheaper to extract that are likely to be developed before work begins in earnest on Camisea. Uruguay's construction of a natural gas storage facility is the key to the Southern Cone loop because producers ideally prefer to pump a consistent amount of gas and store excess supply during the austral summer for use during the winter months. Chile is overwhelmingly dependent on Argentina to meet its oil and natural gas needs. But in recent years Chile has moved to diversify its imports by bringing in oil from Ecuador and Colombia. This has had limited success which also underscores the relative underdevelopment of South America's Pacific ports versus its Atlantic ports and the fact that Colombia's export outlets are concentrated along the Caribbean Sea. The Mercosur countries alone (Argentina, Brazil, Paraguay and Uruguay) account for nine of South America's 19 major international electricity connections that are either in operation, under construction or due to be built (see Table 6.3).

Table 6.3 Major South American international electricity connections

Countries	Location	Tension	Potential	Status
Colombia-Venezuela	Cuetecita-Cuatricentenario	230 KV	150 MW	In operation
Colombia-Venezuela	Tibu-La Fria	115 KV	80 MW	In operation
Colombia-Venezuela	San Mateo-Corozo	230 KV	150 MW	In operation
Colombia-Ecuador	Ipiales-Tulcan/Ibarra	115/138 KV	40/113 MW	In operation
Colombia-Ecuador	Pasto-Quito	230 KV	100 MW	Planned
Brazil-Venezuela	Boa Vista-El Guri	230/400 KV	60/200 MW	In progress
Brazil-Paraguay	Itaipu	220/750 CC	630 MW	In operation
Brazil-Paraguay	Acaray-Foz de Iguazu	132 KV	70 MW	In operation
Argentina-Paraguay	Yacyreta	500/220 KV	800/130 MW	In operation
Argentina-Paraguay	Clorinda-Guarambare	132/220 KV	80 MW	In operation
Argentina-Brazil	Rincon S.M.-Garabi	500 KV	1000 MW	Being built
Argentina-Brazil	Paso de los Libres-Uruguaiana	132/230 KV	50 MW	In operation
Argentina-Uruguay	Anillo de Central Salto Grande	500 KV	1000 MW	In operation
Argentina-Uruguay	Paysandu-Concepcion	150/132 KV	100 MW	In operation
Brazil-Uruguay	Rivera-Livramento	150/230 KV	70 MW	In progress
Brazil-Uruguay	San Carlos-Puente Medici	500 KV or CC	300 MW	Planned
Chile-Peru	Arica-Tacna	66 KV	10 MW	planned
Argentina-Chile	Guemes-Antofagasta	330 KV	200/600 MW	Being built
Argentina-Chile	Mendoza-Santiago	220 KV	150/200 MW	Planned

Source: Andean Development Corporation report on integration routes, August 2000

CASE STUDY

Canadian Hunter International

Founded in 1973, natural gas exploration and exploitation firm Canadian Hunter discovered North America's third-largest gas field the following year. A decade later the fledgling company had become one of Canada's largest gas producers and in 1997 it overhauled its corporate strategy and decided to expand overseas. 'We were looking for regions with ample hydrocarbons, a stable fiscal regime, a stable government and a good legal system,' said George Hart, vice president of international finance at Canadian Hunter International Ltd.[4] 'Russia has ample hydrocarbons but the fiscal regime was not stable, the government wasn't so stable either, and the legal system was a question mark, so we chose the Southern Cone of South America and opened our first office in Argentina in mid-1998.' Canadian Hunter now owns a 23.5 per cent stake in the Sierra Chata and Chihuidos blocks of the northern Neuquen basin in southern Argentina from where it exports natural gas and gas liquids to Chile and Brazil. 'We see Brazil as a big energy hole. Brazil uses natural gas for 3 per cent of its energy needs and we expect it to grow to 10 per cent in 10 years,' Hart added.

Fourth-quarter profits nearly quadrupled in 2000 thanks to surging natural gas prices in North America, in part due to high power generation demand in California. Some analysts believe there are parallels between Brazil's pressing need for energy and California's power crisis. 'What does Brazil need? Electrons or molecules? My guess is a bit of both, so the way to move electrons is with more power transmission lines,' said Hart. The gas company has earmarked $10 million to develop its assets in the Neuquen basin in 2001. Annual natural gas production was expected to grow 14 per cent in 2001 and breaks down as shown in Table 6.4.

Table 6.4 Annual natural gas production

	Canada	Argentina	Total
Natural gas (mmcf per day)	460	30	490
Natural gas liquids (bbls per day)	8,800	165	8,965
Oil (bbls per day)	1,200	0	1,200
Barrel of oil equivalent (6:1)	86,820	5,175	91,995
Barrel of oil equivalent (10:1)	56,000	3,165	59,165

Source: Canadian Hunter (*www.chel.com*)

This production increase forecast was based on internally generated exploration and development prospects. The company was studying other foreign markets in 2001 for its expansion. But executives said they were happy with their first overseas foray. 'We're pleased with the asset but clearly the country (Argentina) is struggling to get out of recession. But it's stable and I don't see it reverting to the days of hyperinflation and military dictatorships,' Hart said. 'It's very, very bureaucratic, like any other Latin American country, but that's just a cost of doing business.' Royalties in 2001 were expected to be 12 per cent in Argentina and operating costs were forecast to be $0.24 per million cubic feet in Argentina. 'We haven't had any problems to date in repatriating funds,' Hart said.

Brazil power struggle

Brazil has long been fighting a losing battle to import less energy. Growth in the country's power demand over the next 15 years is forecast to double or maybe even triple with annual increases in demand ranging between 3.3 and 5.9 per cent. Brazil's ability to keep supply from being rapidly outpaced by this growth in power needs will depend on whether it continues to open the sector to private operators and apply market-based regulations, but either way it will definitely continue to be a net importer, as power rationing that began in June 2001 in the country's most populous and industrialized regions underscores. Potential investors will need to be assured there will be sufficient return on investment in building additional generation capacity and that the national infrastructure is being diversified to include an expanded use of natural gas rather than the traditional heavy reliance on hydroelectric power. Brazil's power market is not as competitive as it could be due to delays in privatizing Electrobras' generation plants and eliminating residual monopolies in the natural gas supply chain.

While Brazil wrestles with developing and perhaps liberalizing its land-based power generation and transportation system it has also been pursuing the development of its off-shore oil reserves. The challenge is that the Campos Basin some 70 miles (120 kilometres) off the shore of Rio de Janeiro state is the deepest oil field in the world. The state-owned exploitation company Petrobras has become one of the best deep-water oil drillers in the world as a consequence, but extraction would probably proceed faster with outside help, which is why Brazil tendered for bids for oil exploration licences on 23 blocks in June 2000. Although the potential reserves of the Campos Basin mean Brazil could produce twice as much oil in 10 years from the 1.24 million barrels per day produced now, analysts believe the world's ninth largest economy will always be a net importer. Brazil has proven oil reserves of 7 billion barrels to supply the needs of its 172.9 million people. There are 17 billion barrels of proven and probable oil and gas reserves. Of its 29 sedimentary basins covering 5.7 million square kilometres – an area more than twice the size of Argentina – about 42.5 per cent of that territory is offshore and at depths of as much as 3.2 kilometres below sea level.

“The urgency in meeting Brazil's growing energy needs has spurred some important changes in its energy sector in recent years”

The urgency in meeting Brazil's growing energy needs has spurred some important changes in its energy sector in recent years. Brazil created Petrobras in 1953 and gave it a monopoly under the nationalist slogan 'The Oil is Ours' until it amended the constitution in 1995. Two years later it created the National Petroleum Agency (ANP) which came into being in 1998 with the mandate of deregulating the sector. The ANP drew up concession contracts and granted Petrobras 397 blocks, of which the state-owned company lined up 32 potential joint ventures for exploration and development. Petrobras returned 28 of those blocks to the ANP in 1999, of which only 12 were converted into relatively minor joint ventures. So the regulator held its first oil licensing round and sold 12 of 27 blocks. A second round was held in June 2000 when 23 blocks were put up for sale.

Taking a step back to see the bigger picture, you will notice that global energy sourcing has gone from solid to liquid and is on its way to relying more on gas. A century and a half ago wood accounted for 90 per cent of world energy use before being surpassed by coal in the 1890s. Coal remained the dominant source of world energy until the 1960s when petroleum displaced it. Now oil accounts for 32 per cent of world energy use and natural gas has climbed rapidly to 22 per cent, edging out coal which has fallen off to 21 per cent. In regional terms, this trend has manifested itself even more dramatically. Central and South America have raised their use of natural gas by 58 per cent in the past decade, with Argentina and Venezuela accounting for the greatest increases in the use of the 'cleanest' fossil fuel. By cleanest, experts explain that natural gas has four hydrogen molecules to every one molecule of carbon, compared with two-to-one for oil.[5] Now serious investments are being undertaken in alternative energy sources. Spanish energy firms Endesa and Elecnor unveiled plans to invest $2.25 billion to create wind parks in Argentina's southern Patagonia region over the next decade through a newly created joint venture, Energias Argentinas S.A. (Enarsa). The first tranche of the project was a $300 million investment to develop wind parks and electrical infrastructure in the windswept southern provinces of Neuquen, Chubut and Rio Negro.

'We must develop other sources of energy, be they solar or wind. It appears on the surface that this is against Venezuela's interests but it isn't. We want to contribute to world development. We proposed to Opec that we establish a budget to study alternative energy sources. Alternative energy sources and the preservation of the environment are in the world's interests and in Venezuela's interests,' said Venezuelan president Hugo Chavez.[6]

But Venezuela is also ensuring its role as a regional supplier of power by offering neighbouring countries in Central America, the Caribbean as well as Suriname and faraway Paraguay oil at a discount from market prices. Once world prices pass a certain varying threshold the balance is converted into debt which those countries do not have to begin repaying until one or two years later and at an interest rate of about 2 per cent. Cuba offered to repay in goods and services and now there are weekly flights from Caracas to Havana carrying Venezuelans to and from Cuban hospitals where they are treated for ailments their own country is either not yet equipped to handle or lacks the capacity to address within a reasonable period of time.[7] Guyana asked late in December 2000 if it could join that energy pact after it accused Venezuela of failing to include it in the deal because of Venezuela's claim over Guyana's mineral-rich Essequibo region.

A growing role in feeding the world

Of all the regions in the world, South America is among those that rely the least on irrigation for the substantial production of food. Agriculture traders like Cargill are well established in South America. You can expect that the volume of food coming from this part of the world will increase in a meaningful way given the recent and rising use of genetically altered crops and fertilizers. In fact, the world's largest pelletized urea fertilizer plant began production in Bahia Blanca, Argentina, early in 2001. Until the Profertil factory started production the Argentines had to import that kind of fertilizer. Now the joint venture between Spain's Repsol-YPF and Canada's Agrium Inc. will produce an average 1.1 million tonnes of pelletized urea each year – it had already exported shiploads of urea to the United States, Brazil and Uruguay within its first two months of operation.

But there are environmental developments that could threaten attempts to raise output here by sapping water from the equation. Scientists may disagree on how much the global climate is warming but they admit temperatures are rising. This is likely to mean greater desertification in the equatorial zones of the planet. South America may be less affected by this process than other regions if logging and forest-clearing practices are reduced in the world's largest jungle. The Amazon rain forest acts as a continental water conduit in the following manner. Trade winds push rain clouds into the Amazon River valley where 75 per cent of rainfall returns to the atmosphere in the form of evaporation while 25 per cent runs off into the river and its tributaries. The cycle sustains itself deep into the Amazon until the rainclouds reach the Andes and then winds divert them southbound into the Argentine pampas where some of the richest farmland in the world can be found. Significant logging and clear cutting could turn this process on its head, with 75 per cent of rainfall at the mouth of the Amazon escaping as runoff and only 25 per cent evaporating and being carried further inland.[8] One of the advantages Argentina and Brazil have is both have a fair amount of water compared to countries in Asia, the Middle East and Africa. Water scarcity is crossing international borders via the world grain trade which is why North Africa and the Middle East are the fastest-growing grain import markets. As populations grow, they divert water from irrigation and import grain because it's the most efficient way to import water. One tonne of wheat is equal to 1,000 tonnes of water. In 2000 the grain imports to that region were equal to the annual flow of the Nile River.

If things are managed right, South America could become an increasingly important supplier of food to the world because of the population to land ratio thanks to their water, if they can stabilize their population growth,' said Lester Brown, then chairman of Washington-based environmental agency Worldwatch Institute.

Soybeans are a prime example of a water-intensive crop in global demand that South America produces in vast quantities. The United States is the world's largest producer of soybeans, an oilseed used for humans and animal feed, followed by Brazil and Argentina. Soybeans account for half of world use of vegetable oils and South America has room to grow its output of that oilseed either through crop substitution or boosting yields. The problem in these two countries isn't so much production as processing. Soybean crushers like US-based Cargill or Norway's Denofa cut operations in Brazil because of low crushing industry profit margins in 2000. The economics of oilseed crushing are complex in any part of the world and profit margins can be razor thin, but the Brazilian market adds its byzantine tax system to the equation as well. A law passed in 1995 added a 12 per cent tax (ICMS) on the movement of processed soy across state lines. Consequently, soymeal exports fell to 9.4 million tonnes in 2000 from 11.56 million tonnes in 1999 while soybean exports rose to 11.3 million tonnes from 3.49 million tonnes over the same period, according to Brazil's Association of Vegetable Oils Industries (Abiove). The US Department of Agriculture estimated Brazil and Argentina would produce record soybean harvests in the 2000/2001 crop year of almost 60 million tonnes and exports of about 17 million tonnes. How much of future exports will be raw materials versus processed oil and meal is up to local policymakers.

Like soybeans, corn in Argentina and Brazil has little to no more room to grow so significant production increases will depend on boosting yields. Corn is a major multipurpose commodity traded worldwide and used in everything from soft drinks to animal feed to consumer products. The United States, Argentina and Brazil rank as the top three producers of this crop (see Table 6.5) and corn is the product most likely to gain or lose ground to soybeans when producers make their seeding decisions in South America. 1996 was a watershed year for Argentina when it started seeding genetically modified soybeans and corn over a significant amount of acreage as well as using fertilizers in a concerted effort to raise production. Soybean output rose to 23 million tonnes in 2000/2001 from 10 million tonnes in 1996/1997 while corn production grew to 15.5 million tonnes in 1996/1997 from 5 million tonnes in 1988/1989. Argentina's share of world soybean production reached 13 per cent in crop year 2000/2001 from 5 per cent in 1982/1983 while Brazil has seen only an incremental rise in the same period to 18 per cent from 16 per cent. The US share of global output, however, has declined to 49 per cent from 64 per cent in the same time frame.[9]

Significant supplies of fertilizers can now be obtained from both the south and north of the continent. In eastern Venezuela, the world's largest nitrogen-based fertilizer plant started shipping refrigerated ammonia to the United States in February 2001. Fertinitro, a joint venture between Petroleos de Venezuela, US-based Koch Industries, state petrochemical firm Pequiven, Italy's ENI SpA unit Snamprogetti and Venezuela's Polar, has an annual production capacity of 1.3 million tonnes of ammonium and 1.5 million tonnes of urea. For a snapshot of South American crop prospects and food supply, you can call up the United Nations Food and Agriculture Organization website at *www.fao.org/giews*.

Table 6.5 World corn exporters and importers in crop year 2000/2001

Exporters	**Millions of tonnes for export**
United States of America	57.0
Argentina	8.5
China	4.0
Importers	**Millions of tonnes for import**
Brazil	1.3
Chile	1.3

Source: United States Department of Agriculture 2000/2001 estimates issued December 2000

Argentina is among the leading wheat exporters in the world (see Table 6.6) and its proximity to Brazil, the world's largest wheat importer in 2000/2001, gives it a distinct advantage in terms of lower freight costs. Brazil, however, does import some of its wheat needs from the United States and Canada to blend higher grade bread wheat for consistent flour quality.

Table 6.6 World wheat exporters and importers in crop year 2000/2001

Exporters	Millions of tonnes for export
United States of America	30.0
Canada	18.0
Australia	15.5
Argentina	12.0
Importers	**Millions of tonnes for import**
Brazil	7.7
Iran	7.2
Egypt	6.2

Source: United States Department of Agriculture 2000/2001 estimates issued December 2000

Consumer fears regarding 'FrankenFoods', as genetically modified crops are sometimes called, curtailed Argentine corn exports to Brazil in 2000. Brazil is the hemisphere's last major competitor to the United States that disallows its farmers from growing and selling genetically altered crops, let alone permitting importers to buy those products. That has been a problem, since Brazil imports corn and some soybeans from the United States and Argentina, the world's No. 1 and No. 2 growers of genetically modified food, respectively. Brazil's refusal to unload a number of cargoes of genetically altered corn may be a precursor of things to come. Argentina has been debating whether to approve mandatory labelling of GM exports in response to fears that undifferentiated crops may be an impediment to entry into the European Union market, which buys 20 per cent of food traded on world markets. The Biosafety Protocol signed in Montreal in January 2000 will allow countries to use precautions when making decisions on imports of genetically modified crops. The Protocol will also have equal standing with World Trade Organization rules that require such decisions to be based on sound science. But the genetic genie may already be out of the lantern in so far as hemispheric trade in food is concerned. States in the south of Brazil, including Rio Grande do Sul, Santa Catarina, Parana and Sao Paulo, are legally barred from importing GM crops, but northeastern states such as Pernambuco are under the jurisdiction of a different regional court. The court in that state ruled late in 2000 in favour of unloading of GM corn from Argentina to supply the region's thriving poultry and hog industry with animal feed and there have been reports of smuggled GM seed found in Brazil's south.

Brazil was the world's largest producer of sugar in 2000 and is expected to harvest a slightly larger sugar cane crop in 2001 and an even larger one in 2002. A discussion later in this chapter about Brazil's Proalcohol programme explains how and why the nation grew to become the top supplier of sugar in the world in the past 15 years and consequently have a significant impact on world prices. Commodity traders and analysts estimate that a 15–18 million tonne market overhang, largely originating in carry-over inventories in India, has weighed on world prices in recent years. But a drought in southern Brazil in 2000 that cut production, and crop problems in Cuba, once a leading producer of sugar, have propped sugar prices back up recently.

“Consumer fears regarding 'FrankenFoods', as genetically modified crops are sometimes called, curtailed Argentine corn exports to Brazil in 2000”

Brazil is also the world's leading coffee producer, supplying an ever larger quantity of the aromatic beans since a harsh frost cut its output in 1994. High world prices between 1994 and 1997 helped Brazil overhaul its coffee industry, moving acreage north nearer the equator to try to avoid frost damage as well as becoming one of the few nations to mechanize the harvest. What has since resulted is an oversupply of coffee beans on the world market that drove prices down 50 per cent between July 2000 and January 2001, to their lowest levels in 30 years. Brazil produces 30–35 million 60 kg bags of coffee each year and responded with a retention plan in June 2000 that withholds 20 per cent of export supply. While the plan enjoyed relatively good compliance from other members of the Association of Coffee Producing Countries (ACPC) it had negligible effects on prices in the first six months. The South Americans' dominance of the coffee market, with production led by Brazilian and then by Colombian growers, and their tentative control of world prices is being chiselled away by the rise of Vietnam as an important source of coffee in the past 20 years. Vietnam has gone from producing virtually no coffee two decades ago to about 11.5 million 60 kg bags today and is rivalling Colombia for second place in output. Peru has been growing in importance as a coffee grower too as it substitutes coca acreage for coffee plants. Central American production varies between 17 and 20 million 60 kg bags out of Costa Rica, El Salvador, Guatemala, Honduras and Nicaragua. Mexico is also a significant producer of coffee.[10]

Brazilian output of cocoa suffered a devastating blow in the mid-1990s when witches'-broom disease swept the tropical crop. Now output is virtually insignificant with most cocoa output concentrated in West Africa and Indonesia. Analysts doubt Brazilian cocoa output will ever rank as the world's second largest export source as it did in the 1970s. Cotton output, however, is seen trending upwards in Brazil, Argentina and Paraguay in the coming years. Producers hedge their crop risk on the New York Board of Trade but cotton is priced on New York delivery so there is interest among South American producers in plans to launch a European cotton market that may be in place later in 2001.[11]

The Southern Cone of South America is also a significant supplier of citrus fruits. Argentina is the leading world producer and exporter of lemons, but had gained access to only a handful of US states in 2000 after years of negotiating access to that market. The US government has granted Argentine citrus fruit exports gradual access to states bordering its own producer states. The Brazilians are already a step ahead. Not only does the Brazilian state of Sao Paulo combined with the US state of Florida account for 90 per cent of the orange juice consumed in the United States, but Brazilian firms have been integrating vertically and buying Florida-based processing firms.[12]

The Economist Intelligence Unit forecast in January 2001 that the price of soft commodities (coffee, sugar, cacao, cotton, etc.) should rebound strongly over the next two years, up almost 11 per cent in 2001 alone, except for beverages. Beverage prices were expected to fall 13 per cent in 2001, led by coffee, and the decline should ease in

2002 when prices are expected to dip only 5 per cent. Grains and sugar were seen posting significant increases in prices in 2001, with grains up almost 23 per cent over the next two years.

Other crops that are grown in abundance in South America include potatoes, tobacco, rice, barley, flax, nuts, bananas, fruit, and wine grapes. Sheep, goats, chickens and hogs are also significant components of the continent's livestock output.

Table 6.7 Production, export and consumption of beef in the US, Brazil and Argentina in 2000

Country	Production (millions of head of cattle)
Brazil	144.153
United States of America	96.595
Argentina	49.342
Country	**Exports (millions of tonnes)**
United States of America	11.4
Brazil	6.5
Argentina	2.8
Country	**Consumption (kg per capita per year)**
Argentina	65.2
Uruguay	60.0
United States of America	42.8
Brazil	34.6

Source: United States Department of Agriculture, Foreign Agriculture Service

More than 190 million head of cattle grazed on the pasture lands of Brazil and Argentina in 2000, or about a quarter of the cattle on Earth (see Table 6.7). Fears that the virus that can lead to the outbreak of foot-and-mouth disease had contaminated regional herds bordering Paraguay in 2000 led to a swift and co-ordinated response by Southern Cone agriculture ministers who ordered the destruction of thousands of cattle suspected of being exposed to the virus. Most western hemisphere importers temporarily closed their markets to Mercosur beef to ensure that the disease, which is fatal to animals but not to humans, did not spread to their national herds. Food security once again became a major market factor in late 2000 and early 2001 when another outbreak of 'mad cow' disease swept Europe, followed by cases of foot-and-mouth disease in Britain. Then, in March, Argentina admitted that cases of foot-and-mouth had recurred on its territory after a six-year absence. The outbreaks cut demand throughout the global beef trade as consumers shunned steak, regardless of origin and health status. It is too early to tell whether these health scares will fundamentally alter consumer demand in the medium to long term, but one thing is certain: cattle in this part of the world graze on pasture land and not on bone meal, which has been identified as the source of 'mad cow' disease, so this facet of food security is more easily controlled here. The Paris-based International Epizootic Office early in 2001 said most Brazilian and Argentine cattle were free of foot-and-mouth disease as long as farmers continued to use vaccinations. These rulings mean greater access to world beef markets for cattle raised in the two countries.

It is unlikely the Brazilian and Argentine herds can increase in numbers very easily. If they did, it would require Brazil to burn off more parts of the Amazon for cattle ranching, but the environmental consequences and poor soil quality make that option unattractive in both the short and the long term. In Argentina's case, it would need to convert crop land into pasture land to accommodate a larger national herd. The only way these two countries could boost tonnage without raising the number of cattle would be through a cultural change in their way of raising livestock: finishing the cattle on feedlots as is the practice in North America. In the United States, more than 30 per cent of the weight on beef raised there is added on at the feedlot. If you are looking for pricing information, Argentina's Liniers Market, one of the world's largest cattle auction markets, launched its internet portal – *www.mercadodeliniers.com.ar* – early in 2001, so users can consult producer data, up-to-date pricing information, livestock movement and historical data.

> **"Fish farming appears to be growing as an industry and may rival cattle ranching in terms of tonnage produced by the end of this decade"**

Fish farming appears to be growing as an industry and may rival cattle ranching in terms of tonnage produced by the end of this decade. Annual world beef output has been steady in the past decade at about 54 million tonnes while fish farming went from virtually nothing in

1980 to 32 million tonnes in 2000. Ecuador is a regional pioneer in fish farming and Peru has been diversifying into the production of fish meal.[13] Anchovies, tuna and crustaceans abound along South America's Atlantic and Pacific coasts but overfishing is a problem, particularly of the South Atlantic hake stock. (Map 6.3)

Looking beyond the 'gilded man'

European explorers scoured the South American continent in search of gold 500 years ago and found plenty of the quixotic metal, but they also found vast amounts of silver. Then they mined tin along the Andean mountain range and extracted nitrates from the world's driest desert, the Atacama. Now miners extract everything from bauxite and iron ore in Venezuela, Guyana and Suriname to copper in Chile and Argentina and aluminum, iron ore and uranium in Brazil. You can find beryl, coal, chromium, diamonds, emeralds, mercury, iodine, mica, manganese, molybdenum, phosphates, lead, platinum, quartz crystal, sulphur, antimony, vanadium, tungsten and zinc in South America's mountains and along its rivers. Latin America's share of world mining investment is forecast to be 41 per cent of the world total in the 1998–2007 period, followed by North America at a distant second at 11 per cent, largely because of its vast and long untapped resources.

Chile's state-owned Codelco, the world's largest copper producer, said it intended to double its profits in 2001, but admitted the target was based on optimistic projections. Codelco owns 20 per cent of known global reserves of the red metal and said it wanted to post a pre-tax profit of $1.4 billion, assuming the average price of the base metal would be about $0.97 per pound. Global demand for copper was expected to rise 2 per cent over the course of 2001, despite concerns of economic slowdown in Asia and the United States. Price weakness in 1998 and 1999 led Codelco to freeze wages and cut thousands of jobs to reduce its cost of production which is now about $0.40 per pound of refined copper from $0.45.

Gold has lost its glamour in recent years. Prices remain well below $300 an ounce as the yellow metal continues to trade under historical levels since the United States dropped the gold standard three decades ago. With the exception of a speculative run-up in prices

Map 6.3 South American Food, Fish and Mineral Concentrations

ahead of the 1991 Gulf War, gold even seems to have lost its status as a barometer of world security. Owing to the weak market price outlook in the short term, Barrick Gold Corp. has delayed plans to start operations at its $950 million Pascua-Lama gold and silver mine that straddles the Argentina-Chile border on the high Andes. The two countries ratified a mining treaty to simplify and converge their mining regulations specifically to attract foreign direct investments like the development of Pascua-Lama. The treaty guarantees fiscal stability for 30 years and both countries allow companies to deduct 100 per cent of prospecting and exploration costs from their income taxes. Chile's mining sector is well developed, but Argentina's potential has yet to be exploited in full and government officials expect that the binational treaty will serve as a blue print that could attract as much as $4 billion in mining activity in the next decade. The story behind Argentina's underdeveloped metal and mineral extraction sector is based in part on the Bajo la Alumbrera project where the provincial government of Catamarca unilaterally increased its take of royalties to the disadvantage of the operator. Diplomats from major mining countries cite that example as the reason why many companies have been wary of doing business in Argentina. If the government of President Fernando de la Rua is serious about attracting world-class miners to Argentina it will do everything it can to assure a more predictable business climate and operators should be rewarded with mineral deposits that, while perhaps not of the magnitude of Chile's reserves, are nonetheless significant.

In addition to Pascua-Lama, Argentina has five major new mining projects on the cards: the $800 million Pachon copper mine and $400 million Veladero gold and copper mine, both in San Juan province; the $124 million Pirquitas silver mine in Jujuy; the $110 million San Jorge gold and copper mine in Mendoza; and the $100 million Agua Rica gold, copper and molybdenum mine in Catamarca province. Argentina's five-year, $20 billion federal infrastructure plan due to begin in September 2001 includes the construction of a high-tension power transport network to feed the mining sector in these remote mountainous regions. But plans to link those areas to the Pacific via the Transandino and Transpatagonico railway lines have yet to be set in motion.

Bolivia has long been an important regional player in the mining sector and the latest installment of its role on the global scene is the development of San Cristobal, tipped as one of the largest silver mines in the world. Backed in part by US financier George Soros, San Cristobal sits in the southwest of Bolivia. The closest route to export is through Chilean Pacific ports to which roads capable of handling heavy truck traffic are being upgraded.

To the northeast, Suriname, Guyana and Venezuela have some of the world's richest reserves of bauxite, a clay-like substance used to convert alumina into aluminium. Bauxite is extracted from Guyana and Suriname and taken by barge into Venezuela along the Orinoco River where it is smelted into aluminum. Brazil also has deposits of bauxite, iron ore and other materials used to make aluminum. The regional challenge to exploiting these minerals is the overcapacity in South America's auto sector, given that many auto parts are made of lightweight aluminum.[14] Auto sector overcapacity in South America is estimated to be as much as 50 per cent and recent plant openings and expansions by Renault, Nissan and other manufacturers in Brazil are bound to weigh on metal prices, while the global auto industry is predicted to see a slump of up to 11 per cent in sales over 2001 and 2002.

Sugar coating the auto sector

Brazil's Proalcohol programme was implemented in 1975 in reaction to the spike in world crude oil prices in 1973. The Opec oil crisis was interpreted as evidence that Brazil needed to limit its reliance on imports of non-renewable energy sources. Brazil in the year 2000 still relied on imports to cover about 20 per cent of its energy needs, but that level would have been higher had it not agressively pursued a policy promoting the production of hydrated and anhydrous fuel alcohol derived from its vast fields of sugar cane. This fuel alcohol import substitution subsidy has also propelled Brazil to the top spot among world sugar exporters, selling 10.67 million tonnes on the global marketplace in crop year 1999/2000 (May/April) up from 1.2 million tonnes in 1975. Sugar is the quintessential example of the distortions caused in the world commodities market, not only because of Brazil's subsidy programme but also thanks to import quotas and regulation in the European Union, United States and Japanese markets. The EU common market divides sugar output into categories and assigns production quotas to each member country, and maintains import agreements with African, Caribbean and Pacific island nations. Sugar is also the last remaining major industry yet to be negotiated into Mercosur after the Proalcohol programme ran into strong resistance from Argentina and Paraguay, and to a lesser extent from Uruguay, at the Common Market Council meeting in Ouro Preto, Brazil in December 1994. As a consequence of managed and subsidized supply, prices have been extremely volatile, running up to $0.50 a pound in 1981 to $0.06 a pound in 1985. Brazil's Proalcohol programme has breached the gap left after the supply agreement between Cuba and the former Soviet Union was dissolved in the early 1990s.

The way Brazil's subsidy scheme works is as follows. Gasoline is taxed heavily and those receipts are transfered to sugar-cane alcohol producers. The net effect of this system is that the subsidy varies with the fluctuations in the price of gasoline and the transferred funds help reduce the fixed costs of Brazilian sugar mills and distilleries, most of which are concentrated in the centre-south states where 80 per cent of the cane is grown. It also ensures an abundant and immediate supply of the raw material as production can either optimize on world sugar prices or world crude prices without having to expand or contract acreage in response to price movement in one commodity market, which is the case with most other cash crops. In other words, if there is a steep drop in the price of sugar, Brazil can extend its alcohol output by raising the proportion in its fuel mixture – that way it cuts sugar output without scaling back on planted area. In the opposite scenario, Brazil can sell its sugar in an appreciating world market paid immediately or in the spot market and buy fuel alcohol on terms of up to 270 days. Brazil has further justified its Proalcohol programme on environmental grounds as well as citing it as a source of net job creation and the development of local technology.

The other variable in the equation is the national fleet of cars that can run on hydrated alcohol and anhydrous fuel alcohol which is combined with gasoline and methanol. Brazil subsidized the development of that technology by its car sector to produce vehicles that ran on hydrated alcohol and at one point there were 4 million running with those types of motors. Now there is a debate on whether to continue using hydrated alcohol and reviving those subsidies to renew the fleet of vehicles or to produce a growing proportion of anhydrous alcohol as a substitute.

Regardless of the decision, Brazil has become an increasingly important player on the world sugar scene, where more than a quarter of global output is traded on foreign markets. Such a large supplier subsidizing its production has raised the ire of not only relatively liberalized sugar producers such as Argentina and Chile but of less open markets like the EU, the United States and Japan. A solution to the bitter sugar battle both at the regional and intercontinental levels will probably be hard to reach.

“Brazil has become an increasingly important player on the world sugar scene, where more than a quarter of global output is traded on foreign markets”

As you have seen in this chapter, South America still has abundant supplies of energy that have yet to be tapped and it could easily increase its production of food. Some countries, notably Venezuela and Argentina, could attract more mining activity and the former has begun to take steps to make its legal and commercial environment more attractive. The next chapter explains what these 12 countries plan to do to make this region an easier place for you to move your goods and services.

Notes

[1]Moore, Mike, secretary general, World Trade Organization, interview in Buenos Aires, 28 November 2000.

[2]Chavez, Hugo, interview in Puerto Ordaz, 20 January 2001.

[3]Andean Development Corporation, 'Accion de la CAF en la infraestructura sostenible de Suramerica', August 2000.

[4]Hart, George, vice president of international finance at Canadian Hunter International Ltd, phone interview to Calgary, Canada, 16 March 2001.

[5]Dunn, Seth (2001) *State of the World 2001*, Worldwatch Institute Report on Progress Toward a Sustainable Society, pp. 83–88.

[6]Chavez, Hugo, interview in Puerto Ordaz, 20 January 2001.

[7]Rangel, Jose Vicente, foreign minister of Venezuela, interview in Caracas, 18 January 2001.

[8]Brown, Lester, chairman, Worldwatch Institute, interview in Washington, D.C., 11 January 2001.

[9]Loewy, Richard, president, AgResource, phone interview to Chicago, 10 January 2001.

[10]Prendergast, Ann, senior soft commodities analyst at Refco, interview in New York, 10 January 2001.

[11]McDougall, Mike, commodities analyst at Fimat, interview in New York, 10 January 2001.

[12]McDougall, Mike, *ibid.*

[13]Brown, Lester, *op. cit.*

[14]McDougall, Mike, *op. cit.*

7

The Latin Marshall Plan

'There are multiple problems and inadequacies with South America's physical infrastructure which means greater costs for operators. There are legal uncertainties with respect to the implementation of accords. Customs procedures are obsolete and there's a lack of understanding regarding future government policies to allow business to draw up their optimum plans,' said Juan Rojas Penso, secretary general of the Association of Latin American Trade Partners (ALADI – *www.aladi.org*).[1]

Imagine trying to offer transport services to move people and cargo through dense Amazonian jungles and over the highest mountains in the western hemisphere with large tracts of land in between that are sparsely populated. Those are the logistics of circulating around South America and why the public sector, be it through army engineers or other government agencies, has played a central role in the development of basic infrastructure in this part of the world until recently. Now that tariff barriers across the continent have been gradually reduced over the past decade (see Table 7.1) and imports have been growing in dollar and relative terms between the South American nations their governments have increasingly come to see infrastructure projects as essential to expanded trade.

Table 7.1 Average South American import tariffs through the 1990s (expressed in percentages)

Country/Year	1990	1998	2000
Argentina	20.9	13.9	13.7
Bolivia	9.7	9.7	9.7
Brazil	30.2	14.6	14.1
Chile	15.0	11.6	9.0
Colombia	15.0	10.9	11.6
Ecuador	32.9	15.5	17.7
Paraguay	16.9	11.5	11.6
Peru	25.9	13.5	13.5
Uruguay	27.7	12.2	12.4
Venezuela	17.6	11.9	12.3
South America:	22.88	12.53	12.56

Source: Inter-American Development Bank *www.iadb.org*

You can see how just as tariffs have been coming down, trade has been on the rise and diversifying. Imports into the continent accounted for 34 per cent of regional GDP in 1997 from 21 per cent at the end of the 1980s. The value of those imports also rose 18 per cent to $280 billion in 1997 from 1990. Trade within the region, meanwhile, had risen to 20 per cent by the end of the 1990s from 12 per cent at the beginning of the decade. Intra-regional trade and investment prior to the Asian financial crisis accounted for 25 per cent of the total in Mercosur and 12 per cent in the Andean Community. Trade and investment between Mercosur and the Andean Community, however, accounted for only 4–5 per cent of the combined total registered in the two trade blocs and the level is even lower with neighbouring Caribbean nations in Caricom or Suriname and Guyana. Another trend in intra-continental trade in goods has been a growing exchange in value added goods. In 1990, about 60 per cent of traded goods consisted of fuel, food, textiles, timber and minerals while 40 per cent were petrochemicals, machinery and electronic goods. By the end of the decade the proportion was closer to 50–50.[2]

“South Americans are keenly aware of how much geography separates them from one another and the outside world”

South Americans are keenly aware of how much geography separates them from one another and the outside world, so in 2000 Brazilian president Fernando Henrique Cardoso asked the Inter-American Development Bank (*www.iadb.org*), the Andean Development Corporation (*www.caf.com*) and Fondo Financiero para el Desarrollo de la Cuenca del Plata (*www.fonplata.org*) to draft some proposals. The three banks submitted a dozen infrastructure project proposals to South America's 12 leaders at the Brasilia summit at the end of August 2000. Preliminary work began on six in 2001 and they are expected to be completed within a decade. 'To our way of thinking, the relationship between the Andean Community and Mercosur should rest on the simultaneous deepening and reinforcement of integration within each group, their growing interconnection, and a rapid movement toward the new common objective. This relationship can prove to be mutually beneficial if we start off by tackling specific tasks such as the harmonizing of standards to link up telecommunication and transportation systems, health measures, customs procedures and other practices that will boost our trade.

We can also take steps toward developing physical infrastructure at the border crossings, thereby making this geographical area a market that is truly active and operating,' said Andean Community secretary general Sebastian Alegrett.[3]

Clearly, road, river and airport infrastructure along with energy transportation systems and telecommunications networks are a high priority for the development and integration of the continent as far as these leaders are concerned. This is perhaps the boldest co-ordinated public works programme ever undertaken in this part of the world but neither government funds nor development bank loans will be enough to pay for these projects. The IADB report argued that although many governments have now pulled back from direct infrastructure management, you must expect a certain level of state involvement, especially in projects whose economic and social dividends will be realized only in the very long term. The world's third-longest natural gas pipeline, from Santa Cruz de la Sierra, Bolivia, to Sao Paulo, Brazil, is a prime example of the move towards joint public-private infrastructure projects. That asset is not only the biggest energy project in Latin American history but also a source of regional development with a steel foundry and petrochemical plant establishing in Puerto Suarez, Bolivia, because of the pipeline. Construction of a road linking Santa Elena, Venezuela to Manaus, Brazil led to $1 billion worth of regional commerce where none existed before. It has helped attract Brazilian tourists to nearby Isla Margarita, Venezuela, and has led to the creation of 21 joint ventures linked to that roadway. 'I believe that what is very important for South American integration are all these sustainable infrastructure projects. There's an ambitious plan to develop the waterways linking the Rio de la Plata to the Amazon and the Orinoco,' said CAF executive president Enrique Garcia.[4] That proposed waterway is more than 30,000 miles (50,000 kilometres) of river networks that stretch from Caracas in the north to Buenos Aires in the south. There is no doubt the need for improved and expanded transportation networks. Average transportation fuel consumption in the urban areas of Latin America increased 5 per cent between 1996 and 1997 compared with 1 per cent in industrialized countries. The streets of Brazil's business capital Sao Paulo, the most populous city of the southern hemisphere, are so congested that the wealthiest residents have taken to the skies. Sao Paulo has the world's third largest helicopter fleet after New York and Tokyo.[5] South America needs more and better transportation routes and that infrastructure is going to be built in large part with financing from investors like yourself, so it's important that you understand how all these plans complement each other.

South America's six-point plan

There is no mention of former US secretary of state George Marshall or the massive reconstruction work undertaken in Europe after the Second World War associated with his stewardship, but the impact of the more than 600 projects drafted by the three development banks could be as important for the South Americans and the people they trade with as the Marshall Plan was for Western Europeans. The key, of course, is financing. When the 12 South American governments assigned priority to these projects they had three principles in mind:

- Is this a project that integrates transportation, telecommunications and energy infrastructures?
- How can the public sector maximize its ability to assist in financing these programmes, many to be undertaken by the private sector?
- How can bureaucracy be reduced and regulations harmonized?

'This is completely new in South America. Every country in South America is involved in financing these programmes in order to improve government fiscality given our limited resources,' said Jose Paulo Silveira, secretary for planning at Brazil's Planning Ministry.[6]

There are six priority integration projects, based on the volume of trade flows (see Table 7.2). They are as follows:

1. Top priority goes to the improvement of roads and railways linking the Mercosur nations because they account for the largest flow of goods and services within the continent. This programme also includes energy and telecommunications projects.
2. The Venezuela-Colombia-Ecuador corridor is another priority programme centred mainly on transportation but includes some energy connections as well.
3. Plans are to pave roads connecting Chile's Pacific ports that go through Bolivia and Brazil's Mato Grosso state on to Sao Paulo, but the bulk of the projects in this programme will concentrate on improving energy interchanges between those three countries.
4. There is also talk of building a 'northern arc' of transport routes and electric power connections uniting Venezuela, Brazil, Guyana, Suriname and French Guyana, of which Venezuela's El Guri power plant connection to Boa Vista, and eventually to Manaus, is an important element.
5. Another east-west link would tie Brazil to Peru through an intermodal transport network linking waterways, roads and ocean ports.
6. The final priority programme is the multimodal cargo shipping lanes tying the Orinoco, Amazon and Rio de la Plata river systems into a 30,000 mile (50,000 kilometre) transcontinental waterway.

Bolivian President Hugo Bauzer inspecting a gas pipeline under construction in the town of Puerto Suarez, at the border of Bolivia and Brazil. Bauzer ordered troops to protect the duct, which is expected to become a key source of income for Bolivia, after workers went on strike to press their demands for special bonuses. *Photo by David Mercardo.© Reuters 2002.*

A pedestrian studies an electronic board showing exchange rates of foreign currency in the heart of Buenos Aires' financial district. *Photo by Enrique Marcarian. © Reuters 2002.*

Stock traders scream out buy and sell orders during the morning session at Sao Paulo's stock exchange on 15 January 1999. Brazilian shares on the Bovespa snapped back from an early nosedive and sailed upwards after the Central Bank allowed the *real* to float freely, traders said. While shares then soared more than 25 per cent by mid-afternoon, the currency was effectively down another 12 per cent by 15 January, more than 18 per cent against the US dollar since the 13 January devaluation. The *real* fell as low as 42 per cent against the greenback in 1999. *Photo by Robson Martins. © Reuters 2002.*

Rio de Janeiro stock exchange president Carlos Alberto Reis (left) and Banco Santander Central Hispano's director of Latin American operations, Marciel Portela, drop the gavel for the winning bid in the auction of Banespa Bank on 20 November 2000. BSCH won Brazil's biggest bank privatization to date with a bid of $3.6 billion, or more than three times the second highest bid. *Photo by Paulo Whitaker. © Reuters 2002.*

A Brazilian worker is reflected in a mirror at the assembly line of the Toyota Corolla car factory in the city of Indiatuba, 110 km northeast of Sao Paulo. The new Toyota Corolla assembly plant, with an initial investment of $150 million and capacity to produce up to 20,000 cars a year, intends to conquer 10 per cent of the market in the Mercosur region. *Photo by Paulo Whitaker. © Reuters 2002.*

Pedestrians walk past the headquarters of Brazil's Central Bank in Brasilia. The bank said it had stopped defending the *real*, allowing it to float freely as of 13 January 1999. The move reverberated throughout South American economies. *Photo by Ruy Baron. © Reuters 2002.*

A woman and child stroll around Buenos Aires' old Abasto central food market on 31 August 1998. The market was being redeveloped into a complex of luxury shops and multiple movie theatres while preserving the building's exterior shell, which was built in 1930, modelled on a Parisian design. The new Abasto is a prominent part of a $5 billion gold rush of property developments that will transform the once splendid but long neglected architectural heritage of Buenos Aires. *Photo by Enrique Macarian. © Reuters 2002.*

Colombia's coffee icon Juan Valdez poses next to a bag containing '100 per cent Colombian Coffee'. Valdez, the fictional spokesman for Colombia's National Federation of Coffee Growers, who became a popular culture icon with his mule 'Lana', celebrated the 40th anniversary of the launch of the 'richest coffee in the world' campaign on 10 September 2000. *Photo by Alberto Lopera. © Reuters 2002.*

The president of Brazilian brewers Brahma Marcel Telles (left) raises a toast with beverage-maker Antarctica president Victorino De Marchi after they announced their merger in Sao Paulo on 30 March 2000. The merger created the world's fifth largest drinks company and fourth largest brewer. *Photo by Paulo Whitaker. © Reuters 2002.*

An Ecuadorean state oil company labourer repairs an oil pipeline after a mechanical failure produced a leak in the Transecuador pipeline in the Chiriboga area (300 km from Quito) on 8 February 1999. *Photo by Guillermo Granja. © Reuters 2002.*

An Ecuadorean woman changes fistfuls of *sucres*, the local currency, for US dollars from a street currency trader in the capital Quito on 14 January 2000. Ecuadorean president Jamil Mahuad began dollarizing his country's economy in an effort to counter galloping inflation. The emergency measure stirred passions in the poor Andean nation where, a week later, peasants and leaders of a rebel army unit ousted Mahuad. *Photo by Andrew Winning. © Reuters 2002.*

Bolivain co-operative miners push an empty cart into one of hundreds of mine shafts tunnelled into the Cerro Rico mountain, containing the world's richest silver deposits. Already believed to have yielded 1–2 billion ounces of silver since an Indian named Diego Hualpa discovered it in 1544 and the Spanish Conquistadores exploited it, the mountain is believed to contain at least as much silver again. *Photo by Antonio Suarez. © Reuters 2002.*

Angry at job losses and floundering prices, thousands of sugar cane labourers protest in front of Brazil's Congress building in Brasilia on 1 June 1999. The workers, who had been burning fields and blocking roads in rural areas for some weeks, marched on Brazil's capital to demand more government support for the can-distilled alcohol industry. Job losses across the cash-strapped sector fuelled the workers' discontent. *Photo by Ruy Baron. © Reuters 2002.*

Brazilian Carlos Peixoto rows among ocean vessels docked in the seaport of Recife in northeastern Brazil. Peixoto, who rows visitors to the ships calling at this port, began a computer course in November 2000 and plans to work in the new 'digital port'. Recife's state governor is investing $19.5 million in the port. *Photo by Paulo Whitaker. © Reuters 2002.*

Table 7.2 Major South American trade partners in 1998 (expressed in $US millions FOB)

Total	$32,298.7
Argentina-Brazil	$14,411.3
Colombia-Venezuela	$2,577.8
Argentina-Chile	$2,413.5
	52.02 pct
Brazil-Chile	$1,851.0
Brazil-Uruguay	$1,815.6
Brazil-Paraguay	$1,598.7
Brazil-Venezuela	$1,367.3
Argentina-Uruguay	$1,338.1
Colombia-Ecuador	$856.5
Argentina-Paraguay	$751.7
	$28,982.02
	77.70 pct

Source: Inter-American Development Bank (*www.iadb.org*)

Building development corridors

One of the best integrated planning projects in South America in recent decades took place in Curitiba, Brazil. Starting early in the 1970s the municipality of Curitiba built several transportation arteries radiating from the city centre. The idea was to create intra-city bus expressways instead of building a much more expensive underground rail commuter service. Zoning laws were passed to encourage construction of high-density housing along these transit corridors. Then extra-long articulated buses were added to the transportation network and advance payment stations were set up at bus stops to ease the flow and speed the pace of the public transport system. The bus routes also link to 90 miles (150 kilometres) of bicycle paths. The result is that even though Curitiba has one car for every three of its citizens, two-thirds of all trips within the city are done by bus.[7] This is what South American policymakers mean when they talk to you about integrated infrastructure projects. Most of the road construction projects under consideration in the proposal drafted by the three development banks are inter-city links and given that an estimated 80 per cent of cargo shipped between Brazil and Argentina is hauled by trucks, the need to improve and maintain roadways will always be of vital importance. In the Andean Community, trucks hauled about a third of cargo tonnage in 1999 which was worth an estimated $1.8 billion or 45 per cent of the total $4 billion worth in goods traded between those five nations (excluding oil and derived products).[8]

Harmonizing customs clearance and transport regulations is key to ensuring a more efficient 'just in time' delivery system that reduces manufacturers' need to maintain large and costly inventories. This is a major problem that has to be solved if South American overland cargo traffic is to move with greater ease. That is not to say that there haven't been improvements, but efforts to streamline customs methods must continue if South American governments are serious about one of the FTAA objectives: a minimum six-hour clearance time for express shipments.[9] Freight forwarders say moving cargo to Sao Paulo from Buenos Aires was a bureaucratic nightmare until the mid-1990s. The entire process would take at least two weeks, but thanks to electronic customs clearance, products arrive within four days now.

“many of these priority projects are a question of connecting the missing links in the highway networks of one country to those of another”

Probably one of the busiest international cargo corridors on the continent is Argentina's National Highway 14 that links Buenos Aires to Sao Paulo. That roadway is so busy it has been named the 'Highway of Death'. But it is more the exception than the rule. Less than 15 per cent of cargo trucks circulating on Brazil's southern highway network that connects to Uruguay, Argentina and Chile cross any of those borders. The same can be said for roads that connect Colombia and Venezuela since trans-shipments by truck were suspended in 2000.[10] (Maps 7.1–7.2) As you can see from maps 7.1 to 7.11 many of these priority projects are a question of connecting the missing links in the highway networks of one country to those of another, such as Cucuta, Colombia to Maracaibo, Venezuela or San Carlos de Bariloche, Argentina to Puerto Montt, Chile. In those and other examples such as the La Paz, Bolivia to Ilo, Peru project, the public works proposed would link hinterland production zones to Caribbean, Pacific or

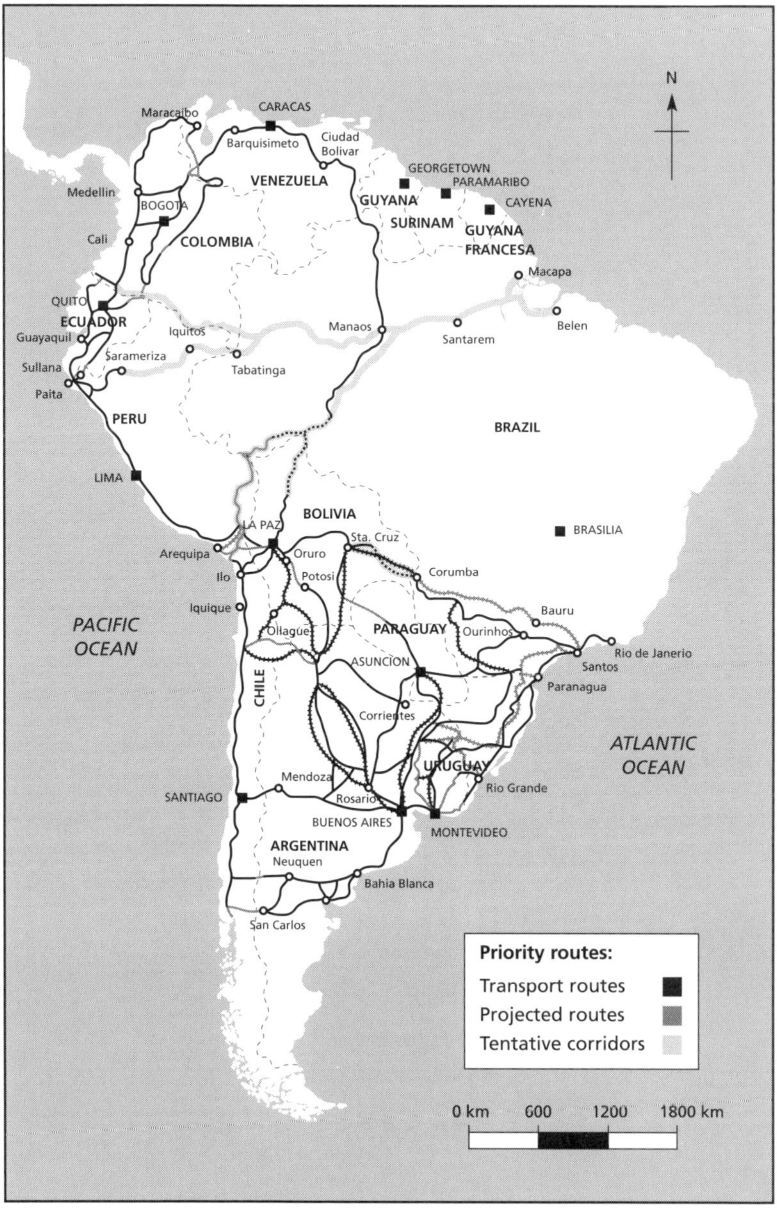

Map 7.1 Priority Transportation Infrastructure Projects for South American Integration

Source: Andean Development Corporation

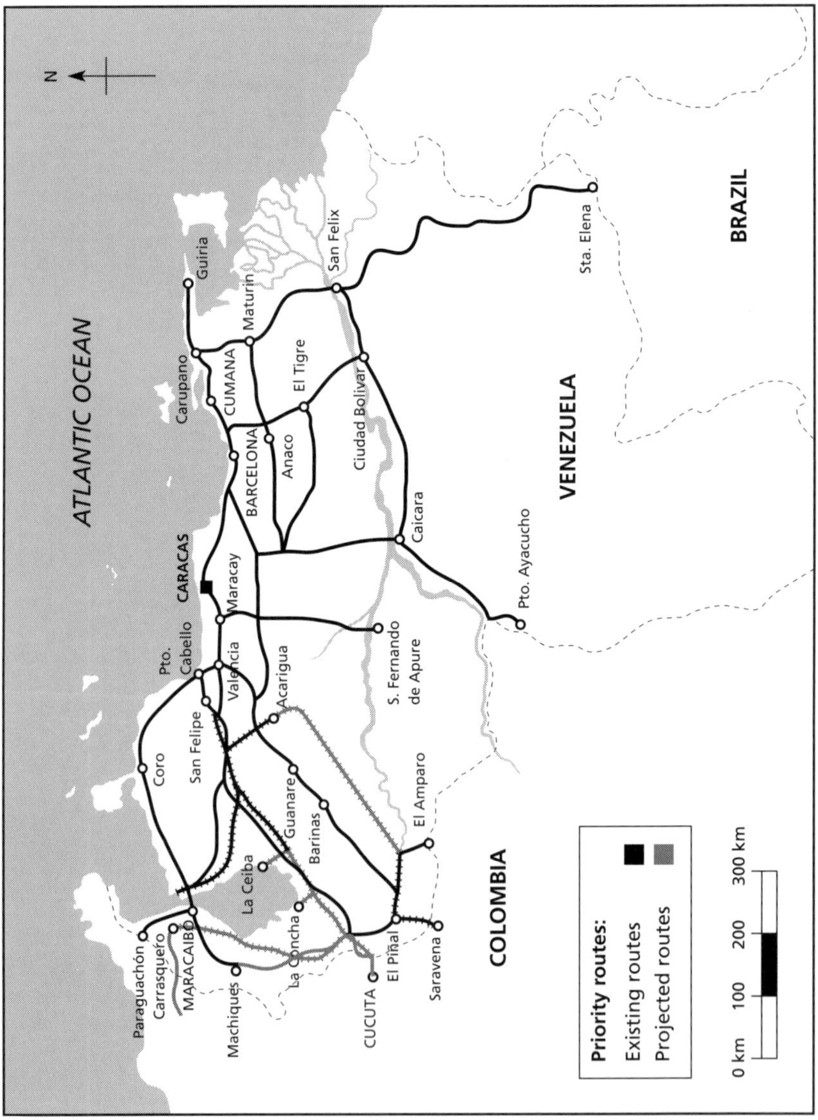

Map 7.2 Venezuela Highway Network

Source: Andean Development Corporation

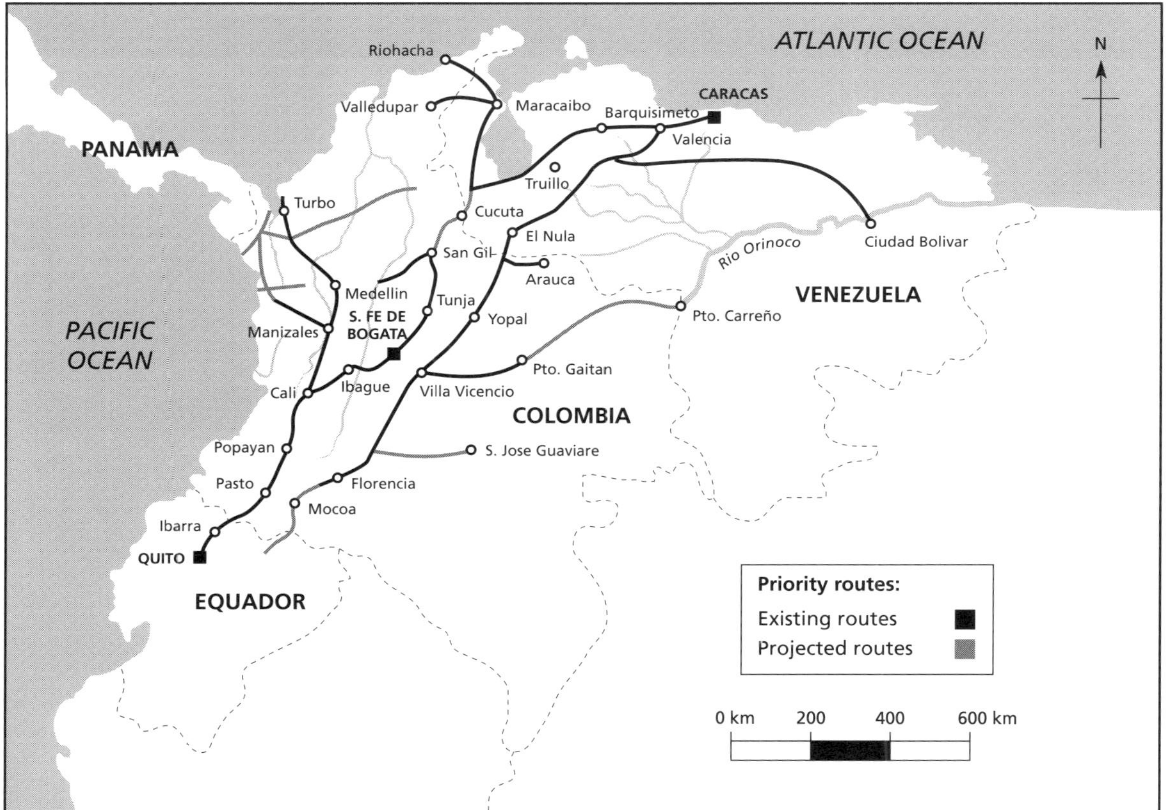

Map 7.3 Colombian Highway Network

Source: Andean Development Corporation

Map 7.4 Ecuadorean Highway Network

Source: Andean Development Corporation

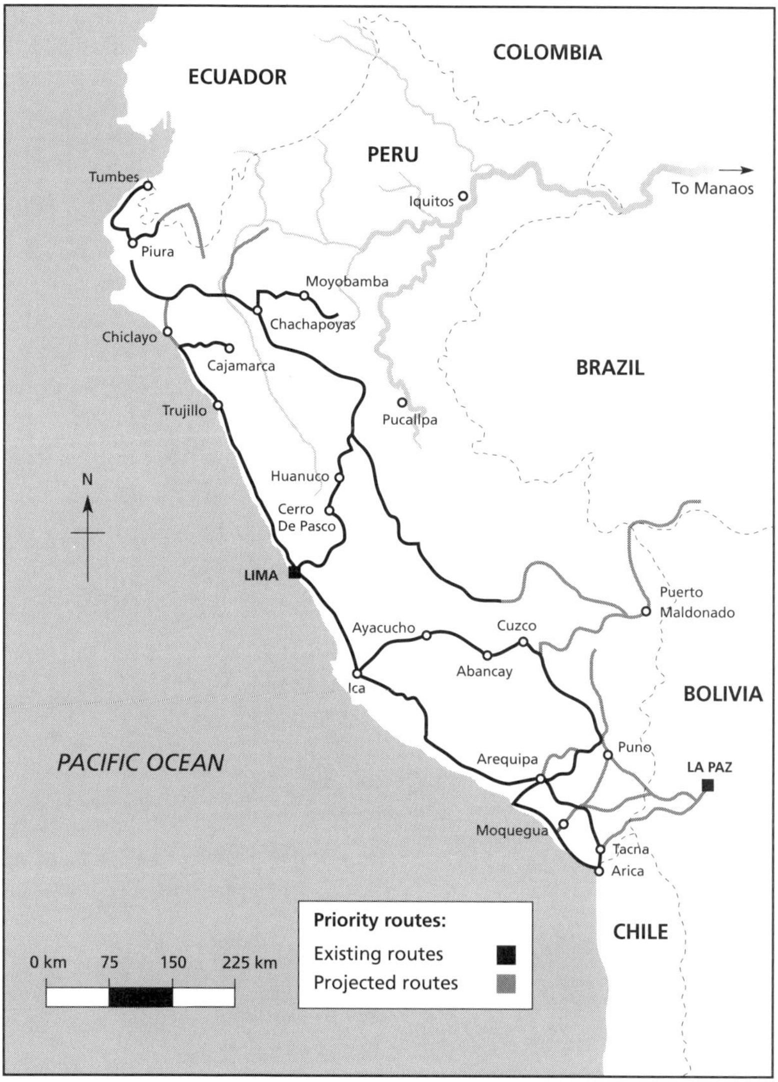

Map 7.5 Peruvian Highway Network

Source: Andean Development Corporation

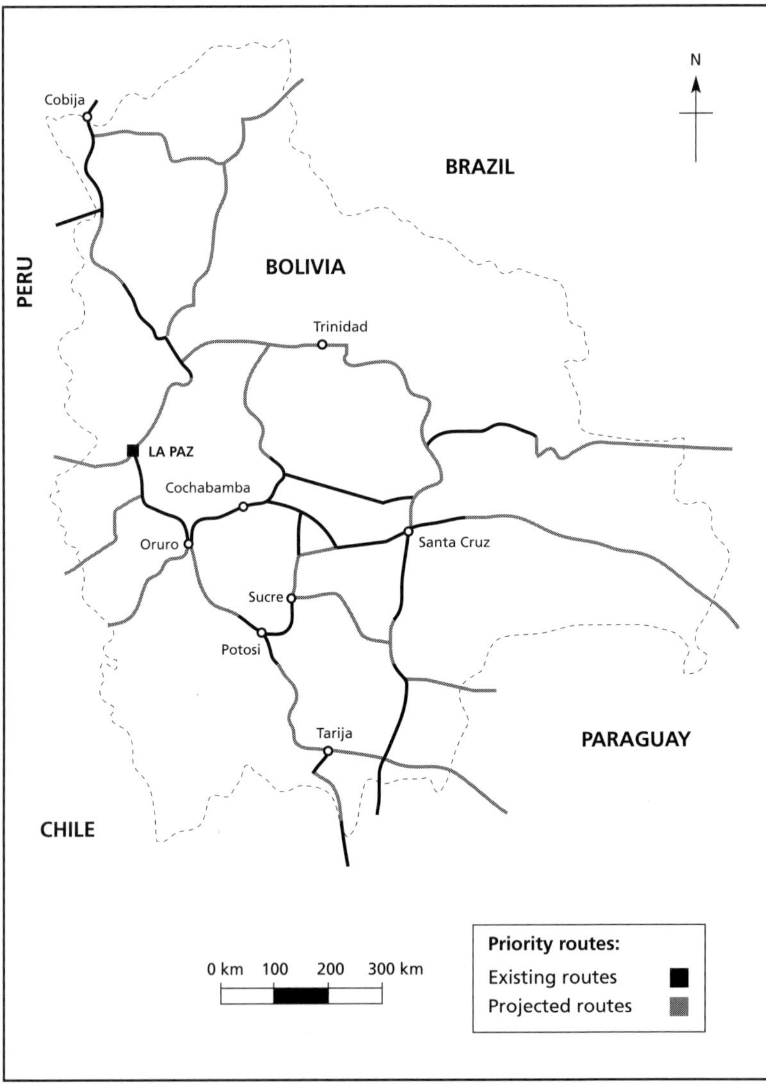

Map 7.6 Bolivian Highway Network

Source: Andean Development Corporation

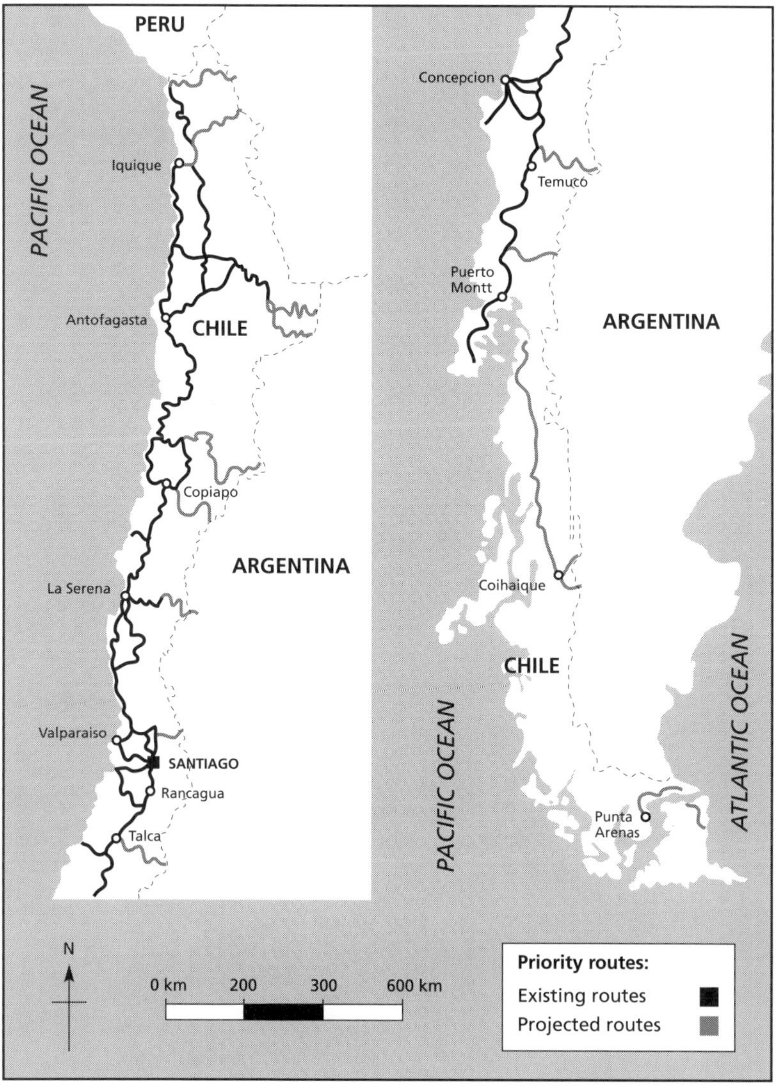

Map 7.7 Chilean Highway Network

Source: Andean Development Corporation

Map 7.8 Paraguayan Highway Network

Source: Andean Development Corporation

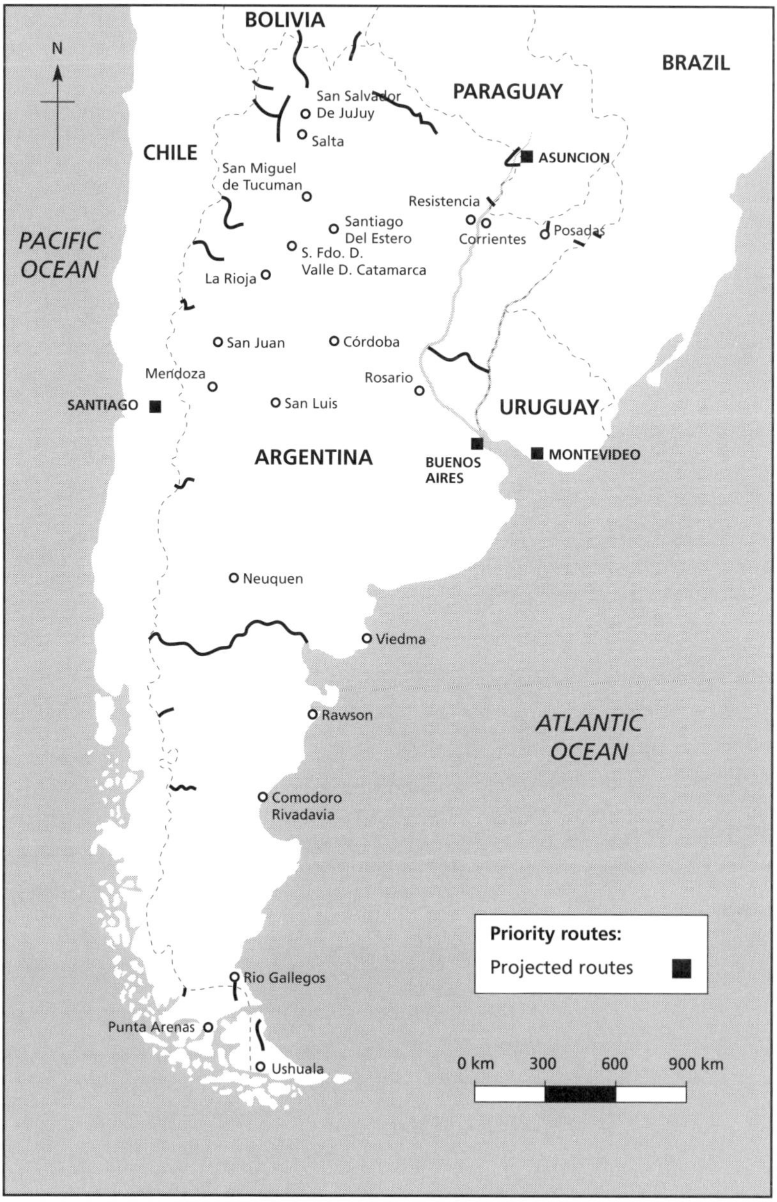

Map 7.9 Argentine Highway Network

Source: Andean Development Corporation

Map 7.10 Uruguayan Highway Network

Source: Andean Development Corporation

Map 7.11 Brazilian Highway Network

Source: Andean Development Corporation

Atlantic export ports. Countries from Argentina to Paraguay have earmarked public, multilateral and private funds for a raft of projects totalling anywhere between 1.5 per cent and 2.5 per cent of gross domestic product to upgrade and add to their national infrastructure. Argentina launched a five-year $20 billion public works programme in 2001, while in December 2000 the Paraguayan government unveiled an ambitious $480 million road improvement and construction plan which is largely financed by multilateral credits. That may not seem like much but the investment is equal to about 2.5 per cent of gross domestic product in a country where about half of the 18,000 miles (29,500 kilometres) of roads are not paved. Public works minister Walter Bower said $190 million would be spent on repaving and improving roads in the remote Chaco forest region of Paraguay. The Inter-American Development Bank will finance about $100 million worth of the total, with the Andean Development Corporation pitching in another $60 million and $30 million being provided by the Paraguayan government. Another $220 million will come from the Japan Bank for International Cooperation to improve roads in Paraguay's western region and the Paraguayan government will contribute $70 million for road work in that region.

There are other roadblocks to international highway transport, however. In 2000, Venezuela suspended trans-shipments of goods by truck across its border with Colombia. The Andean Community's General Secretariat ordered Venezuela to lift the ban but it has refused to do so, the second time and only months after the first in the history of the three-decades old trade bloc that a national government has failed to comply with a Community order. 'We didn't break the accord. It states that there should be equality of conditions and circumstances are not the same in our countries. Venezuelan truckers are getting killed in Colombia. Safety in Colombia won't impede integration but it makes it more difficult,' said Venezuelan president Hugo Chavez.[11] Some of the highway projects approved by individual governments and given priority by the conference of transport, communications and public works ministers of South America are under way. The Paso Jama mountain pass linking Chile and Argentina through the Atacama desert has already been completed on the Chilean side. Others are still being debated and with some strong reservations regarding their economic viability, such as a proposal for what would be one of the world's longest bridges between Colonia, Uruguay and Buenos Aires, Argentina. The following is a list of the projects given priority by the South American ministers.

Venezuela

- Paving the highway from Carrasquero, Venezuela, into Colombia through Playa Bonita, La Yolanda to San Juan del Cesar.
- Widening Highway 6 from La Fria to Machiques.
- Paving the road from Cucuta through Urena, San Faustino and La China to La Fria.
- Building a road from San Cristobal through Rubio on to San Antonio (this segment financed by CAF) then to Urena and Cucuta.
- Paving the roadway from El Pinal through El Nula to Saravena.

Colombia

- Building the Tapon del Darien roadway.
- Constructing the southwestern route from San Miguel to Villagarzon.
- Building the route from La Espriella to Mataje at the Ecuadorean border.
- Erecting a bridge at Quebrada La China.
- Raising a bridge at Tienditas.

Ecuador

- Constructing the road from Catacocha to Macara and Puente Internacional into Peru (financed by CAF).
- Building the road from Puerto El Carmen to Putumayo on the Ecuadorean side of the Putumayo river that runs along the Colombian border (financed by CAF).
- Constructing part of the Esmeraldas highway along the Pacific Coast from Las Penas to Borbon (financed by CAF).
- Building the roadway from San Miguel to Simon Bolivar.

Peru

- Building the road from the southern Pacific port of Ilo through Moquegua, Mumalzo, Mazo Cruz on to Pichupichuni (financed by CAF) then to Desaguadero at the Bolivian border.
- Constructing the route from the coastal city of Matarani to Ilo then inland northeast to Puerto Maldonado at the Bolivian border and north up to Inapari at the meeting of the Bolivia-Brazil-Peru frontiers.
- Building a road from La Tina at the Ecuadorean border west to Sullana.
- Constructing a multimodal facility linking the Pacific port of Paita by road connecting through Lambayeque to Olmos, Corral Quemado up to Sarameriza at one of the sources of the Amazon River, and developing the segment of the river for barge traffic through to Iquitos for transport on to Manaus, Brazil.

Bolivia

- Paving Highway 4 from San Jose de Chiquitos in the Amazonian lowlands to Puerto Suarez which is a river port on the Brazilian border and along the Paraguay River.
- Upgrading Highway 3 on the Altiplano from Santa Barbara to Quiquibey (financed by CAF).
- Paving Highway 8 from Riberalta to Guayaramerin on the border with Brazil.
- Paving the roadway from Yucumo through San Borja to Puerto Almacen.
- Paving the route between Boyuibe and Hito Villazon that connects to Paraguay.
- Paving Highway 1 which leads south to Argentina between Cuchu Ingenio and Tomatas.
- Paving the roadway north of Sucre that leads to Santa Cruz de la Sierra from Puente Sacramento to La Palizada.

- Paving the highway that connects Oruro to Chile between Toledo and Pisiga.
- Building the road between Cuchu Ingenio and Villazon.
- Paving the roads between San Ignacio to San Matias on the border with Brazil.
- Building the route from Concepcion to San Ignacio.
- Constructing cargo depots in Cochabamba and Santa Cruz de la Sierra.

Chile

- Building the road from Pozo Almonte through Huara to Paso Pisiga.
- Paving the routes from San Pedro de Atacama to Paso Sico and Paso Jama (Jama segment inaugurated by the presidents of Chile and Argentina in January 2001). The westbound highway through the Atacama desert leads to the Pacific port of Tocopilla.
- Paving the road from Aguas Negras along the Argentine border to Varillar which connects with the route to the port city of La Serena.
- Upgrading the Chile-Argentina Cristo Redentor mountain tunnel that connects Mendoza, Argentina to the Chilean capital Santiago and the Pacific port town of Valparaiso.
- Constructing the road from Rio del Indio through Malalcahuello to Lonquimay.
- Building the route from Aduana Pajaritos to Limite.
- Paving the road from the Pacific port of Arica near the border with Peru to Tambo Quemado which borders Bolivia.
- Paving the route from Paso San Francisco on the Argentine border to Diego de Almagro which connects to Chanaral on the Pacific coast.
- Paving the mountain pass road linking Argentina to Chile through Pehuenche to Talca which connects to Constitucion on the Pacific Coast.

- Paving the road from Coihaique to Coihaique Alto on the Argentine Patagonian frontier in the deep south.
- Constructing the Phillipi to Monte Aymond road.
- Building the Chimpenaike to San Sebastian route.

Paraguay

- Paving the highway linking Mariscal Estigarribia to Sargento Rodriguez.
- Construction on the Puente de la Amistad between Puerto Presidente Franco and Foz de Iguazu.
- Upgrades to Highway 5 between Concepcion and Pedro Juan Caballero along the Parana river across from Brazil and a feeder route north to Bellavista Norte, also along the Parana river bordering Brazil.
- Building up the road from Mariscal Estigarribia to Pozo Hondo.
- Erecting a bridge over the Rio Apa.
- Building a gravel road from Sanutari to Saltos del Guaira.

Argentina

- Upgrading the highway connecting Paso de los Libres, Argentina which faces Uruguaiana, Brazil through to the Cristo Redentor mountain tunnel into Chile.
- Paving the highways connecting Mision through La Paz to Paso Jama and Paso Sico, Chile.
- Paving the northbound highway from Humahuaca to La Quiaca which borders Bolivia.
- Paving the Patagonian highway linking the Atlantic port of San Antonio Oeste through to Paso Puyehue that borders Chile and connects to the Chilean road that leads south to the port of Puerto Montt.
- Erecting one of the world's longest bridges connecting Buenos Aires, Argentina to Colonia, Uruguay.
- Constructing the road between Vinchina and Pircas Negras, Chile.

Uruguay

- Paving Highway 9 from capital city Montevideo to Chuy which borders Brazil.
- Paving Highways 8, 17, 18 and 26 that connect Montevideo to Rio Branco which faces Jaguarao, Brazil.
- Constructing the road from Montevideo to Fray Bentos.
- Paving Highway 5 from Montevideo to Rivera.
- Paving Highways 1 and 3 from Montevideo to Paysandu.

Brazil

- Paving a 120-mile (200 kilometre) segment of the road connecting Inapari, Peru through Assis Brasil to Rio Branco, Brazil and upgrade 48.5 miles (81 kilometres) of paved road in that same route.
- Paving a segment of Highway 174 from the Amazon city of Manaus through Buena Vista to Santa Elena and erecting the Puente de la Via bridge over the Tacutu River on the Brazil-Guyana border.
- Paving a section of Highway 156 between Trajatuba and Oiapoque.

Danube down under

Less than 10 per cent of cargo, mostly bulk raw commodities, is moved on the extensive river networks that snake across South America. Given that South America has 17 major river systems that interconnect, it is reasonable to expect an expansion of this mode of cargo transport. The United States, for example, moves about a quarter of its grains by barge, 28 per cent by truck and 47 per cent by railway after it invested heavily in developing the Mississippi river as a cargo route in the 1950s. At the moment it is possible to navigate from Boca de los Navios at the mouth of Venezuela's Orinoco river down through the Amazon river system and into the Rio de la Plata waterway through to Buenos Aires. Some people have navigated the entire system, but not for commercial purposes. Operators plying the 2,280 miles (3,800 kilometres) of the Amazon-Solimoes river system haul products from as deep as Nauta, Peru through Brazil's interior to

Atlantic coast overseas export ports. Barges navigating the 715 miles (1,191 kilometres) of Venezuela's Orinoco river do much the same but, president Hugo Chavez wants to integrate that river with Colombia's Meta river and make the shallow Orinoco navigable all year. The Paraguay-Parana rivers of the Hidrovia waterway are an example of how other waterways could be used to further regional integration: the Hidrovia connects Bolivia, Brazil and Paraguay to Uruguayan and Argentine export ports on the Rio de la Plata as well as to processing plants along the way. What all three major river networks need, however, are more signalling systems and multimodal terminals that can link to railways.[12] In the case of the 2,151-mile (3,442 kilometre) Hidrovia waterway linking the Parana and Paraguay rivers to the Rio de la Plata, about $1 billion in dredging and signalling systems is planned. What makes an investment of this magnitude worthwhile is the fact that shipping one tonne of cargo 1,660 miles (2,770 kilometres) from Corumba, Brazil to the port of Nueva Palmira, Uruguay costs $20 by river barge compared with $60 by truck.[13] Presently 800 barges ply the Hidrovia, pushed by 85 tugboats, with US-based ACBL Hidrovias the dominant player with 193 barges and eight tugboats in 2000. The continental infrastructure plan maps out 17 inland waterway development projects as you can see in map 7.12. (see Map 7.12) South America's Atlantic ports handled more than 25 million tonnes of cargo in 1998 but access to the Pacific is what is in need of development.[14]

“Less than 10 per cent of cargo, mostly bulk raw commodities, is moved on the extensive river networks that snake across South America”

CASE STUDY

American Commercial Barge Line Co.

More than two billion tonnes of cargo are carried by river barges worldwide each year. In 1996, the American Commercial Barge Line Co., a major operator on the US Mississippi river system, opened a regional headquarters for the Southern Cone of South America in Buenos Aires because it forecast that the volume of cargo shipped on

Map 7.12 North-South River Waterways

Source: Andean Development Corporation

the Hidrovia would triple by 2003 to 15 million tonnes per year from 5 million tonnes, and perhaps grow to as much as 20 million tonnes. 'Argentina gave us the greatest legal security of the five countries when we set up. It allowed us to bring in used tugboats without having to pay the import tax. The Argentine coast guard is very professional...and the regulations between the five countries are different and a headache, but at last the Mercosur countries are standardizing their rules. In some cases the fines were economically prohibitive,' said Paloma Loewenthal, ACBL Hidrovias S.A. director of institutional relations.[15] The company's study found it could transport grains, oilseeds and their byproducts, sugar, iron ore, manganese, cotton, forest products, cars and parts, tobacco, chilled and frozen beef and containers southbound from deep in the heart of South America and backhaul steel pipes, cement, wheat, fertilizers, processed food, diesel fuel and containers on the journey north. The backhaul alone presented a freight potential equal to 81,000 trucks per year.

The study identified six key export production zones:

- The upper Paraguay river area centred on Caceres, Brazil produces 5–15 million tonnes of soybeans.
- The Sao Simao region of Brazil along the upper Parana river harvests about 2.6 million tonnes of soybeans. ACBL forecast that Brazil's soybean crop may grow as much as 39 per cent by 2005 compared with the 1992–1995 average. Mercosur countries already produce about 29 per cent of the global production of soybeans and could account for 34 per cent by crop year 2002/2003.
- The tropical lowlands of Santa Cruz de la Sierra, Bolivia, have an output of about 1.2 million tonnes of soybeans. ACBL's outlook anticipated a 400 per cent rise in Bolivian soybean output in the years ahead compared with the 1992–1995 average.
- Demand for containers to be transferred to and from trucks in Asuncion, Paraguay.
- Northeastern Argentina's Mesopotamia region is estimated to produce about 2.5 million tonnes of soybeans and 1 million tonnes of wood chips for export.

- Along the western side of the Paraguay river in Argentina another 1–1.3 million tonnes of cotton and soybeans are harvested in the Barranqueras and Reconquista areas.

Further down the Paraguay river is Rosario, the capital of Argentina's key agricultural producing and processing province of Santa Fe, where soybean crushers are located in the city that serves as Argentina's largest agrifood export port. At present, the products transported on the Hidrovia are divided between grains, oilseeds and their byproducts (37 per cent), minerals (26 per cent), containers (23 per cent), clinker (8 per cent) and fuel (6 per cent). By 2003, cargo flows on the Parana-Paraguay system are expected to reach 15 million tonnes. Grains, oilseeds and their byproducts could make up 8 million tonnes (53 per cent) of that total followed by iron ore at 4 million tonnes (27 per cent) and 1 million tonnes of diesel bound for Corumba, Brazil (7 per cent) as well as 1 million tonnes each of wood chips and containers.

'These rivers have been navigable since 1500. It's simply a question of dredging them. There's little fog in comparison to other waterways so we navigate 24 hours a day. We have four months of the year when we can move the crop. We need to develop the Hidrovia in the north and some regions need to learn to use the river rather than the sea. The Paraguayans and Bolivians use the rivers quite a bit. River movement is an economical alternative for moving the crop in that four-month window of opportunity,' Loewenthal said.

The economics of shipping by river barge are such that up to 300 miles (500 kilometres) in distance, trucking has a competitive advantage over inland river transport but after that it becomes much cheaper to move bulk by barge. One truck can haul about 25 tonnes or 28,600 litres of cargo; a railway hopper car carries 50 tonnes or about 60,000 litres (North American hoppers can carry up to twice that load); barges can push 1,364 tonnes or 1.7 million litres of cargo. On one litre of fuel a single tonne of cargo can be trucked about 15 miles (25 kilometres), shipped by train about 52 miles (86 kilometres) or taken 160 miles (268 kilometres) by barge. Specifically in the case of the Hidrovia, ACBL Hidrovias runs 1,500-tonne barges the 1,660-

mile (2,770-kilometre) distance to Corumba, Brazil from Nueva Palmira, Uruguay and then switches to 700-tonne barges further up the Paraguay river which becomes narrower and shallower at that point. About 72 truck containers measuring 20 ft (7 metres) long fit on each of these 1,500-tonne barges and on most of the Hidrovia a tugboat can push up to five barges at a time.

'The Hidrovia is the best form of integration in this region. There is no other more intensive form of integration. The signalling system isn't like the Mississippi which is like a highway but we're in the process of seeking funding from governments to improve that. The Hidrovia will develop regional economies just like the Mississippi did since it was developed 50 years ago and when riverside industry started setting up,' Loewenthal said.

At the other end of the continent, along Venezuela's Orinico river, ACBL de Venezuela C.A. has 90 barges and three tugboats that operate during three to four months of the year when the water level is high enough. They shuttle bauxite from Suriname and Guyana to alumina smelters in Bolivar state that turn out finished aluminium.

Here is a summary of the main inland waterways across South America and development projects given priority by the ministers.

Orinoco river waterway

- The navigable segment of Venezuela's Orinoco river runs 715 miles (1,191 kilometres) from Boca de los Navios to Puerto Ayacucho. Tributaries of the Orinoco system can also be navigated up to 396 miles (660 kilometres) up the Apure river and 150 miles (250 kilometres) up the Portuguesa river to the port of El Baul. Colombia's tributaries to the Orinoco, the Meta, Guaviare, Inirida and Vaupes rivers are also navigable.
- Connecting the Orinoco and Meta rivers was given priority by South American governments.
- Venezuela is studying connecting the Orinoco to Brazil's Casiquiare and Rio Negro rivers and solving the difficult river passes at Atures and Maipures in order to link the Orinoco to the Amazon.

Amazon river waterway

- Large barges can transport goods almost 2,280 miles (3,800 kilometres) from Nauta, Peru to the Atlantic along the Amazon-Solimoes river system.
- The *northern tributary* Rio Negro river is navigable almost 755 miles (1,260 kilometres) from Venezuela. Also to the north is the Rio Branco river which from its confluence with the Rio Negro up to Caracarai is navigable some 265 miles (440 kilometres).
- There are two *eastern tributaries* to the Amazon-Solimoes which are navigable: the Rio Trombetas river is navigable for 155 miles (260 kilometres) and the Rio Jari river is navigable for 90 miles (150 kilometres).
- There are two major *western tributaries*: the Rio Japura-Caqueta which is navigable on the Brazilian side for up to 450 miles (750 kilometres) and the Rio Putumayo-Ica which is navigable for almost its entire length of 1,110 miles (1,850 kilometres).
- Other western tributaries to the Amazon-Solimoes that are partly navigable in short sections are those that link Ecuador to Peru such as the Tigre, Pastaza, Marañon and Santiago rivers.
- Perhaps the most extensive series of navigable rivers that feed into the Amazon-Solimoes system are the *southern tributaries*: the Rio Jurua river is navigable for almost 1,500 miles (2,500 kilometres); most of the 1,980 miles (3,300 kilometres) of the Rio Purus river is navigable, as is 372 miles (620 kilometres) of its Rio Acre tributary up to Brasileia; the Rio Madeira river is navigable the full 660 miles (1,100 kilometres) to Porto Velho and has 960 miles (1,600 kilometres) of its own tributaries that are navigable such as the Rio Mamore and Rio Guapore-Itenez rivers; the Rio Tapajos is currently navigable the 205 miles (345 kilometres) to Sao Luis de Tapajos but should be ready for navigation on as much as 625 miles (1,045 kilometres) in the near future; the Rio Xingu is navigable for 250 miles (420 kilometres).
- Other north-south rivers that are navigable include the Rios Maranon up to Saramiriza and the Ucayali up to the south of Pucallpa in Peru.

Tocantins river waterway

- The Tocantins river is navigable 150 miles (250 kilometres) up to the Tucuri hydroelectric dam and can be navigated for almost 600 miles (1,000 kilometres) upriver from the dam, depending on the ship's draft.
- The Rio Araguaia tributary of the Tocantins can be navigated up to 915 miles (1,525 kilometres).

Sao Francisco river waterway

- The Sao Francisco river is navigable in sections for a total of 1,020 miles (1,700 kilometres) with the final segment being 125 miles (208 kilometres) long between Piranhas and the Atlantic Ocean.

Hidrovia Paraguay-Parana

- This is the most important inland waterway link tying Brazil to Bolivia, Paraguay, Argentina and Uruguay. It spans 2,151 miles (3,442 kilometres) and connects the Parana and Paraguay rivers to the Rio de la Plata.

Hidrovia Tiete-Parana

- The Tiete-Parana river connection, once locks construction is complete, will be the most important east-west inland waterway in Brazil, navigable up to 1,440 miles (2,400 kilometres).

Brazil has developed the Madeira, Tocantins, Araguaia and Sao Francisco rivers as well as the Tiete-Parana network under its Brasil en Accion infrastructure programme. All of these works are scheduled to continue as part of the new public works projects under the Avança Brasil initiative.

Trains across South America

You will find that railway transportation is more developed in the Mercosur countries than in the Andean Community. But even in the Southern Cone, railways' share of the cargo transport sector accounts for a fraction of the volume handled by truck and even barge traffic. The challenge in attracting more use of the South American rail transportation network for trade within the continent or the subregional blocks is considerable given that operators run freight trains on wide-gauge (1.6 metres), narrow-gauge (1 metre) and standard-gauge (1.435 metres) railroad tracks. This is the legacy of competing, privately built and operated rail lines that were laid in the first half of the 20th Century. Railways were built primarily for the export of primary goods overseas, not the movement of products between neighbouring nations. That explains in part why railways handle only about 4 per cent of cargo moved in both Argentina and Brazil. That may change now that the former public rail assets have been opened up to the private sector on the promise of making necessary capital upgrades. There are about 24,000 miles (40,000 kilometres) of narrow-gauge track in Argentina, Bolivia, Brazil and Chile and another 3,600 miles (6,000 kilometres) of standard-gauge track. Both Argentina and Chile also have tracks that are 1.376-metres wide but there is no connection between the two national systems. If they were linked, they would form a 12,000-mile (20,000-kilometre) network.[16]

> **“even in the Southern Cone, railways’ share of the cargo transport sector accounts for a fraction of the volume handled by truck and even barge traffic”**

Brazil privatized its Federal Railway Network (RFFSA) in 1995 and a survey by the Brazilian Transport Ministry in March 2000 found that some concessionaires had ended up investing less in infrastructure than had been expected. But those that did spend more than anticipated, such as MRS Logistica and America Latina Logistica (ALL), have been reaping higher profits. ALL was the first railway to offer a cross-border intermodal link with trucks.

The railroad operator started running 20-unit trains twice weekly as of October 2000 along 1,000 miles (1,700 kilometres) of track linking Sao Paulo via Porto Alegre to Buenos Aires, hauling products manufactured by BASF AG, Colgate-Palmolive, Nabisco, Procter & Gamble and Unilever NV. Formed by the merger of Brazil’s Ferrovia Sul Atlantica (FSA) and Argentine railroads Ferrocarril Mesopotamico and Buenos Aires al Pacifico (BAP), ALL controls about 9,000 miles (15,000 kilometres) of track in the south of Brazil and deep into Argentina. It offers express cargo service by rail to Montevideo, three times a week. The railroad also has multimodal transfer stations in both Argentina and Brazil, making it a prime example of a successful operator in this segment of the transport industry. It plans to invest $80 million in five years to rebuild its infrastructure and rolling stock after securing medium to long-term financing from the Bank of Austria, Citibank and others.

One capital project that began in March 2001 was the construction of a mixed-gauge interchange yard in partnership with Nuevo Central Argentino (NCA) railway. Once completed, the rail triage yard will connect NCA's broad-gauge network to ALL's standard-gauge Mesopotamico line. The interchange yard will link Cordoba and Santa Fe, two of Argentina's most important industrial cities, to Brazil as well as cut three days off current transit times to Mendoza and on through to Chile. In Bolivia, six more locomotives were scheduled to be added in 2001 by Empresa Ferroviaria Oriental S.A., which is controlled by Genesee & Wyoming and UniRail LLC of the United States, to haul more goods from Santa Cruz de la Sierra along 750 miles (1,244 kilometres) of metre-gauge track linking the industrial hub to the Hidrovia port city of Puerto Barrios to the east and Pocitos and Yacuiba in the south. In the north, there are plans to build a railway link from Maracaibo, Venezuela to Cucuta, Colombia and over to La Ceiba, Venezuela. Another Venezuelan railway project would extend track from Saravena, Colombia through El Pinal, Venezuela northeast to Acarigua, Venezuela. Please see maps 7.13, 7.14, and 7.15. ALL and MRS Logistica financed their capital modernization programmes through the issuance of debentures on the Brazilian debt market.

Multimodal terminals may open up more business to railway operators now that South American governments are turning their attention to developing Pacific ports to open up new markets. Be it by truck, river or railway – or more likely a combination of two or all three – South American governments want to make greater use of the Pacific ports. The continent has 214 sea ports, of which 60 per cent are located along the Pacific coast, but these handle only 38 per cent of containers and 28 per cent of general cargo. The east coast ships five times as much cargo as the west coast and of South America's 25 busiest ports, 20 are on the east coast and five on the west. Trends also

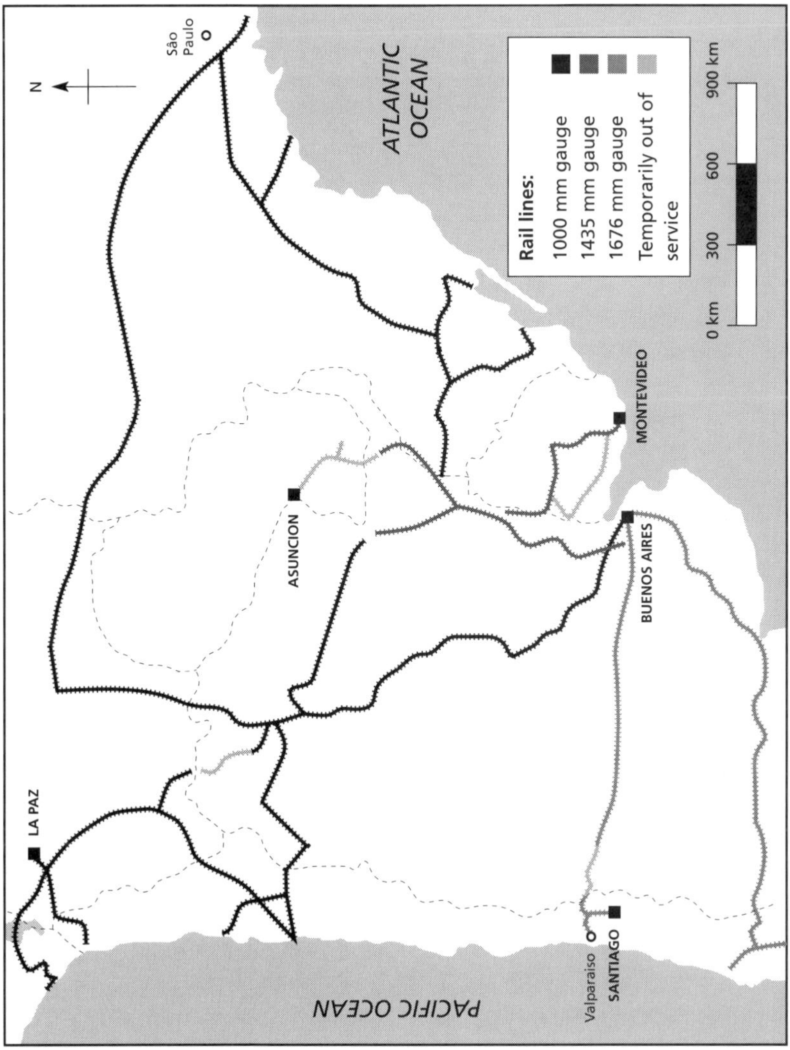

Map 7.13 Basic Intra-Regional Railway Network in the Southern Cone

Source: Latin American Railway Association, courtesy of Andean Development Corporation

Map 7.14 Inter-Oceanic Railway Corridors of Regional Development Interest

Source: Latin American Railway Association, courtesy of Andean Development Corporation

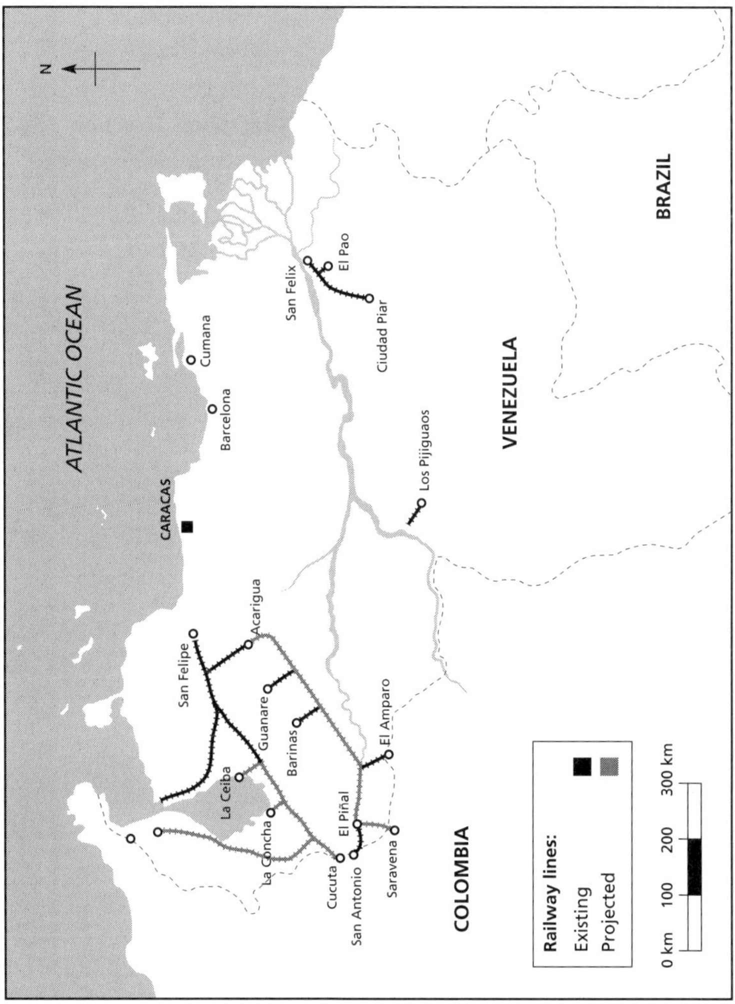

Map 7.15 Venezuelan Railway Network

Source: Latin American Railway Association, courtesy of Andean Development Corporation

indicate that container cargo, about 50 per cent of the 5.36 billion tonnes of cargo shipped by ocean vessels per year, will grow to between 65 and 75 per cent in the second decade of the 21st century.[17] At the end of 2000 there were about 50,000 ocean vessels in the world, two-thirds of which were freighters, a fifth tankers and the remainder ferries. The number of ships in the global fleet has risen about 10 per cent in the past decade and tonnage capacity has increased 35 per cent. Containers can be moved easily and quickly from trucks to either river barges or single or double-stacked trains and then on to ocean vessels. There are three dual-sea corridors that have been given priority:

1. *South Atlantic-South Pacific corridor*: The Sao Paulo-Buenos Aires-Santiago corridor is being rehabilitated to open up access to both oceans via a transport corridor that goes through one of South America's most important industrial belts and concentration of some of the continent's richest residents.

2. *Mid-Atlantic-Mid-Pacific corridor*: The Santos (Brazil) to Matarani (Peru) to Arica/Antofagasta (Chile) corridor has yet to be completed between Aiquiles and Santa Cruz de la Sierra, Bolivia, and the railroad width needs to be standardized throughout.

3. *Pacific-Caribbean corridor*: If the railway link between Colombia and Venezuela were completed it would offer another cargo transport alternative to shipping goods between the Pacific and the Caribbean.

The development of duty-free ports

In addition to these intermodal transportation hubs that are under construction, another asset that could capitalize on trade development is the duty-free zone. Tax-free ports date back to the times of the Roman Empire and have been growing in number in South America in recent years. Take the example of South America's most economically important duty-free zone in northern Chile, the Iquique Free Trade Zone (*www.zofri.cl*). Sixty-five per cent of the imports that are warehoused there duty free come from Asia and the United States. Ninety-five per cent of the products stored by the 1,800 user companies at Iquique's 600-acre (240-hectare) duty-free compound are eventually shipped throughout SouthAmerica.[18] The advantage is that rather than paying import tariffs on the entire cargo upon arrival in port, the importers pay duties on their merchandise only once it leaves the Iquique area. In the case of Iquique, about 40 per cent of the imported goods are gradually distributed throughout Chile, another 30 per cent to Bolivia and the balance is split between Argentina and Peru. The first South American duty-free zone was set up in Colombia in the 1960s and others have since been set up in Peru and Bolivia. 'In terms of economic integration, duty-free zones are a source of conflict. Mercosur decided in 1994 that products from duty-free zones will be treated as imports from third countries. It's so severe that if you import from Brazil and warehouse them in La Plata (an Argentine duty-free port), you will have to pay the common external tariff to bring it into Argentina or other Mercosur countries,' said Guillermo Ondarts, an economist who is an expert in duty-free zone issues.[19] That decision curtailed the growth in Uruguay's plans to position itself as a duty-free import centre in Montevideo. That area was created to help foreign businesses circumvent the region's government-controlled telephone monopolies of the time and offer them affordable international calling rates. The plan was to offer not only duty-free storage but a cheaper business environment and some manufacturing capability. But Mercosur policy makers feared duty-free zones would undermine their newly created customs union. 'I believe that if Mercosur refines its instruments it should change these regulations to be closer to those of the European Union or Nafta. If you assemble a bicycle in a duty-free zone here with 50 per cent of the parts coming from Mercosur you still end up paying 100 per cent of the common external tariff. In the EU and Nafta you only pay the full external tariff on the imported parts,' Ondarts said.

This explains why volume at Argentina's more recent and leading duty-free zone in La Plata, a port city in Buenos Aires province about 50 miles (80 kilometres) south of the capital, is not as high as that in Montevideo. Established in 1997, La Plata's duty-free port handled 90 per cent of imports into Argentina's half dozen 'zonas francas', or about 3 per cent of total imports in the year 2000. Ninety per cent of the $600 million in goods warehoused in La Plata came from Asia, the United States and Europe which were sheltered from Argentina's

21 per cent value added tax, 7 per cent VAT advance payment and capital gains advance payments which vary between 50 and 60 per cent. In a lower tax environment, these duty-free zones could represent important cost savings for multinational manufacturers and retailers like you that operate on just-in-time delivery. 'The virtues of duty-free zones is they're very closely monitored so you can import foreign goods, process them and then export them elsewhere or internally without delay by customs,' Ondarts added. But for now the regulatory environment means duty-free zones are a much less attractive option here than, say, the Caribbean, where there has been a proliferation of tax-free ports.

"The plan was to offer not only duty-free storage but a cheaper business environment and some manufacturing capability"

There are special economic development territories like Manaus in northern Brazil or Argentina's Tierra del Fuego at the tip of the continent. But in Argentina, duty-free zones are not allowed to add value to imports that will be exported to the internal market and in Brazil, which has had a duty-free zone manufacturing law on the books for about 10 years, there are no such territories yet.

Clearing the cluttered southern skies

It is highly unlikely that a market that accounts only for 5 per cent of the world's air transport business can accommodate the number of airlines currently operating in South America (see Table 7.3). There are at least 96 international airports in South America which handled more than 53 million passengers in 1996, of which more than 40 per cent travelled through Brazilian airports.

Nine of the 16 South American airlines flying to other nations were in financial trouble in 2000, meaning the industry is on course for consolidation. On the other hand, we are likely see the emergence of small, local carriers in each country offering services to the interior. Colombia is a good example of this trend. The three largest Colombian airlines, Avianca, Aces and Sam, signed a memorandum of understanding in January 2001 to discuss their merger as a means

Table 7.3 Air passenger traffic within South America in 1999 (expressed in thousands)

	ARG	BO	BRA	COL	CHI	ECU	GUY	PAR	PER	URU	VEN
ARG	0	160.6	573.7	35.1	837.1	5.9	0	109.7	68.7	153.0	29.9
BO	167.7	0	106.8	7.8	92.8	.056	0	27.5	71.8	20.9	12.8
BRA	1266.8	168.4	0	32.8	249.2	14.0	7.2	123.7	58.1	307.5	77.0
COL	40.7	10.2	13.7	0	40.0	30.9	.053	.115	82.5	0	192.9
CHI	852.3	99.8	121.8	25.7	0	20.7	.153	49.9	238.2	83.7	31.6
ECU	12.9	.126	6.8	124.8	41.8	0	0	0	66.0	0	52.5
GUY	0	0	4.6	0	0	0	0	0	0	0	0
PAR	123.4	24.7	54.2	.063	51.4	0	0	0	.202	22.5	.188
PER	88.7	59.2	28.0	74.4	239.3	28.4	0	.518	0	7.5	91.5
URU	1514.6	25.0	304.7	0	80.4	0	0	22.8	7.3	0	0
VEN	32.5	12.7	41.8	157.7	28.1	17.4	0	.214	92.6	0	0

Source: Inter-American Development Bank *www.iadb.org*

to remain profitable in the war-torn country's lagging aviation market. The proposed new airline would have combined assets of $700 million and hold a 50 per cent share of Colombia's international passengers. 'The airlines that survive will be the ones with strategic alliances,' said Latin American Civil Aviation Commission secretary Marco Ospina.[20] He and other analysts agree that Mercosur could sustain two viable regional carriers while the Andean Community could probably afford only one. It is simply not viable for each country from tiny Ecuador on the Pacific coast to behemoth Brazil on the Atlantic to maintain an international carrier.

Argentine flag carrier Aerolineas Argentinas won a reprieve from bankruptcy in 2000 and is trying to reposition itself in the market, while Brazilian international airline Vasp, which owns stakes in Lloyd Aereo Boliviano and Ecuatoriana, continues to struggle with its debt as it undergoes a major restructuring. 'I think there's room to establish regional carriers to feed trunk carriers in South America,' said John MacDonald of Miami-based airline management consultant AvMan Inc.([21]) Regional carriers could connect cities like Santiago to Buenos Aires and on to Sao Paulo, where a trunk airline would handle the domestic leg of the flight to Belo Horizonte, Brazil, for example.

Analysts believe that those airlines that don't adapt to this flight plan are likely to perish. 'It's difficult to find people who want to invest in South America because of its ups and downs: Venezuela is a basket case, its oldest airline Avensa is virtually bankrupt, and God knows where Peru's going,' MacDonald said. Turbulent times are forecast for the whole region, including Chile, which is rated as the hemisphere's lowest-risk nation in which to invest after the United States and Canada. LanChile and its subsidiary, Ladeco, dominate the country's domestic market, but the advent of cut-rate Aerocontinente Chile in May 2000 even had long-distance bus operators complaining about aggressive local pricing. Aerocontinente Chile, 51 per cent-owned by Chilean investors and 49 per cent by Aerocontinente Peru, even offered fares to Miami for $399, well below the $600–$700 asked by competitors. LanChile is widely regarded as one of South America's best managed airlines, and picked up domestic routes in Peru under the banner LanPeru after the collapse of Aero Peru.

Brazil, meanwhile, has more major airlines than any country in the world other than the United States. TAM and Transbrasil announced in May 2000 a joint operational agreement aimed at cutting costs, which TAM officials admit could eventually lead to a merger. A month later Brazil's top airline, Varig, signed a deal with the nation's third-largest carrier, TAM, to create an open-capital internet venture to sell tickets and tourism services. Varig Cargo and Germany's Lufthansa Cargo integrated their air freight activities within a common flight network from September 2000. 'Brazil will need to consolidate down to two carriers. Does Brazil need three carriers serving the US? No. But they need one or two carriers serving the interior of the country. That industry is beginning to grow because manufacturers are building more of that type of aircraft now,' MacDonald said. The region is also bracing for more competition after the US Department of Transportation complained in 2000 that South America is 'lagging behind' in plans to lift flight restrictions with the United States, dubbed 'open skies'. More access for US carriers along with more competition and aggressive marketing could expand the South American marketplace by as much as 3 million passengers, US officials believe.

Electricity generation and transportation

Electricity consumption in South America in 1996 was 544,411 gigawatt hours (Gwh). The Andean Development Corporation expects demand to almost double by 2010 to 1.04 million gigawatt hours, assuming growth in consumption of 4.8 per cent a year. Brazil accounts for roughly 50 per cent of demand while Venezuela and Argentina combined take in another 25 per cent, with the balance split between the remaining South American republics. Annual growth in demand is expected to be above the continental average of 4.8 per cent in Bolivia, Chile, Ecuador, Paraguay and Peru, but is forecast to fall below that average in Argentina, Brazil, Colombia, Uruguay and Venezuela. About 80 per cent of the electricity generated in South America today comes from hydroelectric dams. In fact, Paraguay, Brazil, Peru, Uruguay and Colombia cover more than 80 per cent of their needs with hydro power, in comparison with Argentina and Bolivia which rely on that source for less than 45 per cent of their electric energy needs. What this means is the majority of South American countries are highly vulnerable to weather conditions owing to their dependence on hydroelectric dam turbines to generate their power. Brazil's electrical power crisis in 2001 is a prime example of this.

> **"The privatization of CEMIG illustrates the risks foreign operators can face in this part of the world"**

Market reforms undertaken in the electricity sector in the 1990s (except for Chile which made its reforms in the early 1980s) mean governments have been reducing their role in this sector. As a consequence, operators like US-based AES and Duke Energy have set up power-generation plants in South America to produce electricity. Duke Energy (*www.duke-energy.com*) planned to spend $1.2 billion on generation plants in several South American countries which would more than double its international generating capacity. About 10 per cent of the company's 1999 sales came from outside the United States. By 1999, AES Corp., the No. 1 US power plant developer, had 51 of its 111 facilities in Brazil and had six plants in Argentina. AES began its foray into Latin America in 1993 and took over the formerly state-owned Brazilian electric utilities Light Servicios e Electricidade in 1996 and CEMIG in 1997. The privatization of CEMIG illustrates the risks foreign operators can face in this part of the world. The utility is based in Minas Gerais state which is governed by former Brazilian president Itamar Franco. The nationalist governor has ambitions to return to the presidency and foreign companies have been an easy target to score political points. With CEMIG, the US directors were kicked off the utility's board, sending out a bad signal to other foreign operators thinking of establishing themselves in Brazil.

In 2000 AES acquired four power distributors in Brazil as well as Electrobras' broadband data transmission company, Electronet. Later that year AES bought a 73 per cent stake in Venezuelan electric utility Grupo EDC in a $1.5 billion hostile takeover.

In Venezuela, president Hugo Chavez has said he will not go down the privatization path taken by most of the other South American nations. An avowed admirer of the statist policies of former French president Charles de Gaulle, Chavez prefers to open up the Venezuelan economy to public-private joint ventures.[22]

What you are likely to see happening in the electricity sector in South America in the coming years is a series of infrastructure projects to connect one nation's grid to another's and a proliferation of co-generation plants in nations eager to wean themselves off their hydroelectric dependence. Since there is an abundance of natural gas in South America that has yet to be exploited and the preference seems to be to use it on the continent in order to export more oil, that means industrial power consumers like you will probably rely more on natural gas for your co-generation facilities. There is a definite cost benefit to this scenario. Gas-driven turbines offer 55 per cent electrical efficiency versus steam turbines which are 33 per cent efficient. You may also see some growth in hydroelectric power supply. Down in the Southern Cone, the Yacyreta binational (Argentina-Paraguay) organization said it planned to invest $525 million to raise the level of the hydroelectric dam to its designed height of 83 metres above sea level. Raising the level should double the dam's electricity output to 20,000 GWh. The World Bank and Inter-American Development Bank recently approved the plan and released $130 million in loans earmarked for its completion. Some $200 million is destined to build a new generating station on the Ana-Cua spillway. Five consortia have expressed interest in that project and those which prequalify were asked to submit bids in the second quarter of 2001. Argentina's energy secretary forecast that electricity exports would total about $500 million between 2001 and 2004. The Association of Energy Generators of Argentina (Agreera) estimates expanding capacity to feed Brazilian demand has helped pull domestic prices down to 2.4 cents per kilowatt from 3 cents. At the beginning of 2001 Argentina was midway through a 1,000 megawatt export contract with Brazil, had signed another 1,000 megawatt supply contract with that country, and talks were under way for an additional 2,000 megawatts, according to Agreera. (Map 7.16)

Natural gas network

Natural gas accounts for 22 per cent of world energy consumption and is forecast to grow in importance to 29 per cent by 2020. Argentina has been in the vanguard of South American nations developing this resource and maturing its market, followed by Chile. With more than 70 per cent of South America's proved reserves, Venezuela (see Table 6.2) is among those countries such as Bolivia, Ecuador and Peru that are just beginning to develop the resource. 'The issue with natural gas is transportation. You have to have the infrastructure. Transporting oil is much easier. Eventually, natural gas evolves into a commodity-driven market like in the United States, but building and paying for it is at first a government enterprise, that's why the IADB is involved in Brazil,' said one New York-based energy analyst.

There are two ways to transport natural gas: as a gas or as a liquid. Pipelines can carry the resource in both forms and trucks can haul liquified natural gas as well, and technological advances have made it more economical to transport it. Demand for the energy source in the region grew at an annual rate of 4.7 per cent throughout the 1990s. Global growth in natural gas demand over the next 20 years is expected to average 3.2 per cent, led by Latin America and the developing nations of Asia at 7.5 and 7 per cent respectively. Until recently demand was mainly concentrated in the markets of the major producers but now consumption has been growing in Brazil, Chile and Colombia at annual rates of 9.6 per cent, 7.1 per cent and 6.3 per cent respectively.[23] (Map 7.17) Market reforms throughout South

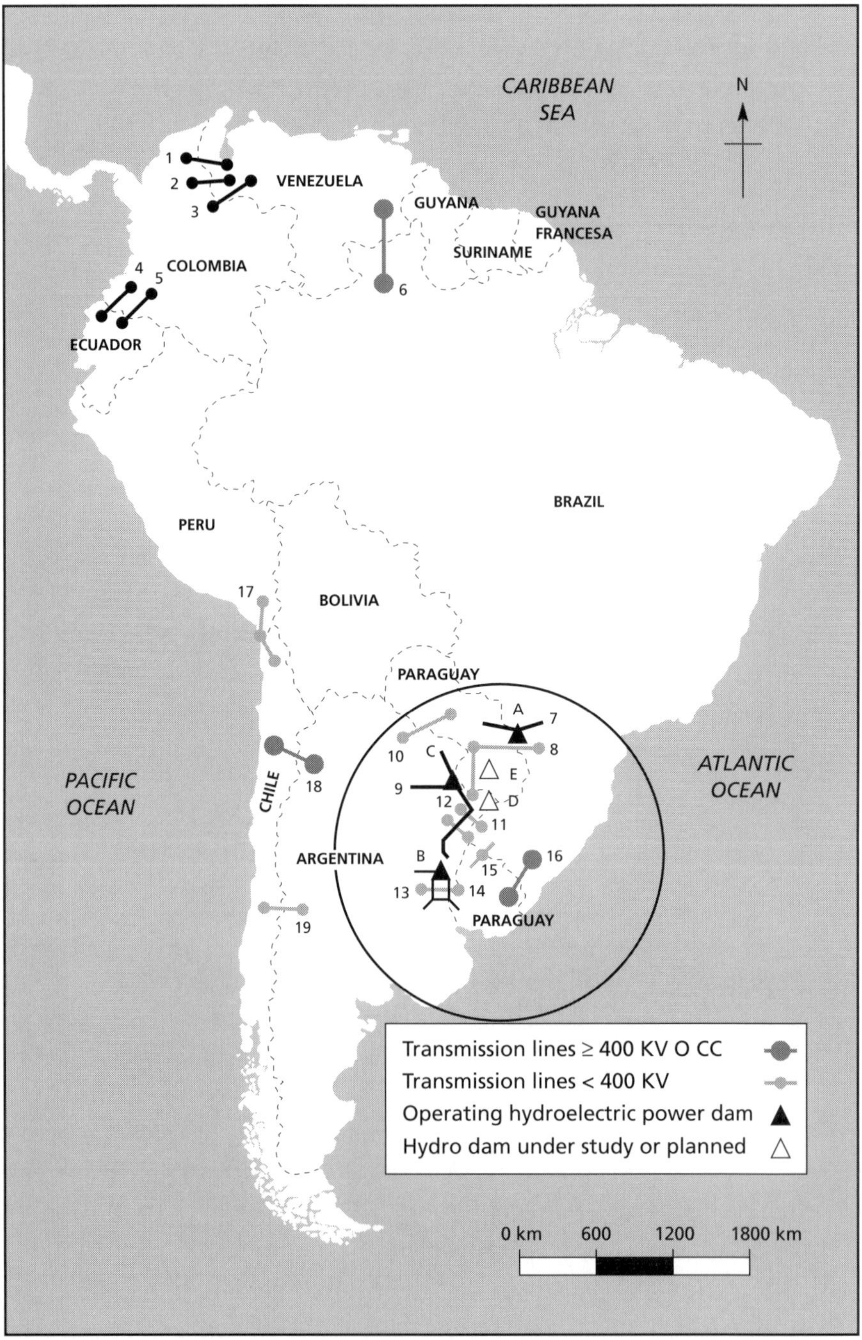

Map 7.16 Main Power Generation Stations and Interconnections

Source: Andean Development Corporation

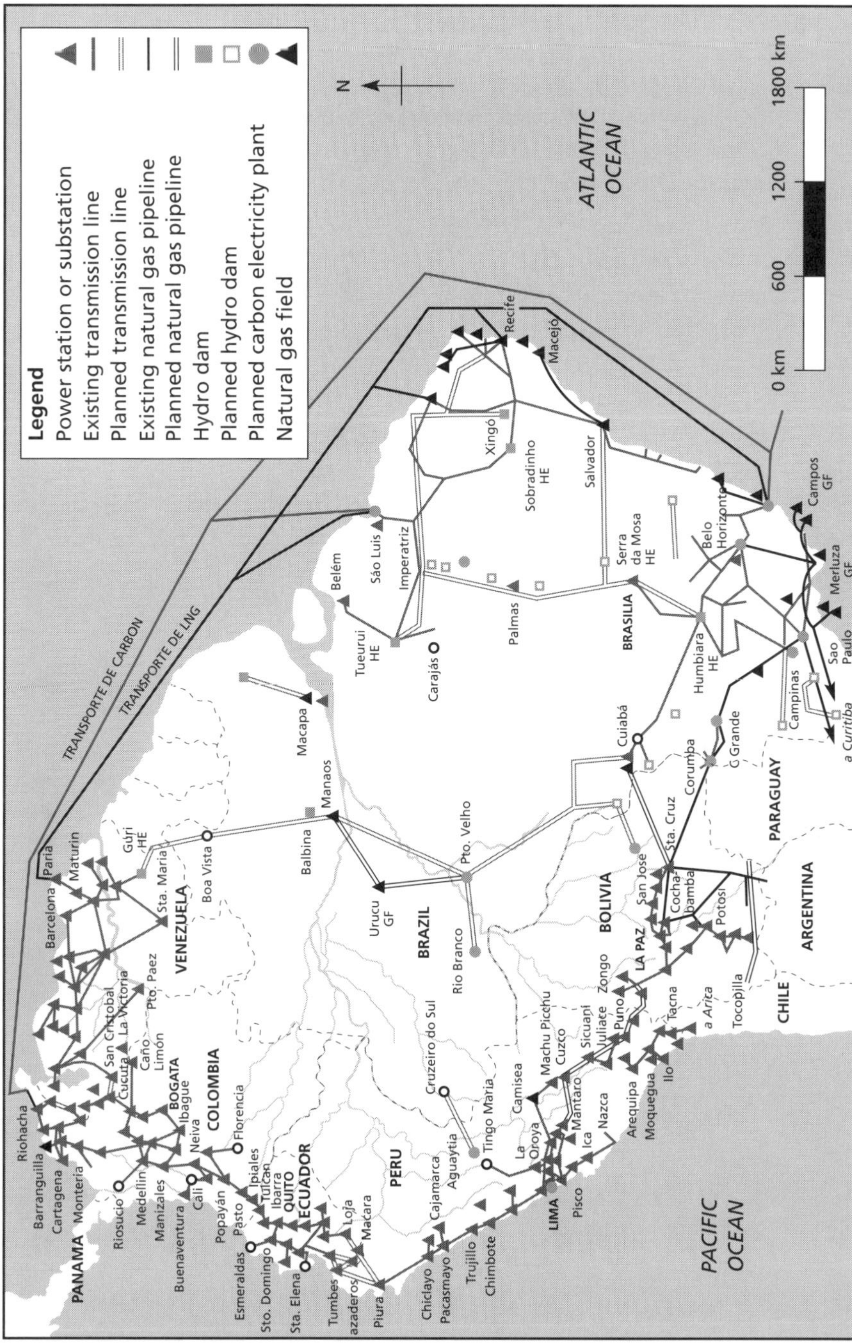

Map 7.17 Energy Integration Projects between Andean Nations and Brazil

Source: Andean Development Corporation

America aimed at fostering a greater role for the private sector in this area should help push resource and market development forward.

Meanwhile, industry's transition to combined cycle plants is likely to rely increasingly on natural gas which offers some of the best efficiencies. Until 1999, South America's international natural gas pipeline network was limited to the Argentina-Chile connection and Bolivia-Argentina connection (see Table 7.4). Brazil will be the most important natural gas market in South America in the coming decades given annual consumption growth forecasts of 11 per cent for the next 20 years and work is already under way to service that market (see Table 7.5).

Table 7.4 Operational natural gas pipelines in South America

Country	Connection	Capacity Cubic feet/day	Length	Start date
Bolivia to Brazil	Santa Cruz-Sao Paulo	1 billion	3,043 km	1999
Bolivia to Argentina	Santa Cruz-Yacuiba	215 million	541 km	1996
Argentina to Chile	Magallanes	72 million	90 km	1996
Argentina to Chile	Gas Atacama	300 million	928 km	1999
Argentina to Chile	Norandino	280 million	530 km	1999
Argentina to Chile	Gas Andes	286 million	776 km	1997
Argentina to Chile	Gas Pacifico	140 million	530 km	1999
Argentina to Uruguay	Entre Rios-Paysandu	88 million	500 km	1998

Source: Andean Development Corp. (*www.caf.com*)

Foreign investor involvement like yours in energy-generation projects can count on some US government support, assuming some capital is repatriated to the United States, to the benefit of the US trade balance. The US Overseas Private Investment Corporation (*www.opic.gov*) signed its first political risk insurance contract in Latin America when it backed a $175 million bond issuance on US capital markets by Argentine natural gas transportation company Transportadora de Gas del Norte (TGN). TGN used the revenues from the bonds to expand its natural gas pipeline system in central and northern Argentina. Thanks to Opic's political risk insurance, TGN's debt instrument was rated investment grade by Fitch IBCA and Standard & Poor's, lowering financing costs. Opic's insurance hedges against

Table 7.5 Natural gas pipelines under construction or study in South America

Country	Connection	Capacity	Length Cubic feet/day	Start date
Argentina-Chile	Magallanes 2	104 million	105 km	being built
Argentina-Uruguay	Cruz del Sur	90 million	215 km	being built
Argentina-Brazil	Gaucho	106 million	440 km	being built
Argentina-Brazil	Yabog	data unavail.	3,541 km	study
Argentina-Brazil	Austral	1.097 billion	3,700 km	study
Arg-Bra-Paraguay	Mercosur	885 million	3,115 km	1999
Bolivia-Peru	La Paz-Ilo	145 million	400 km	study
Bolivia-Chile	Villamontes-Tocopilla	212 million	700 km	study
Bolivia-Brazil	San Miguel-Cuiaba	140 million	530 km	being built
Bolivia-Brazil	Transchaco	244 million	846 km	study

Source: Andean Development Corp. (*www.caf.com*)

the risks of a reduced ability to convert local currency into dollars and to transfer dollars out of the host country to service payments of principal and interest on the debt raised in the capital markets. Typically, Opic's political risk coverage will be issued to a US-based trust, which will hold the insurance for the bondholders. In order for you to qualify for the coverage, at least 50 per cent of the funding for the bonds must come from US financial institutions which must hold those funds for at least 40 days. Some of the TGN pipelines fed natural gas all the way to Uruguaiana, Brazil, where another Opic-supported energy project was inaugurated, 10 months ahead of schedule. AES built a 600-megawatt natural gas-fired, combined cycle power-generation plant in Uruguaiana, of which 140 megawatts were brought online on 22 January 2001. This is the first major energy integration project between Brazil and Argentina. It is estimated that Brazil has an 11,000-megawatt power deficit, or that electricity demand exceeds supply by 16 per cent. Opic provided $115 million in investment guarantees for the AES power-plant project because it expected repatriated profits to benefit US balance of payments by about $75 million. The plant will also create an estimated 392 US jobs and 40

“This is the first major energy integration project between Brazil and Argentina”

Brazilian jobs as well as the purchase of local construction materials to the tune of about $128 million over five years, plus generating annual tax revenues of about $59 million.

Telecommunications links

Until the 1990s, most South Americans had to wait years before their state-owned telephone monopolies would assign them a phone line. Now that nine of the 10 major South American countries have allowed private operators to enter that sector (although Bolivia, Ecuador and Paraguay have not yet fully deregulated) the situation has been turned on its head with a proliferation of cybercafes and more than 27 million South Americans using cellular phones as of 1999. There are now more mobile phones than fixed lines in Venezuela and Paraguay. Only Uruguay has yet to privatize and deregulate. Telephone market penetration doubled in South America during the course of the 1990s to 14 per cent from 7 per cent. One study forecasts market penetration to reach 60 per cent within the next decade, meaning every adult living in an urban area may have access to a telephone.[24] All the major North American and European telecommunications companies and fibre optics manufacturers are present in South America and market deregulation has been reducing the costs of international telecommunications. Both government and business will be the drivers of growth in this sector. (Maps 7.18 and 7.19)

This description of the South American version of the Marshall Plan should help you appreciate the relative economic importance of these various infrastructure projects in the context of expanding trade flows within the region as well as facilitating the movement of goods and services into and out of this continent. Between the forecasts for growing demand for energy and a summary of financial assistance available to you, it is clear there are some opportunities in this region worthy of deeper analysis.

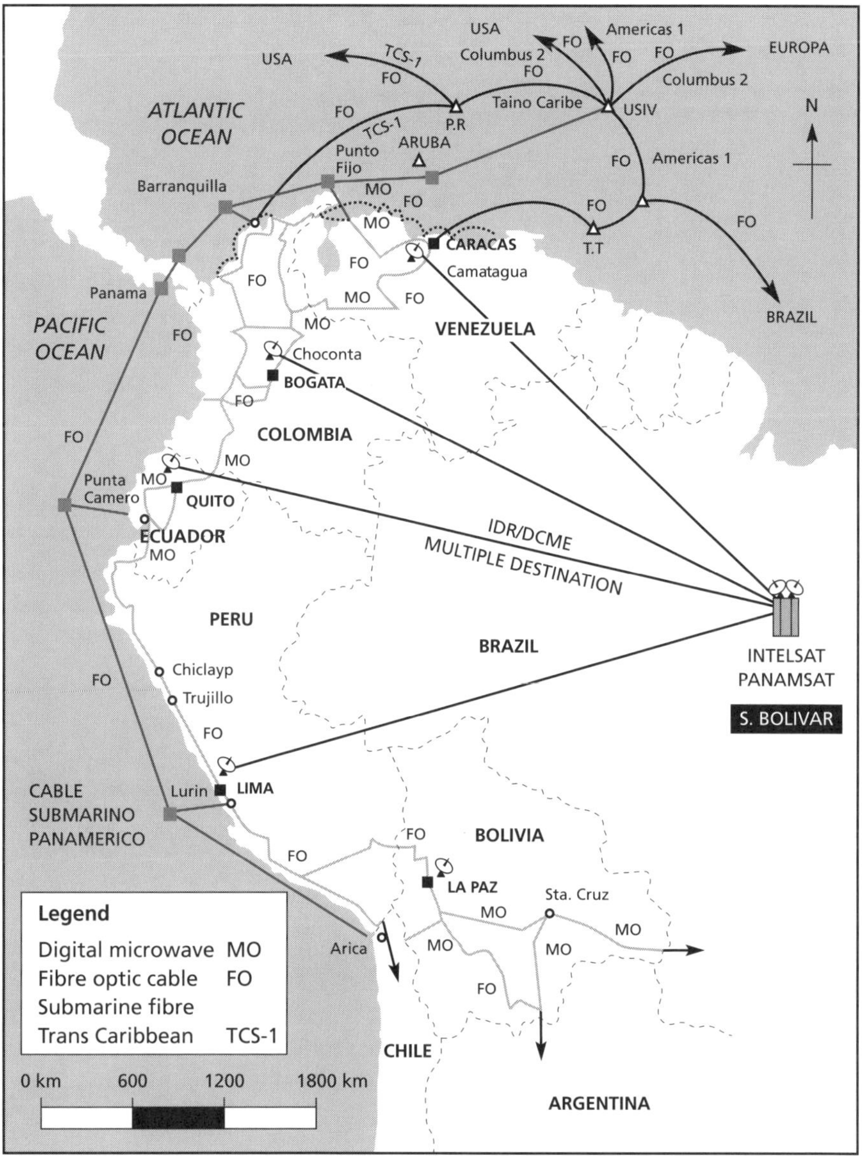

Map 7.18 Andean Corridor of Digital Telecommunications

Source: Andean Development Corporation

Map 7.19 Submarine Fiber Optic Cable Network

Source: Andean Development Corporation

Notes

[1]Rojas Penso, Juan, secretary general of the Association of Latin American Trade Partners, interview from Montevideo, 21 March 2001.

[2]Inter-American Development Bank (2000) 'Un nuevo impulso a la integracion de la infraestructura regional en America del Sur', pp. 1–2, 12, 20.

[3]Alegrett, Sebastián, Andean Community secretary general, interview with Bolivian newspaper *Presencia* published 1 October 2000.

[4]Garcia, Enrique, executive president of Corporacion Andina de Fomento, interview in Caracas, 17 January 2001.

[5]O'Meara Sheehan, Molly, in *State of the World 2001*, Worldwatch Institute Report on Progress Toward a Sustainable Society, pp. 109–111.

[6]Silveira, Jose Paulo, secretary for planning at the Brazilian Planning Ministry, phone interview to Brasilia, 16 January 2001.

[7]O'Meara Sheehan, Molly, *op. cit.*, page 117.

[8]Andean Community of Nations, General Secretariat website *www.comunidadandina.org/estadistica/sgdi261/sgdi261.htm*, viewed 19 January 2001.

[9]Smith, Mark, US Chamber of Commerce, Latin America and Caribbean section, interview in Washington, D.C., 12 January 2001.

[10]IADB report, *op. cit.*, pp. 15 and 33.

[11]Chavez, Hugo, interview in Puerto Ordaz, 20 January 2001.

[12]IADB report, *op cit.*, page 35.

[13]Ibanez, Carlos, head of special area regimens in Argentina's foodstuffs division of the federal agriculture department, interview in Buenos Aires, 3 August 2000.

[14] IADB report, *op. cit.*, page 30.

[15]Loewenthal, Paloma, institutional relations director, ACBL Hidrovias S.A., interview in Buenos Aires, Argentina, 18 December 2000.

[16]Andean Development Corporation (2000) 'Vias para la integracion', IADB report, page 41.

[17]*Ibid*, pp. 44–47.

[18]Iquique Free Trade Zone website, *www.zofri.cl*, viewed 28 February 2001.

[19]Ondarts, Guillermo, economist specializing in duty-free zone issues, interview in Buenos Aires, 27 February 2001.

[20]Ospina, Marco, secretary of the Latin American Civil Aviation Commission, a division of the International Civil Aviation Organization, phone interview to Lima, 21 July 2000.

[21]MacDonald, John, analyst at airline management consultant AvMan Inc., phone interview to Miami, 21 July 2000.

[22]Chavez, Hugo, interview in Puerto Ordaz, 20 January 2001.

[23]Andean Development Corporation, *op. cit.*, pp. 72–74.

[24]*Ibid*, pp. 79–85.

8

The twilight of national currencies?

Where are all these integration efforts leading? Leaders in both the Andean Community of Nations and Mercosur say they want to turn their regions into common markets comparable to the European Union, even though at present both of South America's largest trade blocs are far from even being perfect customs unions. The Andeans have a large body of harmonized regional legislation while the Mercosur nations have concentrated on the economic architecture of their trade bloc. But the truth is neither bloc can succeed in creating a common market without integration in both the economic and legal areas. The Andean Community has a common jurisprudence but the macroeconomic indicators of its five members are widely divergent (see *www.comunidadandina.org/estadisticas* and Table 8.1). The debt and deficit to GDP ratios of Mercosur member nations are more comparable (see *http://gmm.mecon.gov.ar* and Tables 8.3 to 8.6) and their inflation levels are shrinking. The Mercosur member states still have a significant amount of work to do to harmonize their tax collection systems, streamline their financial services sectors and bring their industrial and labour policies into line. Still, the macroeconomic convergence targets unveiled in 2000 are a significant step in the right direction.

Table 8.1 Average Andean Community inflation through the 1990s (expressed in per cent)

	1991–1995	1996–2000
Andean average	46.93	24.36
Bolivia	12.02	6.32
Colombia	24.72	15.61
Ecuador	39.71	47.89
Peru	113.30	6.91
Venezuela	44.90	45.10

Source: Andean Community (*www.comunidadandina.org*)

'Everything builds on trade. Economic convergence, regulatory convergence, a common energy or transport policy give better future fine points to business. I think it's a good thing because it helps business understand what it is about and helps business make decisions which are three, four, five to ten years from now,' said European Union trade commissioner Pascal Lamy, adding that Mercosur macroeconomic convergence was 'looking quite good'.[1]

South American central bankers have argued that price stability is the basis for levelling the poles-apart foreign exchange regimes. Argentina and Brazil have talked about the possibility of creating a common currency, and synchronizing the levels of their inflation, debt and deficits to ensure their economies march at the same pace before heading for monetary union, as Europe's 1992 Maastricht Treaty mandated for European Union member nations. This chapter evaluates the South Americans' progress towards creating a common market and assumes this means an evolution towards a continental economy with fewer foreign currencies, be it through the successive adoption of the dollar or the creation of a regional currency.

A snapshot of South American integration

To be fair, it seems reasonable to criticize a three-decades-old trade bloc like the Andean Community whose internal trade in goods and services is less in percentage terms out of total trade than 10-year-old

Mercosur. It's also fair to be sceptical of Brazilian and Argentine officials who have talked about creating a common currency at such an early stage. At the same time, there is no denying that these two regional trade blocs have progressed towards their stated goal, albeit at their own pace and from their own particular tack. The newspaper headlines may herald the end for both these integration movements, but you just have to think back to the sometimes halting and fitful evolution of the European Union and its Europessimism period to realize these are complex and time-consuming projects to implement. 'Mercosur's macroeconomic co-ordination is important for convergence. This is a very important signal to the world about Mercosur's efforts to stabilize its economies. As far as a Mercosur currency goes, we don't think it's proper to discuss that now. We need to strengthen our currencies. We are beginning to converge but the conditions are not there, so we don't feel it's appropriate to discuss that at this time,' said Rubens Barbosa, Brazil's ambassador to the United States.[2] South American government officials and economists as well as US analysts agree that whatever form any potential regional common currency may take, any such development is decades away (see Table 8.2). That is owing mainly to the legal and economic ground work needed to prepare for that kind of fundamental change in monetary policy. But perhaps the most difficult challenge to overcome, as experienced in the European Union, is not a factor in most of these countries: the cultural acceptance of a new currency. Hyperinflation has led many South American governments to retire one currency to make way for the creation of another, while some countries have junked their national money altogether to adopt the US dollar. Panama, Ecuador and most recently El Salvador have taken to the greenback while South America's second-largest economy is three-quarters dollarized since Argentina established a currency board system that swaps dollars for the local currency at par since 1991.

“There is no denying that these two regional trade blocs have progressed towards their stated goal, albeit at their own pace and from their own particular tack”

Table 8.2 The evolution of trade blocs

	European Union	Mercosur	Andean Community
–6 yrs	1951 – Treaty of Paris on coal and steel		
–5 yrs		1986 – Integration and Economic Cooperation Program (PICE)	
–2 yrs		1989 – Treaty on Integration, Cooperation and Development	
Origin	1957 – Treaty of Rome	1991 – Treaty of Asuncion	1969 – Cartagena agreement
+4 yrs		1995 – Customs union formed	1973 – Venezuela joins
+7 yrs		1998 – Common currency talk	1976 – Chile withdraws
+8 yrs		1999 – Series of trade rows	
+9 yrs		2000 – Macroeconomic targets set	
+10 yrs		2001 – Argentina's temporary import tariff changes	1979 – Andean parliament and foreign ministry council created
+11 yrs	1968 – Customs union		
+12 yrs	1969 – Common currency discussed		
+14 yrs			1983 – Andean Court created
+21 yrs			1990 – Presidential Council
+22 yrs	1979 – European Monetary System to stabilize foreign exchange volatility		
+23 yrs			1992 – Peru temporarily suspends liberalization plans
+24 yrs			1993 – Free trade zone among Bolivia, Colombia, Ecuador and Venezuela
+25 yrs			1994 – Common external tariff
+28 yrs	1985 – White Paper for a common market and adding new members		1997 – Peru to be gradually added to free trade zone
+29 yrs	1986 – Integration objectives set		1998 – Peru-Ecuador peace and free trade agreements
+30 yrs			1999 – Andean-Brazil tariff preference deal
+31 yrs			2000 – Andean-Argentina partial economic complementary deal
+35 yrs	1992 – Maastricht Treaty on macroeconomic convergence goals		
+36 yrs	1993 – Common Market: customs union and the free flow of labour and capital		
+42 yrs	1999 – Monetary Union: the euro		

It is fair to say that creating an Andean, Mercosur or 'Amercosur' currency for the entire continent would be premature at this time if you evaluate the South American market through the optic of Nobel Laureate Robert Mundell's 1961 Theory of Optimum Currency Areas.

Mundell's theory examined the convenience of a shared currency among the western European nations using two criteria: the intensity of trade and the mobility of the regional labour force. A number of economists will often argue in favour of dollarization, given the high level of trade with the United States, especially in the northern half of the continent. In the southern half of the continent trade is more evenly split between the United States and the European Union, with a significant amount of commerce taking place with Asian nations as well. What you also have in the Southern Cone are the region's two largest economies whose financial sectors have been consolidating and stabilizing. Both Brazil and Argentina have seen a reduction in the number of banks in the past two decades, liquidity requirements have risen to about 20 per cent of deposits which exceeds Bank of International Settlement guidelines, and a growing number of foreign banks are offering domestic depositors what is essentially a home-based safe haven for their capital. Administrative costs, however, remain persistently high, exceeding 5 per cent of total assets, and the delinquency rate on loans still surpasses 10 per cent. To achieve monetary union within Mercosur the member nations would need to ensure the absolute freedom of capital flows – which is still not the case in Brazil – as well as minimal harmonization of banking regulations and open access to all banks across the region.[3]

'In the past few years Mercosur and the Andean Community, the two most dynamic subregional integration blocs in Latin America, gradually started reforms theoretically necessary for creating a common currency: macroeconomic convergence is increasing; subregional trade is expanding...but there remains the need to liberalize flows of capital as well as harmonize tax, labour and capital markets laws,' said Juan Rojas Penso, secretary general of the Association of Latin American Trade Partners.[4] 'The creation of a common currency would require years to nurture credibility whereas the adoption of an existing currency (the dollar) would create significant benefits, such as avoiding the cost associated with waiting for the common currency to gain credibility. However, dollarization introduces certain inflexibilities for countries in the region which would lose their lender of last resort as well as income from seigniorage fees and interest on foreign reserves.'

The maturing of the Brazilian and Argentine financial sectors could also create conditions favourable for other forms of monetary union. You will often find the next most common argument regarding a common currency would be one that is indexed to the dollar and euro since Mercosur's trade flows are more evenly split between those two markets. Economists who specialize in foreign exchange admit that tracking a hybrid currency is more difficult for markets, but on the other hand it would be a form of exchange that more accurately reflects the region's dealings with the outside world. Whichever option these trade blocs choose, there is no doubt monetary union brings advantages to its members. Reducing exchange rate volatility increases trade, although not to the extent monetary union does. Countries with the same currency trade more than three times as much with one another as countries with different currencies. There are more than 100 countries, official dependencies or overseas territories in the world that are members of common currency schemes. Three of the five largest currency unions in terms of number of participating countries, dependencies and territories are tied to a G7 currency. At least 18 countries, territories and dependencies use the US dollar, nine French overseas departments and territories and Monaco use the French franc, and eight territories and dependencies use the British pound. There are two other large currency union groups: one combines 15 western African nations that use the same currency and the other involves six territories and countries using the Australian dollar. These five groups are either countries with common land borders, language or regional trade agreements, or colonizers and former colonies in geographically dispersed regions of the world. What they have in common is that they all share disproportionately intense trade. A study of these and smaller common currency groupings found that the statistical significance of sharing the same currency over simply reducing exchange rate volatility was one standard deviation, or in layman's terms it made an economically meaningful difference.[5] This alone should explain the South Americans' interest in a shared currency at some future

> **"Most of the Andean nations still depend heavily on price-volatile oil to earn the foreign exchange they need to repay their foreign debt obligations"**

point, but the trend towards regional trade agreements worldwide adds another incentive. There are about 170 regional trade deals in place at present, half of which have been concluded since 1990. Another 70 are being negotiated.

'If we have too many regional arrangements with too many varying rules and dispute resolutions then that's a problem. Regional trade agreements can be a good thing, as Mercosur has spectacularly demonstrated over the past 10 years ... intra-Mercosur trade has jumped from 9 per cent in 1990 to over 20 per cent in 1999,' WTO director general Mike Moore said.[6] 'The darkest future would be a repeat of the 1930s and a world spiralling into defensive, even hostile, regional blocs.'

Bumpy road to a common market

It is undeniable that most South American governments in the 1990s were able to significantly reduce their inflation rates thanks to macroeconomic adjustments. Inflation in Mercosur as a bloc was more than 25 per cent in 1995, just under 25 per cent for the Andean Community and 15 per cent for Latin America as a whole. Five years later, inflation remained at just under 25 per cent in the Andean Community but at about 5 per cent for Mercosur compared with just under 10 per cent for all of Latin America.[7] Most of the Andean nations still depend heavily on price-volatile oil to earn the foreign exchange they need to repay their foreign debt obligations. Ecuador has an extremely high debt-to-GDP ratio and Colombia is enmeshed in armed combat to wrestle an area the size of Switzerland from rebel forces. These are some of the reasons why the Andean Community simply has not advanced as quickly towards integration in tangible, commercial and economic terms as has Mercosur (see Table 8.1). The biggest trading relationship between a Mercosur member nation with that of an Andean Community country (Brazil-Venezuela) represented only 3.6 per cent of total trade within South America in 1998 (see Table 7.2)[8]. There clearly remains a lot to be done to draw the two blocs closer. At the same time, free trade talks between the Andeans and the Southern Cone countries could create commercial opportunities for you. 'The European experience has inspired us. We hope one day to have monetary union, the free circulation of labourers and a common passport. If we don't have this political push, then the integration process will freeze itself into something strictly economic and commercial and become a routine, dealing only with trade issues,' said Venezuelan foreign minister Jose Vicente Rangel.[9]

'At this point in time, it's too soon to talk about adopting the dollar or a common currency. Of course, some countries are more dollarized than others. Ecuador adopted the dollar and that's a strong decision. You first have to have macroeconomic stability. Our finance ministers have agreed that our region needs to lower inflation below the double digits,' said Andean Community of Nations secretary general Sebastian Alegrett.[10] 'Our Andean fund (Fondo Latinoamericano de Reservas) could serve one day as an Andean Central Bank. It's existed for 20 years so the potential's there for creating a regional central bank,' Alegrett added.

The Latin American Reserve Fund (FLAR, *www.flar.net*) was conceived more than two decades ago as the Andean Reserve Fund. Since the fund began functioning in mid-1978 its charter has been modified to allow other countries to join and it now includes Costa Rica in addition to the Andean Community countries. The fund's mandate is to assist in correcting payments imbalances through loans with terms of up to four years. It offers guarantees to its members and helps coordinate their monetary, exchange and financial policies. One of its long-term objectives is perfect monetary and exchange rate stability. But in order to achieve that the five Andean nations have a lot of work ahead of them in synchronizing their macroeconomic variables. If you look at the Andean Community through Mundell's optimum currency area theory, you have to conclude that progress in terms of open mobility of capital and labour within the trade bloc has been modest in comparison with the European Union countries. 'We're trying to improve the customs union so the Secretariat is drafting a new common external tariff, since Peru's been outside of it for a long time and Ecuador and Bolivia have special treatment,' Alegrett said.

Obviously economic and political instability have hamstrung the integration process in the Andean Community. Once the individual countries eventually stabilize their situations they will have at their disposal all the institutional instruments to follow through on their common market aspirations, assuming they share a common vision and political will to do so. 'The Andean Community is very institutionalized but we can learn a lot from Mercosur's vitality,' Alegrett said.

In the case of Mercosur, all the member nations with the exception of Paraguay enjoyed greater political stability throughout the 1990s which allowed their central governments and banks to focus on economic stability and development. That is why the Southern Cone countries were able to agree to a series of macroeconomic targets before the Andeans when they met in Florianopolis, Brazil in December 2000. The targets take effect starting in 2002. They are:

- *Fiscal flow* – this is defined as the variation of the consolidated net public sector fiscal debt, which is equivalent to the borrowing requirements, measured according to the below-the-line criterion. A common target beginning in 2002 of a maximum 3 per cent of GDP is set for all the countries. In the years 2002 and 2003 (conformity period), a maximum value of 3.5 per cent of GDP is established.

- *Fiscal stock variable* – the tracking variable is defined as the three-year average (2002–2004) of the ratio of the consolidated net public sector debt (net of international reserves) to nominal GDP. Starting in 2005, based on the average for the years 2002–2004, a descending path for subsequent three-year averages is set, except for countries for which the result for this indicator falls below 40 per cent. Starting in 2010, a maximum limit will be imposed on the countries at 40 per cent of GDP. The countries can individually set a limit lower than the jointly established maximum limit.

- *Inflation* – a maximum value of 5 per cent is set for the years 2002–2005. By inflation the Southern Cone countries mean core inflation, which will be defined and published from 2003. Starting in 2006, the maximum value for the core inflation is set at 4 per cent per year. Also starting in 2006, the trend of core inflation cannot exceed 3 per cent per year. Paraguay agreed to reduce during each year a quarter of the difference between the observed inflation in 2002 and the maximum value of each year. The conformity period will be in effect up to 2006. In Brazil, where national laws take precedence over foreign agreements, the law has previously fixed an interval of two percentage points around its inflation target for 2002 of 3.5 per cent.

- *Procedures for correcting deviations* – any country which in a given year deviates from those targets will have to explain at the first following meeting of that year of the Macroeconomic Monitoring Group (GMM) the corrective measures it plans to undertake to bring its economy back into line with the established goals. The correction must take place no later than by the end of the year after that country's presentation to the GMM. Corrective measures must at least include the following points:
- macroeconomic projections for the period of return to the targets;
- macroeconomic policy measures;
- structural measures, whenever warranted.

The GMM then has to analyze that country's presentation at a technical level before taking its evaluation to the meeting of economy ministers and central bank presidents for discussion. This forum may issue commentaries considered relevant.

Tables 8.3 to 8.6 are official Mercosur baseline statistics issued by the Brazilian Central Bank on 3 January 2001 that are used in calculating the macroeconomic convergence targets.

'It's been 10 years since we sat down to create a customs union and in that time we've made significant progress. Trade has increased 20 per cent with the world and threefold within Mercosur,' said Argentine president Fernando de la Rua.[11] 'Now, predictable goals in public spending are a fundamental pillar to freer trade.' The result of the so-called 'little Maastricht' agreement, dubbed after the treaty that set convergence targets for the European Union, should be a more attractive economic environment for foreign direct investment and lower spreads on those countries' international bonds. Some of the countries already met certain convergence requirements by the time the targets were unveiled in Florianopolis in mid-December 2000, as Table 8.7 shows. Could the next step be a common currency? 'Scholars and think-tanks are studying that question at this point. We're working on fiscal disciplines and fiscal balance goals that can be achieved. The idea of a common currency is the icing on the cake,' said Jose Alfredo Graça Lima, Brazil's undersecretary for trade and commercial affairs.[12]

Table 8.3 Argentina – official country statistics

Fiscal results (accumulated in 12 months)				
Concept	**Harmonized methodology**			
	June 2000		**December 1999**	
	In millions of pesos	**as % of GDP**	**in millions of peso**	**as % of GDP**
National government primary result	52	0.0	–324	–0.1
National government nominal result*	–7,016	–2.5	–7.067	–2.5
Consolidated public sector net debt				
With international reserves	99,194	34.7	95,000	33.6
Without international reserves	126,569	44.3	122,831	43.4
National government net debt				
With international reserves	85,303	29.9	82,348	29.1
Without internatonal reserves	112,678	39.5	110,179	39.0
Fiscal net debt change	9	3.2	8,255	2.9

*Fiscal results were calculated according to the cash citerion
Annual pension fund reform cost: 17% of GDP
Up-to-date transfers to the private system (AFJP) are 20,242 millions of pesos.
Only deposts by the provinces int he financial system are included in the provincial governments' assets. Other possible assets are under revision.

Consumer Price Index				
Period	**Index value**			
	Base year 88=100	**Monthly**	**Annual**	**12 months**
Dec 1999	319,87	–0.1	–1.8	–1.8
March 2000	320,88	–0.5	0.3	–1.1
June 2000	318,69	–0.2	–0.4	–1.1

Table 8.4 Brazil – official country statistics

Fiscal results (accumulated in 12 months)				
Concept	**Harmonized methodology**			
	June 2000		**December 1999**	
	In millions of reais	**as % of GDP**	**in millions of reais**	**as % of GDP**
National government primary result	29,975	2.9	26,417	2.7
National government nominal result	–18,868	–1.8	–65,100	–6.8
Consolidated public sector net debt				
With international reserves	510,010	47.5	468,149	45.0
Without international reserves	560,865	52.2	533,135	51.3
National governemnt net debt				
With international reserves	304,718	28.4	272,338	26.2
Without internatonal reserves	355,573	33.1	337,324	32.4
Fiscal net debt change	42,525	4.2	96,158	10.0

Federal state companies are considered for the above-the-line criterion

Consumer Price Index				
Period	**Index value**			
	Base year 88=100	**Monthly**	**Annual**	**12 months**
Dec 1999	1,588.56	0.6	8.9	8.9
March 2000	1,604.01	0.2	0.9	6.9
June 2000	1,614.61	0.2	1.6	6.5

Dollarization domino effect?

It is very tempting for many Latin Americans to contemplate taking on the US dollar as the national currency. After all, Panama did that almost a century ago and recently so did Ecuador (2000), then El Salvador (2001). But just ask your average Argentine and they'll be the first to admit that dollarizing an economy is no panacea. South America's second-largest economy was in the throes of hyperinflation in the late 1980s with consumer prices rising as much as 200 per cent a month in 1989. To stop inflation dead in its tracks and ensure no return to inflationary fiscal measures, the Argentine government passed a so-called 'Convertibility Law' in 1991. Basically, the legislation junked the austral, launched the peso and required the Central Bank to maintain

Table 8.5 Paraguay – official country statistics

Fiscal results (accumulated in 12 months)				
Concept	**Harmonized methodology**			
	June 2000		**December 1999**	
	Millions of guaranies	**as % of GDP**	**Millions of guaranies**	**as % of GDP**
National government primary result	–808,382	–3.2	–426,087	–1.8
National government nominal result	–947,218	–3.7	–537,064	–2.2
Consolidated public sector net debt*				
With international reserves	4,339,115	16.9	3,037,365	12.5
Without international reserves	7,659,380	29.9	6,368,105	26.4
National government net debt				
With international reserves	4,339,115	16.9	3,037,365	12.5
Without internatonal reserves	7,659,380	29.9	6,368,105	26.4
Fiscal net debt change	550,653	2.1	755,624	3.1

*State governments and municipios are not included in the consolidated public sector net debt

Consumer Price Index				
Period	**Index value**			
	Base year 88=100	**Monthly**	**Annual**	**12 months**
Dec 1999	236.0	0.5	5.4	5.4
March 2000	247.4	2.1	4.8	9.6
June 2000	249.0	–0.6	5.5	10.3

a matching number of US dollars in reserves for every peso in circulation. The government coined the measure 'convertibility' to reassure the population they could go to the bank at any time and swap as many pesos as they wanted for an equal number of dollars. What it meant for the federal government was the supply of money to the domestic economy was handcuffed to the level of dollars in reserves so there was no way to artificially boost the size of the economy nor was there the danger of a devaluation. But it also meant relinquishing one of the Central Bank's main roles and control of a key pressure valve in stabilizing the economy: the power to set interest rates.

In theory this strategy may appear to hold a certain level of promise

Table 8.6 Uruguay – official country statistics

Fiscal results (accumulated in 12 months)				
Concept	**Harmonized methodology**			
	June 2000		**December 1999**	
	Millions of pesos	**as % of GDP**	**Millions of pesos**	**as % of GDP**
National government primary result	–5,289	–2.2	–3,983	–1.7
National government nominal result[1]	–10,758	–4.4	–9,002	–3.8
Consolidated public sector net debt				
With international reserves	63,850	26.4	52,792	22.1
Without international reserves	96,358	39.8	81,214	34.1
National government net debt				
With international reserves	59,242	24.5	48,513	20.3
Without international reserves	91,750	37.9	76,934	32.3
Fiscal net debt change[2]	11,034	4.6	9,428	4.0

[1]Cost of penison fund reform
[2]Preliminary data, subject to revision

Consumer Price Index				
Period	**Index value**			
	Base year 88=100	**Monthly**	**Annual**	**12 months**
Dec 1999	124.15	0.9	4.2	4.2
March 2000	125.80	0.6	1.3	4.5
June 2000	127.57	0.5	2.8	4.8

Information for unrestricted disclosure. It is not intended to bind Banco Central do Brasil in its monetary or foreign exchange policy actions. For more details see *http://gmm.mecon.gov.ar*. Questions and comments to *gci.bacen@bcb.gov.br*.

Table 8.7 Mercosur economic indicators in June 2000

Country/indicator	**Inflation (pct)**	**National debt (pct of GDP)**
Argentina	–1.1 pct	44.3 pct
Brazil	+6.5 pct	52.2 pct
Paraguay	+10.3 pct	29.9 pct
Uruguay	+4.8 pct	39.8 pct

Source: Central banks, economy ministries and national statistics bureaus

for an economy in deep trouble. But adopting a foreign currency as the national money or pegging the local currency to another through a currency board makes sense if there is a significant amount of trade between the two countries and if their economies are in relative synchronicity. Looking at it from this point of view then, it would make more sense for Canada and Mexico, whose markets and economic cycles are much more closely tied to that of the United States, to dollarize their economies.[13] A case in point, once again, is Argentina which underwent its steepest economic contraction in a decade in 1999 just as the United States was going through its eighth consecutive year of growth. The US Federal Reserve Board had raised its bellwether Fed funds overnight bank lending rate to as much as 6.5 per cent by 2000 in an effort to keep US inflation under wraps. The Argentine economy, meanwhile, stagnated as financial liquidity dried up. To be sure, there were other factors at play, but interest rates are a key component in the functioning of an economy and this example underscores the dangers of pinning a country's hopes on the dollar.

“Dollarization simply forces a country to balance its budget since it eliminates the possibility of resorting to inflation to do that”

Dollarization simply forces a country to balance its budget since it eliminates the possibility of resorting to inflation to do that. It is no substitute for a strong financial sector with an appropriate number of commercial and retail institutions as well as sound regulations based on guidelines from the Bank for International Settlements and its Basle Accord guidelines. A 1999 study by the Argentine Banking Association found that of the four Mercosur trade bloc member states Uruguay lagged the furthest in complying with Basle Accord banking supervision guidelines but that most regulations were in place. While notoriously corrupt Paraguay repatriates more US $100 bills than the nominal value of its legitimate economy, the landlocked nation lacks the sophisticated financial services to be a major money laundering centre.[14] So it appears that most of the economic policy makers in South America understand that dollarizing is no panacea and are aware of the need for sustained fiscal discipline regardless of what their monetary policy may be.

'The underlying trend is, with ups and downs, what you see in the 1990s is a general improvement in the quality of macroeconomic policy and structural reforms. There's been a fundamental change in the quality of policy makers with a better understanding of the benefits of good macroeconomic policies and structural reforms,' said Claudio Loser, director of the western hemisphere at the International Monetary Fund.[15]

As discussed earlier in this chapter, there are tangible trade benefits for countries that share the same currency. After Brazil's steep 1999 currency devaluation, the desire to control or even eliminate foreign exchange volatility between neighbouring, trading nations has gained more support and was a prime mover in drafting the Florianopolis macroeconomic targets. The stock exchanges in Santiago, Buenos Aires and Sao Paulo have been negotiating an agreement that would allow brokers to trade electronically in equities from each other's nations. Some participants are talking about various Mercosur markets to combine efforts and maximize volume. Agriculture ministers from Brazil and Argentina met in Buenos Aires in February 2000 and agreed to study the possibility of creating a Mercosur commodities market as a counterweight to the Chicago Board of Trade.

Could and should South America dollarize?

The answers are that yes, some South American countries are in a better position to dollarize than others, but if they do, they certainly should not do so just yet. 'As I have said on many occasions, I don't believe the issue is so much dollarization but rather the trend is towards a reduction in the number of currencies and for me there is no doubt that Latin America and the world in general is headed in that direction,' said Inter-American Development Bank president Enrique Iglesias.[16] IADB chief economist Guillermo Calvo said Latin America could develop its own independent currency as a group but warned that it would end up 'shadowing the dollar and be a sort of bastard currency if you are not careful'.[17]

Popular support for Latin American economic integration is strong. A poll taken in Mexico and the Southern Cone of South America showed 63 per cent of Mexicans were in favour of integration, 70 percent of Argentines supported the idea, as did 66 per cent of Paraguayans, 64 per cent of Uruguyans and 62 per cent of Brazilians.[18] 'We always have to keep in mind how strong the political will was in Europe (to create a common currency) and you need that for something like that to happen. Latin America hasn't had any kind of intra-Latin American war which is a big reason why we have the euro. So, saying it's not on the radar screen now is correct for right now but it's also probably correct to say that the process Mercosur is going through, its logical end game, is a common currency. Some of these countries, not Brazil, but some of the other countries like Mexico for instance, they're showing that they're not that nationalistic about their currency. That's a thing Europeans have a hard time trying to understand. A lot of these guys are quite willing to give up their currencies, like Ecuador did to adopt the dollar. I don't see a common currency at all as impossible, maybe not in 10 or 15 years, but I'd say in two or three decades,' said Tomas Jelf, vice president of foreign exchange emerging markets at Lehman Brothers.[19]

Peru is a good example of a candidate for dollarization. Central bank reserves of foreign currencies at the end of 1999 stood at $8.5 billion while the supply of the national currency, the nuevo sol peruano, was equal to about $6 billion. About 78 per cent of loans are made in dollars and 68 per cent of deposits are in dollar-denominated accounts.[20] An argument could be made for Chile eventually dollarizing since the United States is its largest trade partner and the two are negotiating a bilateral free trade agreement. So what you are facing in Latin America are two possible scenarios:

1. a dollarization domino effect where a growing number of smaller economies that have a significant amount of trade with the United States eventually adopt the dollar; versus
2. those countries that are within the economic orbit of Brazil fuse their markets ever more closely and in two to four decades see more merit in a regional currency rather than maintaining national ones.

Trying to create an independent currency and then managing it is one theoretically possible way to go, but one which I think would be much slower than integrating around the dollar. You could create a central bank for Mercosur and that currency could be backed by the dollar or euro, but the dollar is more important for Latin America.

If you had a Mercosur dollar, the (US) dollar would be the basis. If you created a new currency for Mercosur it should be based on and related to the dollar and that currency could be used throughout Mercosur. Then of course, theoretically, if it turned out that the US became too deflationary that currency could be devalued against the dollar or if it became inflationary it could be appreciated against the dollar, so you'd have an escape valve-type mechanism. That, to me, would be the likelier option to monetary stability,' said Robert Mundell.[21]

Of course, whether these countries adopt the dollar or issue their own common currency, it would not remedy the risk of crises precipitated by significant fluctuations in the dollar-yen-euro exchange rates. 'I think they (Mercosur) could do it. It's a process they could work on. They'd have to adapt Maastricht but you can't have a common market with flexible exchange rates. The end of what they're doing is certainly correct. There's also the issue of labour mobility which is a big part of the European Union. If the principal goal is monetary stability, there are alternatives to the Maastricht approach that don't involve the same high degree of political integration, (such as) stabilizing their currencies relative to the dollar with safeguards like a currency board for very large countries,' said Mundell.

Notes

[1]Lamy, Pascal, European Union trade commissioner, interview in Buenos Aires, 22 September 2000.

[2]Barbosa, Rubens, Brazilian ambassador to the United States, interview in Washington, D.C., 12 January 2001.

[3]Fundacion Capital (1999) Convergencia Macroeconomica en el Mercosur: 'Un camino critico', pp. 137–138.

[4]Rojas Penso, Juan, secretary general of the Association of Latin American Trade Partners, interview from Montevideo, 21 March 2001.

[5]Rose, Andrew K., professor at University of California at Berkeley, presentation to the Argentine Central Bank conference, Buenos Aires, 24 August 2000.

[6]Moore, Mike, director general of the World Trade Organization, interview in Buenos Aires, 28 November 2000.

[7]Andean Community of Nations website, *www.comunidadandina.org/document/repor/infla-01.htm*, viewed 19 January 2001.

[8]Inter-American Development Bank (2000) 'Un nuevo impulso a la integracion de la infraestructura regional en America del Sur,' page 20 (*www.iadb.org*).

[9]Rangel, Jose Vicente, foreign minister of Venezuela, interview in Caracas, 18 January 2001.

[10]Alegrett, Sebastian, secretary general of the Andean Community of Nations, phone interview to Lima, 8 March 2001.

[11]De la Rua, Fernando, closing remarks to the XIX meeting of Mercosur's Common Market Council in Florianopolis, 15 December 2000.

[12]Graca Lima, Jose Alfredo, undersecretary of trade and commercial affairs for Brazil, phone interview to Brasilia, 9 March 2001.

[13]Calvo, Guillermo, chief economist, Inter-American Development Bank, interview published in the *New York Times* 26 January 2001.

[14]Able, Alan, money laundering expert with PricewaterhouseCoopers and member of the US Bank Secrecy Act Advisory Group, interview in Buenos Aires, 15 June 2000.

[15]Loser, Claudio, director of the western hemisphere, International Monetary Fund, interview in Washington, D.C., 12 January 2001.

[16]Iglesias, Enrique, president, Inter-American Development Bank, interview in *Pulso*, the Grupo de Diaros America monthly newsletter, December 2000.

[17]Calvo, Guillermo, *op. cit.*

[18]Fundacion Capital (1999) Convergencia Macroeconomica en el Mercosur: 'Un camino critico', page 4.

[19]Jelf, Tomas, vice president of foreign exchange emerging markets at Lehman Brothers, interview in New York, 9 January 2001.

[20]Du Bois, Fritz, economist at Instituto Peruano de Economia, interview in *Pulso*, the Grupo de Diaros America monthly newsletter, December 2000.

[21]Mundell, Robert, economist and author of the 1961 Theory of Optimum Currency Areas, phone interview to Sienna, Italy, 8 February 2000.

9

Striking the Latin stance

What is probably most appealing to South Americans about the idea of a nascent Brazilian hegemony is that it is now conceivable that the world's ninth-largest economy could in the foreseeable future enter the select circle of countries rated 'investment grade'. Chile, Uruguay and most recently Mexico have been rated investment grade and enjoy lower interest rates as a result, a vital factor in reducing capital costs on businesses there. Their Latin neighbours have benefited from the reallocation of higher-risk capital throughout the region as well as seen through their example the rewards for years of austerity and adjustments. Investment-grade status is the gold card of international finance that gives a country access to credit from banks, pension funds and other institutional investors on favourable terms. Creating a regional and perhaps continental geopolitical and economic front of 6–12 countries rallied around a world heavyweight with this kind of prospect is what makes the United States and European Union stand up and take note. US President George W. Bush delivered a major campaign speech on Latin America with the help of advisor Robert Zoellick, who was later named his US trade representative. The European Union dispatched both its trade and external affairs commissioners to South America in late 2000 to show the priority it has given free trade talks with Mercosur.

'The critical problem is: will Brazil be willing to give up some sovereignty like France and Germany did to push integration ahead?' said Riordan Roett, of Johns Hopkins University.[1]

The answer? Brazil is probably prepared to be flexible in order to realize its dream of becoming a regional leader in world affairs. 'Brazil has a more longer-term perspective. We think Mercosur is important not only for geopolitical reasons but also for commercial reasons. We don't mind having (trade) deficits with Argentina because this will help them. The short-term approach Argentina has is because of trade: they need to export more and Brazil is there. They need our market. Free trade between Mercosur and the Andean Community is a priority. It will be difficult to achieve that by January 2002 but we'll try. The domestic situation in some (Andean) countries and the reluctance to negotiate by some countries who think Brazil will benefit most from reduced tariffs will be a challenge,' said Brazil's ambassador to the United States, Rubens Barbosa.[2]

“This region is one of the few in the world with which the United States enjoys a trade surplus so it is in the interests of the US government to build on that commercial relationship”

In matters of political economy, South American affairs are invariably gauged in their relation to the United States. What you should also keep in mind is the fact that the United States has a deep and growing interest in Latin America. This region is one of the few in the world with which the United States enjoys a trade surplus so it is in the interests of the US government to build on that commercial relationship. Add to that the fact that Hispanics are poised to make up the single largest minority group in the world's biggest economy and you can appreciate why the US administration is increasingly turning its attention south. In fact, Canada was so alarmed that president Bush decided to make his first foreign trip to Mexico instead of the traditional trip north that it dispatched its foreign minister, defence minister and prime minister to meet their Bush administration counterparts and remind them that they are the other country in the world's largest trading partnership. A day after Bush dined with Canadian prime minister Jean Chretien, US administration officials announced plans to open US highways to Mexican trucks.

Trade officials suggest that what the North Americans want most are assurances on legal guarantees for their companies operating in South America, specifically in the areas of intellectual property and patents. The Europeans, who have a much more developed and sophisticated government procurement sector, are keen for concessions in this area. In return, governments on this continent want the United States to ease its anti-dumping measures and the European Union to grant their farm products freer access to that market, which accounts for about 20 per cent of world food trade. This chapter tries to map out for you the South Americans' trade positions and political strategies in these ongoing trade negotiations so that you have an idea of how circumstances may evolve.

Argentina as FTAA ambassador

The 34 countries negotiating the Free Trade Area of the Americas at present represent about one-third of global economic output, 22 per cent of world exports, with only 13 per cent of the planet's population. Argentina took over as chairman of the FTAA talks from Canada after a ministerial meeting in Toronto in November 1999 and its tenure ended with the third Summit of the Americas in Quebec City in April 2001. 'In these negotiations, we're not only dealing with the classic trade in goods issues, like tariff and non-tariff barriers. We're also discussing services, agriculture, subsidy policies, how investments are treated as well as intellectual property and conflict resolution plus competition policy. This accord will create a more favourable trade environment and greater investment flows,' Argentine deputy foreign minister Horacio Chighizola said.[3]

FTAA negotiations began in earnest after a ministerial meeting in San José, Costa Rica, in March 1998 where 34 of the hemisphere's 35 countries agreed to discuss market access. The Hemispheric Guide on Customs Procedures, containing information on all 34 nations, was updated in November 2000 and was disseminated through the FTAA home page at *http://www.ftaa-alca.org*. The ministers responsible for trade also agreed that the Negotiating Group on Market Access should periodically update information on tariffs and trade flows through the 'Hemispheric Trade and Tariff Data Base for Market Access' at *http://alca-ftaa.iadb.org/eng/NGMADB_E.HTM*. The guidelines set out for the Negotiating Group on Market Access were as follows:

- Negotiate to eliminate tariff and non-tariff barriers and other measures having equally restrictive effects on hemispheric trade.
- Put all tariffs up for discussion.
- Different liberalization timetables may be negotiated.
- Facilitate the integration of smaller economies for their full participation in FTAA talks.
- Develop an efficient and transparent system of rules of origin to ease the trade in goods without erecting unnecessary barriers to trade.
- Simplify customs clearance to ease trade and cut bureaucratic costs.
- Create a system like a standardized electronic customs clearance mechanism in order to exchange information.
- Create a system to detect fraud and illicit customs activities.

By the end of 2000, the Negotiating Group on Market Access had met 11 times and the agriculture group had met 10 times. Market access has the broadest mandate of all the nine groups and was charged with designing a hemispheric regime that would address tariff and non-tariff barriers (as well as other equivalent measures), rules of origin, customs procedures, safeguards, and standards and technical barriers to trade.

The 1990s were marked by a significant proliferation of trade liberalization agreements throughout the Americas, either between two countries or among regional groups of countries. These agreements should help facilitate progress in trans-continental free trade talks.[4] Here are the tasks ahead of the FTAA negotiators.

Canada will have to negotiate the removal of duties with Central America, the Andean Community, Mercosur, the Dominican Republic and Panama. The *United States'* Generalized System and Preferences annual import tariff exemption programme for developing countries could serve as a basis for its negotiations with Central America, Caricom, the Dominican Republic and Panama, but complex talks lie ahead with the Andean Community, Mercosur and Chile. *Mexico* was negotiating free trade with Panama, Peru and Ecuador as of the end of 2000 so it would only need to engage in talks with Caricom, the Dominican Republic and Mercosur to enjoy liberalized trade throughout the FTAA zone. It already enjoys free trade in some sectors of the Brazilian and Argentine economies. *Central America* has a significant amount of work ahead of it. It was negotiating free trade with Canada and Panama as of the end of 2000 but remains to reach agreements with the United States, Caricom, the Andean Community and Mercosur.

Caricom has the peculiar distinction of enjoying a number of preferential access agreements in foreign markets without matching many of those commitments itself. Other than the free-trade deals with Colombia, Venezuela and the Dominican Republic, Caricom has no examples to follow, so simultaneous negotiations would probably be the quickest route to hemispheric free trade for this trade bloc. The *Dominican Republic* had by the end of 2000 negotiated free trade with Central America and Caricom, meaning it will need to engage in talks with the remainder of the FTAA nations, as is the case with *Panama* which was negotiating free trade with Central America and Mexico as of the end of 2000. The *Andean Community* was negotiating free trade with Mercosur as of December 2000 and remains to engage in what should be complex talks with Canada and the United States. 'The new US administration has an enormous interest in Latin America but we'll have to wait and see what they do. They certainly have a strong political interest in trade with our region,' said Andean Community secretary general Sebastian Alegrett.[5] Colombia and Venezuela's agreements with Caricom could serve as a basis for a deal with the entire trade bloc. The Andean Community also remains to negotiate with the Dominican Republic and Panama.

Mercosur is the key to combining South America and North America into a bi-continental free-trade zone. The Southern Cone countries will have to make concessions to Canada, the United States, Mexico, the Dominican Republic, Panama, Central America and Caricom. Talks with the Nafta nations in select sectors will prove challenging. 'We have to be at least equally ambitious in terms of market access. We're interested in the liberalization of goods and services, but we're concentrated on goods,' said Brazilian undersecretary for trade and commercial affairs Jose Alfredo Graça Lima.[6] 'Agricultural products are our number one priority. We want a reduction in tariffs, the elimination of non-tariff barriers and we want subsidies to be eliminated,' Graça Lima added. *Chile* has negotiated market access agreements with all but three of the FTAA countries and one trade bloc: the United States, Panama, the Dominican Republic and Caricom.

The 'country of the future' comes of age

Brazil, the 'country of the future', has come of age. In the world of diplomacy, there are no true friendships, simply common interests. In the case of Brazil, one of only three countries in the world that fronts 10 or more nations, there are many common interests. The man at the helm of Itamaraty – the Brazilian Foreign Ministry – is Celso Lafer, who replaced the brash and combative Luiz Felipe Lampreia who stepped down as foreign minister at the end of 2000. Lafer is at the vanguard of Brazilian intellectual society and is a personal friend of President Fernando Henrique Cardoso. South American political analysts maintain Lafer understands the value of nurturing alliances to promote common interests on the international arena. Born in Sao Paulo, Lafer has been a lifelong supporter of state intervention in Brazil's industrial development and will not be easily displaced by neo-liberal arguments. Lafer is well aware of the state interventionism, subsidies and tariff barriers used by East Asian economies in recent decades or the United States more than a century ago to shelter emerging industries, or how the United Kingdom closed its borders to Commonwealth imports during the 1930s to protect its manufacturing sector. The end game is to consolidate the Brazilian hegemony over the South American continent and political analysts believe Lafer is a refined enough diplomat who understands the necessity of making concessions to Brazil's neighbours and partners to achieve that objective. As he is so often fond of saying: 'The FTAA is an option, Mercosur is our destiny.'

The Brazilians insist on negotiating the FTAA as a member of the Mercosur bloc and not as an individual country. The Argentines have repeatedly affirmed their commitment to negotiating alongside Brazil after Chile announced it would barter for a bilateral free trade deal with the United States. 'As a consequence of a decision adopted at the beginning of FTAA negotiations, Mercosur countries have presented a united position and have co-ordinated throughout the whole negotiation process on a political and technical level,' said Argentine foreign minister Adalberto Rodriguez Giavarini.[7] Foreign trade officials in both countries admit that there remains a certain level of suspicion and mistrust on either side of the border and some people would not be surprised if Argentina broke ranks to negotiate one-on-one with the United States. But others say that's not likely. 'I have no evidence the United States would extend the same offer to Argentina that it made to Chile. Chile had been waiting in line for 10 years,' said Jose Alfredo Graça Lima.[8]

“Often criticized by some US officials and observers as being too passive in continental affairs, other diplomats maintain the Brazilians prefer to work behind the scenes”

Brazil subscribes to a lower-profile kind of diplomacy, what US president Teddy Roosevelt once called 'walk softly and carry a big stick'. Often criticized by some US officials and observers as being too passive in continental affairs, other diplomats maintain the Brazilians prefer to work behind the scenes, be it during Peru's marred 2000 elections or in acting as middleman trying to ease tensions between the United States and Venezuela's Hugo Chavez, perceived by some as the new US enemy in Latin America. The Inter-American Dialogue think-tank rightly concluded in December 2000 that 'on many of the most important issues in hemispheric affairs, the United States simply will not be able to make much headway without the backing of Brazil'. In fact, some academics believe the United States would be wise to tap Itamaraty for its insight on hemispheric affairs. 'It would pay off well for the United States to call on Brazil and its desire to be a significant partner in diplomatic initiatives. The Brazilians are particularly preoccupied with the lack of sensitivity regarding Chavez and they're worried the Colombian conflict will spill over into northwestern Brazil,' said Riordan Roett.[9] In the final days of his presidency, Bill Clinton said that in his opinion 'Brazil's influence extends well beyond Latin America'.

Chile's 'stab in the back'

The reality today is that there is no such thing as a South American bloc or socio-economic monolith. Nothing underscored that more than Chile's decision in November 2000 to go ahead with long-stalled free trade talks on its own with the United States, without the fast-track approval of the US Congress. Brazil's foreign minister at that time, Luiz Felipe Lampreia, branded the move a 'stab in the back' and suspended talks to make Chile a full member of Mercosur. Officials in Brasilia were clearly annoyed by Chile's action but, as president Fernando Henrique Cardoso said, 'it's a fact of life we have to live with'. Chilean president Ricardo Lagos, a practical man who cuts to the chase, wasted no time in smoothing over ruffled feathers when he attended a Mercosur presidential summit in Florianopolis, Brazil a month later in mid-December 2000. 'To negotiate together with Mercosur we would need to have Mercosur's tariffs, while we have a 9 per cent tariff and Mercosur has a 14 per cent tariff and it's easier to reach a free-trade agreement when you start with a 9 per cent tariff rather than 14 per cent,' he said. From this point of view, we have commercial autonomy to negotiate independently of the Mercosur countries. This is why we are negotiating with the European Union and Japan.

> It's not that we're stronger or weaker. We're together on the issues, but here we're talking about free trade. In other words, what are your tariffs and what are mine and what do we do to lower them? We're interested in belonging to Mercosur because it's a regional bloc in which we want to integrate politically, economically, socially and culturally.[10]

Still, diplomats and academics agree that not having Chile incorporated as a full member of Mercosur is a blow to the geopolitical image of the bloc. Lagos made full Mercosur membership a promise during the 1999 presidential campaign. One reason was to be part of the Common Market of the South, but the socialist leader also had a domestic motivation. Mercosur's 1998 democracy clause and the bloc's behind-the-scenes diplomacy has had a proven track record in easing political instability in Paraguay. That could prove an ace in the hole for the Chilean leader as he handles the ongoing issue of kidnapping and murder charges against former dictator General Augusto Pinochet which has split the 15 million Chilean citizens right down the middle. For these reasons there is hope yet for Chile's full inclusion in Mercosur. The Brazilians practise a lower-profile form of diplomacy than do foreign affairs officials from the United States and there have been two prevailing attitudes coming out of Itamaraty since Chile's trade talks began with the United States. One is that Chile will eventually become a full member of Mercosur and the other, as Brazil's Mercosur ambassador Jose Botafogo has said, is to observe Chile to see what the United States is ready to give in exchange for free trade with them. President Cardoso expressed his government's view in a more colourful way, saying Chile's negotiations with the United States would be like the lead float coming out of Rio de Janeiro's Sambodromo during Carnival, heading the hemispheric free trade discussions between South and North America. Business and academia tend to agree that Mercosur would gain more from having Chile join as a full member than vice versa. 'I think Chile in particular has always been several steps ahead of everybody else and not just in the region but in the hemisphere save for the United States and Canada. It's had fairly decent economic growth over the last 10 years, a very respectable succession in political change, its economic policy is fairly sound and that's why it's been recognized...The whole trading bloc could stand to gain something by following the example of Chile. It's harder for Chile perhaps to make its point to the rest of the group which is driven by Brazil and Argentina. In some cases just driven by Brazil. The problems they face are those of a very large economy that has its own agenda and its own kinds of constraints. Would Chile be able to somehow influence that kind of large economy like Brazil, I don't know,' said Miami-based international trade lawyer Tony Santos.[11]

Freer trade from Ellesmere Island to Tierra del Fuego?

US trade representative Robert Zoellick told his confirmation hearing before the US Senate Finance Committee that the Bush administration needs 'fast-track' trade negotiating authority to push forward on the US government's first big trade initiative: the creation of the Free Trade Area of the Americas. Fast-track, or trade promotion authority means the US Congress agrees to either accept or reject the trade proposal drafted by the administration rather than ratify it line by line. Arguing that the 1993 North American Free Trade Agreement 'contributed to the longest period of economic growth in US history', Zoellick stressed the importance of creating a free-trade zone from Canada to Argentina. Latin America is one of the few regions of the world with which the United States enjoys a trade surplus, so US trade officials are understandably eager to preserve these circumstances.

'This is one of those points in history where we have an unparalleled opportunity to shape the international trade world...If other countries go ahead with free-trade agreements and we don't, I can't blame them. It's our mistake,' Zoellick told the Senate committee in veiled reference to European Union talks to create the world's largest free-trade zone between Western Europe and the Southern Cone of South America.[12]

US secretary of state Colin Powell testified at his confirmation hearing that the United States has made excessive use of unilateral trade sanctions in the past decade and pledged to review many of the punitive measures in place. This too could bode well for forging a free-trade area spanning two continents. 'If the United States could get fast-track authority by the end of this year (2001), then it would be feasible to accomplish FTAA by 2003,' said Brazil's Graça Lima said.[13] But economists and diplomats believe Brazil may be reluctant to ink the hemispheric free-trade deal since its car, high-technology and other industrial sectors would be at a competitive disadvantage to their US counterparts. FTAA, first proposed by Bush's father when he was US president in 1990, has been under negotiation since 1998 with nine working groups discussing everything from intellectual property rights to government procurement. The transition cost is perhaps highest for Brazil of any of the 34 American hemisphere countries involved in the negotiations. In 2000, 28 per cent of Brazilian exports went to the European Union, 24 per cent to South America and 23 per cent to the United States. The remaining quarter went mainly to Asia. Overall, the Americas accounted for 51 per cent of Brazilian exports.[14] What that means is Brazil, one of the developing world's most industrialized economies, stands to potentially lose market share in its biggest export region if it locks into FTAA. Developing countries argue that the G7 economies used tariffs, subsidies and non-tariff barriers to shield their industries when those sectors were establishing themselves, so why can't they do the same now.

A case that illustrated Brazil's market share fears was the trade dispute between Brazil and Canada over subsidies to their respective regional jet manufacturers. Canada first complained to the World Trade Organization in 1996 that the low-interest loans offered by Brazil's government export credit agency, ProEx, to airlines that buy aircraft manufactured by Empresa Brasileira de Aeronautica S.A. (Embraer), the world's fourth-largest jet aircraft maker, were illegal. Brazil responded that Canada was no better because it did the same with Montreal-based Bombardier Inc. The WTO ruled in March 1999 that both countries offered illegal subsidies and ordered them to change their export credit programmes. Canada complied but Brazil, according to the WTO, did not. Result: Bombardier's share of the 50-seat aircraft market fell to 43 per cent in 2000 from 65 per cent in 1999 while Embraer's stake rose to 57 per cent from 35 per cent, according to the Canadian government. So, in December 2000, the WTO awarded Canada the right to impose the biggest WTO-sanctioned trade penalties up to that date worth about $1.37 billion (C$2.06 billion) over six years on Brazilian imports ranging from shoes to coffee and sugar to steel. Trade experts said commerce between Brazil and Canada is small enough to run the risk of a trade war for the broader goal of ensuring WTO members respect the rules – trade between the two nations amounted to about $2 billion in all 1999 compared with the $1 billion in goods and services that cross the Canada-US border every day.

“The high-profile battle threatened to add another obstacle to hemispheric trade talks as each country upped the ante in the dispute”

But the high-profile battle threatened to add another obstacle to hemispheric trade talks as each country upped the ante in the dispute. Canada announced in February 2001 a temporary ban on Brazilian beef imports on fears the products may be tainted with mad cow disease. The Brazilians were incensed by the move, having never recorded a single case of mad cow disease on their territory. Although Brazil stopped importing breeding cattle from Europe in 1996, the Canadians had asked in May 1998 for documents proving the world's largest herd was not contaminated with mad cow disease. Canada received the information only after announcing the import ban in February 2001. While the official Canadian position was that the ban was imposed for purely phytosanitary reasons, no one really believed that since the decision came one day after Brazil scored a victory before the WTO in the ongoing aircraft subsidy battle. Even two unnamed scientists in the Canadian health department were quoted as saying the move was motivated more by politics than by health concerns. Regardless of the motive, the effect was that this temporary measure applied to the entire Nafta trade bloc. In other words, Canada's decision also closed the US and Mexican markets to Brazil. President Cardoso, in an interview on 8 February 2001 with TV O Globo, the nation's largest network, capped a series of threats by warning Canada to lift the ban within 15 business days or else to prepare itself for a trade war and that given the 'current climate' between the two countries, Brazil might skip the third Summit of the Americas set for Quebec in April 2001. Agriculture minister Marcus de Pratini Moraes added his voice to the chorus, saying the ban 'threatens' the creation of the FTAA. There was no doubt that the Brazilians were frustrated with Canada's actions, but foreign minister Celso Lafer moved quickly to reaffirm Brazil's commitment to hemispheric trade talks: 'The summit is not a bilateral meeting between Canada and Brazil. It is a previously scheduled meeting of all the countries of the region and it would be inconsiderate if we did not attend. Brazil will go to the meeting in Quebec.' Canadian agriculture minister Lyle Vanclief dispatched an inspection team to Brazil and said that imports would resume immediately if the group could ensure that Brazilian monitoring and enforcement was sufficient to detect the disease. 'In a situation like this, one does not retaliate without first exhausting all negotiation possibilities,' said Lafer. The Canadians cleared the

Brazilian herd of mad cow disease within Cardoso's 15 business day deadline, pulling the two nations back from the brink.

The Canada-Brazil clash was not the first between the two countries. A century earlier a Toronto-based company now known as Brascan ran telephone, streetcar, electricity and gas distribution services in Rio de Janeiro and Sao Paulo. Rioters in the capital of the northeastern state of Bahia destroyed Canadian-run street cars in Salvador in 1909, branding Canada the 'Great octopus of the north' after Brazilian companies that wanted the concession whipped up local nationalist fervour. Brascan eventually sold its stakes in public services back to the Brazilian government in the 1970s for about $2 billion. That also caused a scandal, with critics charging that the Brazilian government should have waited until 1989 when Brascan's concessions in Rio and Sao Paulo expired and then taken the services back for free.

A development that augurs well for progress in trade talks, however, is the fundamental difference between the Clinton and succeeding Bush administrations in the handling of commercial relations. The Brazilians take a favourable view of the fact the current administration does not appear to want to insist on including environmental and labour regulations in trade talks. The so-called WTO-Plus agenda of the Clinton administration lumped in intellectual property, environmental rules, labour standards, government procurement and the services sector as essential parts of the trade talks. Developing countries often complain that insisting on applying the same guidelines to them in those areas is unfair since they are still nurturing their industries to full maturity in order to compete in a globally liberalizing marketplace. Their argument is harder to defend when developed countries start citing cases of child labour. Still, many people in Brazil and some other South American countries oppose 'early harvest' and are perfectly content with the outermost deadline of 2005 to create the FTAA. Trade officials in various South American countries consider early harvest, or partial and temporary accords in one sector, to be too complicated and that it is unrealistic to try to isolate a sector which will ultimately be tied back together with the entire market package under what is commonly referred to as the 'single undertaking'.

The Brazilians, Argentines and Chileans consistently say one of their top objectives in free trade talks with the United States is to score concessions on that country's anti-dumping measures. During a lengthy exchange between the Southern Cone presidents at the December 2000 Mercosur summit, Brazilian president Fernando Henrique Cardoso warned Chilean president Ricardo Lagos about 'bad experiences' Brazil had known in the past. Although the Brazilian leader didn't name names, experts interpreted his cryptic comment as a reference to punitive anti-dumping measures allowed for under 'Super 301' instituted by United States Trade Representative Carla Hills during the Ronald Reagan and George H.W. Bush administrations that imposed heavy duties on Brazilian steel.[15] US steelmakers have been pressuring their government to impose tougher import controls since 1998 when imports of hot-rolled steel and iron straps increased more than 70 per cent from the previous year's record high while the average price on those products fell almost 20 per cent. Many of those imports came from emerging markets that bore the brunt of the recent financial crisis and which tried to keep their economies running by taking advantage of their currency devaluations to export their now more competitively priced products.

It was also in this context that the controversial 'Byrd amendment' was approved by the US Congress late in 2000. Named after its chief sponsor, West Virginia Democratic senator. Robert Byrd, the amendment allows US industry to collect the proceeds of anti-dumping and countervailing duties imposed on imports. Those revenues used to go into the US Treasury. Many US trading partners have strongly protested the change in policy because they fear the new policy will encourage US industry to bring anti-dumping and countervailing duty cases to their government. Trade experts admit it would probably take a WTO ruling to make Congress repeal or change the amendment. The 15-nation EU and 10 individual nations on 23 August 2001 convinced the WTO Dispute Settlement Body to set up a formal panel to investigate the US anti-dumping law.

The United States has also been seeking improvements in the treatment of intellectual property rights in South America where software pirating is common and pharmaceutical patents are a major point of conflict. US industry considers Argentina to be the major sore point in its handling of intellectual property while it sees the Brazilian statute as adequate but enforcement as lacking. US pharmaceutical manufacturers also question a Brazilian presidential decree that opened up their patent rights on drugs to treat Acquired Immuno-Deficiency Syndrome (AIDS) after the Brazilian government declared the illness a national emergency. Brazil's death rate was estimated at 9.37 per 1,000 population in 2000 compared with the world death rate of 9 per 1,000 population. AIDS is believed to account in large part for Brazil's excess mortality. Neighbouring Argentina's death rate is 7.59 per 1,000 and Uruguay's is 9.06, while Paraguay's rate is 4.81 per 1,000 population. In the copyright area, US industry submitted a brief to the USTR in late 2000 arguing in favour of stripping Brazil of its Generalized System and Preferences (GSP) status. GSP is voted on by the US Congress every year and if approved it pays to eliminate tariffs on imports from specific developing countries.[16] Agriculture, of course, is high on the list of priorities of everyone's agenda. The US sugar industry is strongly opposed to Brazil's Proalcohol subsidy programme and South American grain and oilseed exporters complain US farm subsidies have been on the rise. 'Brazil is part of Mercosur, considers Mercosur an essential part of its foreign policy and trade policy. Mercosur shouldn't isolate itself, but should integrate with the Andean Community, Mexico and the Free Trade Area of the Americas. If we integrate at a regional level, we can then take greater strides. The WTO is about practising free trade but we do not have free trade in agriculture. We do not have access to markets in agriculture. We will not accept exceptions,' Brazilian president Fernando Henrique Cardoso told delegates at the World Economic Forum's conference on Mercosur in Rio de Janeiro in 2000.[17] A study published by the OECD in June 2000 found farm subsidies in the United States had risen to 24 per cent of gross farm receipts from 14 per cent in 1997, despite deregulation of the sector earlier in the decade. EU subsidies to its farmers were equal to 49 per cent of gross farm receipts. 'What is up for debate is the symmetry of the globalization process. The world usually thinks of the G7 or G8 with Russia but now we have the G20 with emerging nations. Mercosur is giving the world an example of when countries share common views they can flourish,' said Cardoso.

The Europeans' return

The European Union's trade strategy regarding Latin America has been to start with a free-trade deal with Mexico and follow that up with talks with other key markets in the region. Up until the middle of 2001 the EU negotiators had met four times with their Mercosur counterparts to deal with technical issues and non-tariff barriers to trade. The politically charged part of the talks began in July when negotiators met in Montevideo, Uruguay to discuss tariffs. 'We haven't set a deadline, unlike FTAA, but there is a certain amount of parallel between the two negotiations,' said Vittorino Allocco, the EU's head of delegation in Argentina.[18]

The loss of 7 per cent of Mexican market share in the space of four years after Mexico entered Nafta in 1992 was a painful wake-up call for the Europeans. The EU accounts for about 40 per cent of foreign direct investment in the Mercosur countries and European diplomats want to ensure they do not relinquish any of their stake in this market. In fact, commercial attachés at a number of EU member nation embassies in the region say companies based in their countries are more concerned with cutting down the mountains of Mercosur red tape than with the trade bloc's common external tariff. 'We, in these negotiations, want to gain greater access for our industrial goods and services and Mercosur wants more access for its processed foods. Their success will depend on their ability to produce quality, certified products,' said Allocco. The Europeans' drive for greater market access will depend entirely on their willingness to grant the South Americans more access to their agriculture markets, negotiators there have countered. 'For the Europeans and the Americans, the intellectual property rules are needed because those rules are not as strong here. But we are all members of the WTO and our top priority is access for agricultural products through the reduction of tariffs, the elimination of non-tariff barriers and eliminating subsidies. We know (European) reform of CAP (the Common Agricultural Policy) will not come about from these negotiations but we will make it clear that if there is no willingness to do this, it will be less desirable for us to engage in free trade with them. The Europeans are aware FTAA is around the corner,' said Jose Alfredo Graça Lima.[19] By July 2001, the EU had made a unilateral comprehensive offer to phase in free trade with Mercosur over the next decade while the Bush administration was still trying to obtain Congressional approval for trade promotion authority. Two months later, in September 2001, US trade officials met with their

> **“The EU accounts for about 40 per cent of foreign direct investment in the Mercosur countries and European diplomats want to ensure they do not relinquish any of their stake in this market”**

Mercosur counterparts in Punta del Este, Uruguay, to advance their free trade agenda. Mercosur called the EU offer 'positive' and promised to reply with an offer of its own by no later than the end of October 2001.

Bridging the southern divide

The developed world is accustomed to thinking of the developing world in north-south terms, but there are concrete steps under way to create a south-south dialogue on issues of common interest, both commercial and political. The six Southern Cone countries signed a framework agreement in December 2000 with South Africa to begin free-trade talks with their trans-Atlantic neighbour. 'We have consistently stressed the need for a fundamental restructuring of the world economic order as a central condition for the reversal of underdevelopment,' South African president Thabo Mbeki told his Southern Cone counterparts after signing the framework agreement.[20] 'In reality, our progress has been slow and our collaboration inconsistent. As developing countries we have to radically restructure our economic relations and increase economic co-operation, investments and trade flows between our countries in addition to the existing historical patterns of economic interaction with the developed countries of the north,' Mbeki said.

The driver, literally, behind these free trade talks is the auto industry, said Brazil´s undersecretary of trade and commercial affairs Jose Alfredo Graça, Lima. There is more to these talks than just autos and parts. After all, South Africa´s market is relatively small in comparison with Mercosur, with a gross domestic product of $135 billion versus $1.17 trillion. 'President Mbeki has expressed a common position regarding the next round of World Trade Organization talks and there are strong links between Africa and Brazil,' said Brazilian president Fernando Henrique Cardoso. The South African leader called on his South American counterparts to act as a bloc on issues of common interest before the WTO and the G20.

There is a range of areas where the outcome of previous multilateral negotiations has been weighted against the developing countries. This is not only restrictive of our development but will soon also be a restraint on the continued growth and prosperity of the world economy,' said Mbeki

The view from Venezuela

'As far as Venezuela is concerned, the Andean Community is not enough. The Andean Community is a step towards a greater integration process,' said Venezuelan foreign minister Jose Vicente Rangel.[21] 'Up to now, integration hasn't emerged from its economic and commercial parameters. Venezuela sees itself as the link between the Andean Community, Mercosur and the Greater Caribbean to build an alternative pole, rather than live in a unipolar or bipolar world so that you could have the European pole, the North American pole, the Asian pole and the South American pole,' Rangel added. This isn't simply rhetoric on the part of the government of populist leader Hugo Chavez, at that time the *pro tempore* president of the Andean Community of Nations. The Andean Development Corporation (CAF), the bloc's most effective institution, espouses a pan-Latin view given that its 12 nation shareholders are all Latin American. 'Our financing policies respond to our priorities and not to those of the Japanese, Germans or the United States. It has advantages and disadvantages. The Inter-American Development Bank and the World Bank are very much influenced by industrialized countries in setting their agendas. They have AAA ratings because they're backed by the United States but we have a single A rating which is the highest and best risk rating of the region,' said a high-level official with the Caracas-based development bank.

Diplomats interpret Venezuela's position as indicating it wants to integrate with Mercosur before it goes forward with the Free Trade Area of the Americas, while Colombia's position is more analogous to that of Chile's. One thing can certainly be said for the South American continent as a whole: there is the political desire to pursue integration with one another. 'The integration of the Andean Community and Mercosur is absolutely necessary in preparation for the FTAA and I share Cardoso's view of equality and unity before the FTAA talks so we need to pursue political integration in South America. I'm not talking about erasing borders and founding a South American capital, that's utopian. In (Simon) Bolivar's time it would have been possible. The European Union is an interesting model and a very good example for the creation of a South American federation,' said president Hugo Chavez.[22]

The *pro tempore* head of the Andean Community acknowledged Mercosur-Andean free trade talks got bogged down in technical difficulties in 1998 but that he and Brazil's Cardoso agreed to redouble their efforts with a view to clinching the deal by January 2002.

'At this time, I'm not pessimistic. I'm realistic. The Andean Community-Mercosur negotiations are complex and difficult but it's so important we can't abandon the project or leave it strictly in the hands of trade negotiators because this is about political will. We're seeking a multipolar world. We're not saying South America will be the next empire but it can be an important region in geopolitics because we share a common culture and view of the world,' Chavez added.

The suspicious south

So, why are South Americans who are so eager to trade among themselves so tentative about free trade with their northern neighbours? It probably has a lot to with the 1980s debt crises. Of course, to a large extent South American governments have themselves to blame for what happened then, but they are also right to point out that lenders in the north did not necessarily have their best interests at heart either. The Bretton Woods institutions failed to warn these sovereign debt issuers or the bondholders who invested in that debt about the long-term unsustainability of their borrowing until it was too late. Like the old adage that says you know your debt is high when the bank starts to worry about you, Latin American governments were given longer amortizations and slightly better terms under the Brady debt swap arrangements of the 1980s. The United States' use – or abuse, depending on the point of view – of economic sanctions also makes these governments sceptical of rosy assessments of the benefits globalization could bring. In the past decade the United States has slapped sanctions of one kind or another on 75 of the world's 193 countries. US secretary of state Colin Powell's plans to review these sanctions could assuage fears of the United States as a selfish hegemon able to wreak havoc on the economies of the region at will. This may not be an image widely held in the halls of power, but important segments of South America's political class that are in opposition feed this image to the masses. For free-trade talks to succeed with South America, be it with the North American Free Trade Agreement countries or the European Union, the developed world will have to reassure these developing nations that their industries will not be steamrollered as a consequence of opening up their markets. The South Americans on the other hand will have to convince northern hemisphere investors that they are putting lax macroeconomic management and arbitrary treatment of foreign firms behind them.

Notes

[1]Roett, Riordan, Sarita and Don Johnson professor and director, Western Hemisphere Program, Johns Hopkins University, interview in Washington, D.C., 11 January 2001.

[2]Barbosa, Rubens, Brazilian ambassador to the United States, interview in Washington, D.C., 12 January 2001.

[3]Chighizola, Horacio, deputy foreign minister for Argentina, guest column published in *La Nacion*, Argentina, section 5, page 8, 13 March 2001.

[4]Organization of American States-Brookings Institution Press (2001) Towards Free Trade in the Americas, Chapter 5.

[5]Alegrett, Sebastian, secretary general of the Andean Community of Nations, phone interview to Lima, 8 March 2001.

[6]Graca Lima, Jose Alfredo, undersecretary of trade and commercial affairs of Brazil, phone interview to Brasilia, 9 March 2001.

[7]Rodriguez Giavarini, Adalberto, foreign minister of Argentina, press briefing in Buenos Aires, 7 March 2001.

[8]Graca Lima, *op.cit.*

[9]Roett, Riordan, *op.cit.*

[10]Lagos, Ricardo, interview in Florianopolis, 15 December 2000.

[11]Santos, Tony, lawyer for US and European telecommunications, high-technology and internet firms, phone interview to Miami, Florida, 18 July 2000.

[12]Zoellick, Robert, United States trade representative, testimony before the US Senate Finance Committee, week of 29 January to 2 February 2001.

[13]Graca Lima, *op.cit*.

[14]Barbosa, Rubens, *op.cit*.

[15]Redrado, Martin, chief economist at Fundacion Capital, interview in Buenos Aires, 4 January 2001.

[16]Smith, Mark, US Chamber of Commerce, Latin America and Caribbean section, interview in Washington, D.C., 12 January 2001.

[17]Cardoso, Fernando Henrique, opening address to the World Economic Forum's conference on Mercosur in Rio de Janeiro, 7 May 2000.

[18]Allocco, Vittorino, chief of the European Union's delegation in Argentina, interview in Buenos Aires, 15 March 2001.

[19]Graca Lima, *op.cit*.

[20]Mbeki, Thabo, address to the Mercosur presidential summit in Florianopolis, 15 December 2000.

[21]Rangel, Jose Vicente, foreign minister of Venezuela, interview in Caracas, 18 January 2001,. *www.mre.gov.ve*.

[22]Chavez, Hugo, interview in Puerto Ordaz, 20 January 2001.

10

'Ordem e Progresso'

Perhaps the motto on Brazil's flag, 'Ordem e Progresso' (Order and Progress), best summarizes southern South America's transformation during the 1990s. This was a time when most republics concentrated on stabilizing their economies and nurturing their nascent democracies. These countries are reaching out to each other and to North America, Central America and the Caribbean, not to mention the European Union. They have already begun to expand and diversify their trade flows which have generally helped stimulate growth at home. Many of these nations have also been weaning different sectors of their economies off subsidies, tariff and non-tariff protections and preparing those sectors for more open competition. This in large part explains the developed world's desire to bridge the north-south divide by negotiating the Free Trade Area of the Americas and the European Union-Mercosur free trade agreement. South America has already begun to reap the rewards of its increased stability, more sustainable growth and improved competitiveness. The result has been the assignment of a growing amount of investment capital for this region.

FDI (foreign direct investment) inflows to Latin America should keep their momentum as countries continue to pursue changes in the regulatory frameworks to attract FDI in banking, commerce, telecommunications and energy among other industries', said Fiorina Mugione, project officer at the United Nations Conference on Trade and Development (Unctad's) division on Investment, Technology and Enterprise Development.[1]

'In addition, FDI raised through privatization or M&A (mergers and acquisitions) should not be seen as one-off deals but as catalytic transactions with a potential to generate new FDI through the medium term. Peru is a case in point,' said Mugione.

Bear in mind that except for Chile and Uruguay, these are still emerging markets that are prone to volatile shifts in the balance of their budgets and terms of trade, so investing in this part of the world comes with a certain level of risk. But each risk carries its own rewards, just as a crisis means both the danger of financial ruin or opportunity to begin to address deeply rooted problems as has been the case recently in both Brazil and Argentina. Trends in the past decade indicate many of the largest economies in this region are serious about tackling market fundamentals such as containing inflation, reeling in their deficits and trying to shift debt financing more on to domestic capital markets. That means some of the riskiest factors are increasingly coming under control and that means a more predictable future. Foreign investment and retail banks have noticed and that is why they have raised their stakes in these markets. This chapter summarizes the main points made throughout this book to demonstrate how trends in the past decade suggest South America is becoming an increasingly attractive place for you, your business and your clients to invest because of greater stability, better prospects for growth and clearer rules of competition.

United in freer trade

'It's possible the South American nations could form a joint negotiating bloc on trade matters,' said ALADI general secretary Juan Rojas Penso.[2] ALADI member nations exported $157 billion in goods and services to the United States in 1999. By 2007, the date by which the US Department of Commerce estimates US exports to Latin America will be greater than those to the European Union and Japan combined, ALADI countries' exports to the United States are forecast to grow at least 60 per cent to between $250 billion and $258 billion. 'The rapprochement of the Andean Community and Mercosur, and at the same time the association with Bolivia and Chile, open interesting possibilities for the South American countries to co-ordinate a similar negotiating position before international meetings,' Rojas Penso added.

Brazil's leadership in calling for improved transportation, energy and telecommunications links across the continent could prove to be the catalyst of this union. These projects will undoubtedly improve conditions for you to do business here. Negotiations are under way to liberalize trade in goods and services between the Andean Community and Mercosur. Granted that leaders admit they may not be able to meet the January 2002 deadline for creating a free-trade zone combining the north and the south of the continent, but the political will to clinch this deal is firm. So this book is a snapshot of South America's evolution towards more open market economics and legislation. As the region's history indicates, or the example of the European Union would suggest, the integration process is not a smooth, linear process. It is a halting, two-steps-forward, one-step-back evolution driven as much by external as internal factors but which does eventually achieve its goal if there is sufficient political will. In the case of the Andean Community progress has been stalled by bureaucratic delays, regional security concerns and domestic problems so pressing that integration has been relegated to the back burner.

Mercosur's ambitions to expand suffered a significant setback in 2000 when Chile announced the beginning of bilateral free trade talks with the United States, putting plans to include it as a full member of the Common Market of the South on hold. That may have been a blessing in disguise since Mercosur member nations really need to harmonize their legislation first if they want to work together more closely. Some government officials have suggested Argentina might follow Chile and negotiate a free trade agreement with the United States on its own, sounding a death knell for the Common Market of the South. But three successive presidents of South America's second-largest economy have made Mercosur the centrepiece of their foreign policy and the current administration of president Fernando de la Rua is negotiating its entry into the Free Trade Area of the Americas not as an individual country but as a member of the Mercosur bloc.[3] The Brazilians and Venezuelans are firm in their desire to form a common geopolitical bloc so they can speak with one voice on world affairs. There is mounting evidence that despite many

“As the region's history indicates, or the example of the European Union would suggest, the integration process is not a smooth, linear process”

macroeconomic, legal and infrastructure imperfections in this part of the world, circumstances are improving. 'The political and social upheavals that we have seen throughout Latin America in the last five years have not risen to a level that would reverse the liberalization of the economies and democracy – but we have come close to it,' US Overseas Private Investment Corporation president and chief executive George Muñoz told 150 business leaders in Houston, Texas. 'There are no guarantees that being in the western hemisphere will assure economic success or a decent standard of living. But with the progress toward free markets and democracy, the codifying of free trade in treaties, and the promise of globalization to transform an old economy to a new one given the right frameworks, I would say that right now is the time to look at Latin America as a long-term growth investment.' [4]

> 'It is urgent that the Free Trade Agreement of the Americas (sic) be concluded in the next three to four years. It is only with the security of an international treaty that the commitment of countries to free trade can be relied upon.'

Free trade throughout the western hemisphere would go a long way to creating a lower-risk environment and attract longer-term foreign direct investments to Latin America, and the South Americans are by and large ready and willing to negotiate free trade on fair terms. 'We'd like to have legislation that is transparent and applied universally to all countries in the FTAA, including the largest partners. We don't want this to be used as a protectionist instrument,' said Andean Community secretary general Sebastian Alegrett.[5]

Improved stability

Between 1996 and 2000, inflation in Latin America and the Caribbean as a whole was cut by more than half to 7.8 per cent in 2000 from 19.6 per cent in 1996.[6] This means the purchasing power of the region's nascent middle classes is not being eroded by compounding consumer prices. As we saw in Chapter One, most of these countries learned painful lessons during the hyperinflation era of the 1980s and have taken the necessary steps to ensure their people are less likely to suffer this phenomenon again. Argentina, the focus of world financial market attention in mid-2001 as it completed a third year of recession and moved to stop a slow motion run on bank deposits, finally woke up to the fact it must spend within its means and root out endemic tax evasion – or risk an economic collapse that would shrink its middle class further. In fact, senior officials at the International Monetary Fund estimate the region's macroeconomic management has undergone a palpable change for the better. Now there is evidence of growth in the ranks of the middle class in some of the region's most dynamic economies, as you read in Chapter Three, and this is one reason why Banco Santander Central Hispano and brewer AmBev are banking on a bright future there. 'If (Brazilian) GDP grows 4 per cent then the consumption of beer will grow 6 per cent. With respect to South America, the same relative growth possibilities exist through growth in income and per capita consumption,' said Victorio De Marchi, co-president of the world's fourth-largest brewer.[7]

While it is true that about a third of South America's 346 million people live on $2 a day or less, microcredit is spreading across the continent as one tool in the fight against abject poverty. Bolivia is a pioneer in this radical form of financing that is described briefly at the end of Chapter Five. It is also very likely, as shown in Chapter Eight, that foreign exchange volatility will be less of a destabilizing factor in South America in the coming two to four decades as more countries either adopt the US dollar or develop their own regional currency derived from the greenback and possibly the euro as well. Add to that the fact that most of the continent's key economies have renegotiated their debt obligations over a longer amortization under the Brady plan of the 1980s and are continuing to do so in the form of exchanges for global bonds and you have a region that is equipping itself with a more sustainable borrowing profile. Of course, there is still much work to be done in this area, but Brazil and Chile are regional leaders in nurturing domestic capital markets and Argentina, Latin America's largest foreign borrower, is close behind in shifting its borrowing burden to the local from the overseas market. Nevertheless this part of the world is still quite vulnerable to external shocks and local crises of confidence that can dramatically drive up the interest rate costs on debt financing, throw current accounts further out of balance or sap liquidity from perilously leveraged markets. Fortunately, the IMF learned the value of preventive action after Thailand's financial crisis and subsequent devaluation in July 1997 set off an emerging market domino effect. The Washington-based multilateral lender put together aid packages for Brazil in November 1998 and Argentina in December 2000 that are widely credited with pulling the region back from the precipice of their potential worst-case scenarios, and again for both those countries in August 2001.

This is also a relatively peaceful part of the world where the last full-blown border conflict, between Ecuador and Peru, was solved in 1998. In early 2001 the decades-old civil war in Colombia appeared to have entered a new phase of peace talks, but its neighbours worry about the military facet of Plan Colombia and its potential for destabilizing the northwest of South America. The ethnic tribalism that has escalated into full conflict and social breakdown from Rwanda and Southeast Asia to the Balkans and the former Soviet republics is virtually inconceivable in South America. Mexican philosopher Jose Vasconcelos wrote in his 1925 book *La Raza Cosmica* (*The Cosmic Race*) that the Latin American mestizo, or person of mixed Spanish and Amerindian ancestry, would herald a new post-racialist era in human development. That's not to say racism is not a fact of life in South America, but it does not seem as prevalent as in many other parts of the world, perhaps thanks to ethnic and racial mixing. There are people in northeastern Brazil who have green eyes and black skin who speak Portuguese with a Dutch lilt. Ninety-five per cent of Paraguayans are mestizo and 55 per cent of Bolivians are of Quechua or Aymara native extraction. Eight in every 10 Colombians are of mixed races, as are 65 per cent of Ecuadoreans. More than one in three Brazilians and Peruvians are of mixed blood while only Argentina and Uruguay have populations that are more than 90 per cent caucasian. A generation ago it was unusual for citizens of many South American countries to travel to a neighbouring country, but as you saw in Chapter Seven intraregional travel for business or pleasure has grown and is likely to continue. Fervent nationalism among most South Americans appears to have been shuffled into the past along with the military dictatorships that fanned those sentiments.

“There is no doubt that applying trade sanctions under the democracy clause in the case of a military coup in Brazil would be to the detriment of the other countries”

While Peru, Paraguay, Ecuador and Venezuela are not paragons of democracy, they and the other South American republics are relatively new to this form of government. Behind the scenes diplomatic pressure by the region's governments is credited with pulling many of the weakest democracies back from committing more flagrant violations of constitutional rule and democratic institutions. The Introduction and Chapters Two and Nine describe this lower-profile way of exercising influence in the region. Mercosur, for example, ratified the Ushuaia Protocol in 1998 establishing the trade bloc's democracy clause in direct response to one of the coup attempts staged by former Paraguayan cavalry general Lino Oviedo. The Ushuaia Protocol sets trade sanctions approved by international bodies as the maximum penalty for violating a nation's democratic institutions and is a way of upholding the regional policies of non-intervention at the same time.

But the idea of suspending the 'most favoured nation' status of a Mercosur member nation that violates its democratic institutions may only be an effective deterrent for some supporters of a potential coup in the smaller countries. There is no doubt that applying trade sanctions under the democracy clause in the case of a military coup in Brazil would be to the detriment of the other countries. The reality is that Brazilians constantly reiterate their commitment to democracy and one of the principal excuses used for justifying coups in the past, inept public administration, is a diminishing concern now that the government has reeled in tax evasion and succeeded in fighting corruption to a certain extent.[8] In Argentina's case, its military has been completely discredited after the disappearance of perhaps as many as 30,000 people during the 1976–1983 'Dirty War' dictatorship, its humiliating loss to Britain in the 1982 Falklands War, and the junta's poor record of economic management. For a military coup to succeed and last it needs the support of at least a significant segment of society and in the case of South America's two largest economies, conditions are not at all amenable to that, nor are they burdened with large rebel movements.

Higher growth prospects

You don't need to study demographic charts to figure out that South America's population is younger than that of North America and Western Europe. Just walk down any street in most cities in this continent and you'll see the high proportion of youth here with your own eyes. These are the consumers and labourers of the future and for companies evaluating regions outside North America and Western

Europe for their expansion, this is an attractive place in which to establish themselves. 'We were looking for regions with ample hydrocarbons, a stable fiscal regime, a stable government and a good legal system,' said George Hart, vice president of international finance at Canadian Hunter International.[9] 'Russia has ample hydrocarbons but the fiscal regime was not stable, the government wasn't so stable either, and the legal system was a question mark, so we chose the Southern Cone of South America and opened our first office in Argentina in mid-1998,' he said. 'We see Brazil as a big energy hole. Brazil uses natural gas for 3 per cent of its energy needs and we expect it to grow to 10 per cent in 10 years.'

Chapter Three shows how a growing number of the region's people are joining the ranks of the middle class and chapters Five, Six and Seven show how these people work, what kind of products and services they use, and how they distribute what they make. Take three sectors to extrapolate your market forecasts for this region: retail franchising, health care, and mining. Brazil is the world's third-largest franchising market, with 863 brands and 48,000 locations, of which only 73 are foreign brands. Argentina has 168 franchise brands, Uruguay has 138 and Chile has 74, most of which are US restaurant, hotel, car rental, fast-food and dry-cleaning networks. Annual billings in the Mercosur nations are estimated at $20 billion and yearly market growth in Brazil and Argentina is 25 per cent and 20 per cent. These kinds of market profiles and growth forecasts suggest an attractive investment opportunity for you in this region. Of course, any retail franchiser interested in this region will have to be sensitive to its particularities. Cariocas, the residents of Rio de Janeiro, like to put ketchup and mustard on their pizza. McDonald's had to open upscale espresso bars in its restaurants to attract porteños, the people of Buenos Aires. Growth in discretionary income is why an estimated 4.5 million computers were sold throughout Mercosur in 2000. The regional market for health care equipment is estimated to be worth $5 billion per year. Latin America's share of world mining investment is forecast to be 41 per cent of the world total in the 1998–2007 period, followed by North America at a distant second at 11 per cent. 'Let's face it, South America has only opened up in the last 10 years while North America's been run several times over, so there's not as much left to find,' said Alan Hill, executive vice president of development at Barrick Gold Corp.[10] 'I think it (economic integration) is a good thing because it helps business understand what it is about and helps business make decisions which are three, four, five to ten years from now. Everything builds on trade. Economic convergence, regulatory convergence, a common energy or transport policy give better future fine points to business,' said Pascal Lamy, the EU's trade commissioner.[11]

While debt swaps are likely to continue making front-page news in South America for the years ahead, harvest reports may make the headlines in more countries than just China, India and Russia in the near future.[12] Food security has never been far behind in the list of factors ensuring political stability, be it from the hordes of starving Mongols invading the Roman Empire to food riots outside the gates of Versailles. In a world where 30 per cent of the 6 billion people on the planet today are aged 14 or younger it is reasonable to expect that increasing food demand will be met in a meaningful way only through an increase in yields since there is little room left for expanded acreage in arable land. Other than South America, there are few other parts of the world, save Russia and eastern Europe, that can potentially increase their production yields in any significant way. Nearly all of the 3 billion people to be added to the world population by the middle of the century will be born in developing countries. Some analysts argue there is not enough land to feed everyone and make way for enough roads and parking lots based on the current rate of car sales. For this reason future food security depends on restructuring transportation budgets now – investing less in highway infrastructure and more in railways.[13]

Building more roads, railways and inland waterways isn't just talk. The Inter-American Development Bank teamed up with private sector banks in March 2001 to create the Inter-American Corporation for Infrastructure to fund small to medium-sized infrastructure projects throughout Latin America.[14] The 12 South American governments agreed to pick the highest-priority projects and start building them between now and the end of the decade. This continent has been fragmented for centuries by its own geography, be it the highest mountains in the Americas, the largest tropical rain forest in the world or simply by decrepit railways and roads. That's not going to change overnight. But instead of individually pursuing infrastructure plans geared for the export of goods overseas, the South American integration plan described in Chapter Seven aims to connect neighbouring countries. The idea is to facilitate the flows of services, goods and people to build on the momentum described in chapters Two and Nine of commerce brought on by the explosion in regional free trade deals through the 1990s.

Fine-tuning competitiveness

What many of the trade deals that were negotiated in Latin America in the 1990s represented was a break from the protectionist and isolationist import substitution policies of the past to embrace a more open form of regionalism. As you saw in chapters Two, Four and Five, several of these free trade agreements are in line with World Trade Organization standards. That means there is common ground or a foundation upon which free trade talks with North America and western Europe can be built. There are a number of complex issues to be harmonized and points of disagreement to be resolved, but there is without doubt a willingness to discuss all of these matters.

'If we were to combine Chile, Mercosur and the Andean Community, we would be speaking of a market of 340 million persons, which would place Latin America's integration in a different class and set in motion new prospects not limited to the area of trade. The progressive alignment of the two subregions will open up a harmonious and balanced area that will place us in a more competitive position within the international economy where we can unquestionably make our political weight felt,' said Andean Community secretary general Sebastian Alegrett.[15]

The South Americans' idea of globalization is one that is 'multipolar', where developing countries have a voice in determining the architecture of the world financial system and the way to be heard is by forming alliances, one form of which is a trade bloc. In the trade context you can be sure the South Americans will argue for more time and exemptions to nurture their industries to maturity, just as the Group of Seven industrialized nations were able to develop their manufacturing sectors in a relatively sheltered marketplace. Brasilia is a leading champion of this view and the inability of Washington or Brussels to reach some kind of compromise on this matter will doom free trade talks. Civil society may be able to play an important role in forging a bridge between the developed and developing world. Chapter Five offers one example of a non-governmental organization suggesting an alternative policy choice in the polarized pharmaceutical patents debate. Oxfam has asked the World Trade Organization to change its patent rules to allow developing countries to produce low-cost versions of drugs that treat AIDS, respiratory tract infections and childhood diarrhoea. The NGO, based in Oxford in the UK, suggested creating a $5 billion international fund to assist in disease research and subsidize drug distribution in poor countries. Trade officials suggest that what the North Americans want most are assurances on legal guarantees for their companies operating in South America, specifically in the areas of intellectual property and patents.

"Trade officials suggest that what the North Americans want most are assurances on legal guarantees for their companies operating in South America, specifically in the areas of intellectual property and patents"

The Europeans, who have a much more developed and sophisticated government procurement sector, are keen for concessions in this area. Both trade groups appear willing to be flexible in other areas if the South Americans are prepared to give some ground in those categories. In return, governments on this continent want the United States to ease its anti-dumping measures and the European Union to grant their farm products freer access to that market, which accounts for about 20 per cent of world food trade.

It is conceivable that chronically high regional unemployment and underemployment could be eased in part in a continental marketplace freer of impediments to trade and competition. Economic development policies, international public-private partnerships and what the Inter-American Development Bank calls 'axes' – transportation corridors that foster the development of an array of regional industries such as those beginning to sprout up along the Santa Cruz-Sao Paulo natural gas pipeline or the Hidrovia waterway described in Chapter Seven – will probably change the labour market and business climate in South America for the better. If you look at South America and compare it with many other emerging markets you must admit that this region has a fairly well-educated workforce that speaks two languages and shares the same roots, and this region is gradually progressing in socio-economic terms. This part of the world certainly has its share of challenges to overcome, but generally speaking it is neither going backwards nor is it the worst place to invest. That is probably why this region was the fastest-growing market for US exports between 1992 and 1998.

What is certain is that this is one of the few regions of the world with which the United States has a trade surplus and it is forecast to export more to Latin America by 2007 than Japan and Europe combined. The US Department of Commerce estimates exports to Mercosur almost tripled between 1990 and 1999 and that US investment in the trade bloc over the course of the 1990s had reached $40 billion by 1998. The United States, in turn, was the fastest-growing destination of all Mercosur exports between 1995 and 1999, growing at four times the rate of intra-Mercosur exports (an average 6.1 per cent per year versus an average 1.6 per cent per year).[16] 'Inflows to Latin America continued to expand in 1999 to reach $90 billion,' said Unctad's Fiorina Mugione.[17] A significant amount of that foreign direct investment came in the form of mergers and acquisitions, and privatization programmes also contributed significantly to the increased flow of FDI into the region. 'Direct investors seem indifferent to short-term macroeconomic difficulties experienced by several countries in the region with relatively stable institutional and policy frameworks, such as Argentina, Brazil, Bolivia, Chile and Peru. Long-term growth prospects in these countries were not substantially affected by the recent economic slow-down. Inflows to Brazil are expected to maintain high levels. In contrast, investors are reducing their involvement in countries with unstable institutional frameworks, such as Paraguay, Colombia, Ecuador and Venezuela. However, given the investment potential of these countries, particularly in the oil industry in the case of the Andean countries, inflows should resume rapidly as stability and predictability increase,' said Mugione.

Perhaps the late Victor Paz Estenssoro, elected president of Bolivia four times and who died of a heart attack at 93 on 7 June 2001, best personifies South America's transformation in the period from the Cold War to fall of the Berlin Wall. During his first term in 1952 he expropriated Bolivia's tin mines, then the country's chief export, and extended the vote to indigenous Bolivians. He also implemented land reforms in one of the western hemisphere's poorest countries with a large peasant population. But in his fourth elected term that started in 1985, facing the collapse of tin prices on world market and hyperinflation of 23,500 per cent, Paz Estenssoro shut the mines down and implemented painful economic austerity measures to prepare his people and country for the 21st Century.

Notes

[1]Mugione, Fiorina, project officer at the United Nations Conference on Trade and Development's division on Investment, Technology and Enterprise Development, interview from Geneva, 12 March 2001.

[2]Rojas Penso, Juan, secretary general of the Association of Latin American Trade Partners, interview from Montevideo, 21 March 2001.

[3]Rodriguez Giavarini, Adalberto, foreign minister of Argentina, press briefing in Buenos Aires, 7 March 2001.

[4]Munoz, George, president and chief executive of US Overseas Private Investment Corporation, speech to the Greater Houston Partnership on 11 January 2001, posted on website *www.opic.gov.* viewed 20 February 2001.

[5]Alegrett, Sebastian, Andean Community secretary general, phone interview from Lima, 8 March 2001.

[6]International Monetary Fund 2001 outlook, issued in Washington, D.C., 10 August 2001.

[7]De Marchi, Victorio, co-president of AmBev, interview from Sao Paulo, 14 March 2001.

[8]Swinarski, Christophe, human rights consultant and former human rights observer of the International Committee of the Red Cross to Argentina, Brazil, Uruguay and Paraguay (1987 to 1991) as well as Bolivia and Chile (1989 to 1991), interview in Buenos Aires, 18 December 2000.

[9]Hart, George, vice president of international finance at Canadian Hunter International, phone interview to Calgary, 16 March 2001.

[10]Hill, Alan, executive vice president of development at Barrick Gold Corp., phone interview to Toronto, Canada, 16 March 2001.

[11]Lamy, Pascal, European Union trade commissioner, interview in Buenos Aires, 29 September 2000.

[12]Brown, Lester, chairman, Worldwatch Institute, interview in Washington, D.C., 11 January 2001.

[13]Brown, Lester, *ibid*, briefing note, 14 February 2001.

[14]Inter-American Development Bank statement, issued at its annual meeting in Santiago, 20 March 2001.

[15]Alegrett, Sebastian, Andean Community secretary general, interview with Bolivian newspaper *Presencia*, 1 October 2000.

[16]Ashby, Christopher, US ambassador to Uruguay, speech to the 'Doing business between Mercosur and the United States' seminar, 25 September 2000.

[17]Mugione, Fiorina, *op.cit*.

Recommended reading and websites

Salazar-Xirinachs, José Manuel and Robert, Maryse (eds.) (2001) *Toward Free Trade in the Americas*, General Secretariat/Organization of American States and Brookings Institution Press, Washington D.C.

Stephenson, Sherry M., (ed.) (2000) *Services Trade in the Western Hemisphere, Liberalization Integration and Reform*, General Secretariat/Organization of American States and Brookings Institution Press, Washington D.C.

Worldwatch Institute (2001) *State of the World 2001*, W.W. Norton & Company, New York, London.

Campbell, Jorge (ed.) (1999) *Mercosur, Entra la Realidad y la Utopia*, Centro de Economia Internacional & Nuevohacer Grupo Editor Latinoamericano.

Nweihed, Kaldone G. (1999) *Bolívar y el Tercer Mundo*, Universidad de los Andes, Ediciones del Rectorado, Consejo de Publicaciones.

Rodriguez Mendoza, Miguel, Low, Patrick and Kotschwar, Barbara (ed.) (1999) *Trade Rules in the Making, Challenges in Regional and Multilateral Negotiations*, General Secretariat/Organization of American States and Brookings Institution Press, Washington D.C.

Meirovich de Aguinis, Ana Maria (1992) *Empresas e Inversiones en el Mercosur*, Abeledo-Perrot, Buenos Aires.

Chudnovsky, Daniel, *Investimentos Externos No Mercosul*, Universidade Estadual de Campinas Instituto de Economia & Papirus Editora, Sao Paulo.

Inter-American Development Bank (2000) Integracion & Comercio 35 anos INTAL, Numero Especial, Instituto para la Integracion de America Latina y el Caribe, Buenos Aires.

Schaposnik, Eduardo C. (1997) *As Teorias da Integracao e o Mercosul*, Estrategias, Editora DA UFSC, Florianopolis.

Krischke, Paulo J. (2000) Ecologia, Juventude e Cultura Politica, A Cultura da Juventude, A Democratizacao e a Ecologia nos Paises do Cone Sul, Editora DA UFSC, Florianopolis.

Journal of Applied Economics (1999) Vol. II, No. 1, May.

Brooklyn Journal of International Law 'Harmonization of Competition Policies among Mercosur Countries', (1998) Vol. XXIV No. 2.

Almeida, Antonio Jose (1997) *Mercosul, Integracao e Impacto Socioeconomico*, Editora Vozes, Petropolis.

Consejo Argentino para las Relaciones Internacionales & Fundacion Popular Iberoamericana (1995) *Union Europea y Mercosur*, Jornadas de Reflexion, Buenos Aires.

World Bank (2000) *Trade Blocs*, Oxford University Press, New York.

World Bank (2000) *World Bank Atlas 2000*, Communications Development Inc., Washington D.C., with Grundy & Northedge, London.

Corporacion Andina de Fomento (2000) *Vias para la Integracion*, Grupo La Galaxia, Caracas.

Fundacion Capital (1999) *Convergencia Macroeconomica en el Mercosur: Un Camino Critico*, Buenos Aires.

Websites

www.monde-diplomatique.fr/
www.gazetamercantil.com.br/
www.lanacion.com.ar/
www.europa.int.com/
www.schinvestment.com/
www.unctad.org
www.undp.org
www.mecon.gov.ar
http://gmm.mecon.gov.ar
www.ibge.gov.br
www.ipea.gov.br
www.dieese.org.br
www.iuperj.br
www.stn.fazenda.gov.br
www.redmercosur.org.uy
www.cafedecolombia.com
www.observatorio.net
www.agronegocios-e.com.br
www.fao.org/giews
www.bolsa1.com.br
www.iadb.org/intal
www.intercommercial.com
www.aladi.org
www.sugaronline.com
www.boucinhas.com.br
www.rubbernetwork.com
www.comunidadandina.org
www.caf.com
www.avman.com

Glossary of terms

American Depository Receipt (ADR): Shares of a foreign company listed for trading on the New York Stock Exchange. An American Depository Share (ADS) is essentially the same thing but instead of being in circulation on a stock market it is held in a bank.

Andean Community of Nations: The Andean Community is an economic and social integration organization with an international legal status. Bolivia, Colombia, Ecuador, Peru, and Venezuela are member nations.The Community is administered by the Andean Integration System (SAI). Its beginnings date back to 1969, when a group of South American countries signed the Cartagena Agreement, also known as the Andean Pact. The purpose of the agreement is to promote the balanced and harmonious development of its members, accelerate the growth of the Andean countries and the creation of jobs, and facilitate participation in the regional integration process to eventually create a Latin American common market. The agreement also aims to help reduce members' external vulnerability and improve their position in the international economic context and define social policies oriented toward improving the quality of life of different subregional groups.

Over the past three decades, Andean integration has been through a series of stages, going from a closed concept of inward-looking integration based on the substitution import to a form of open regionalism. The direct intervention of the presidents in the leadership of the process within the new model spurred integration and made it possible to attain the main objectives set by the Cartagena Agreement, such as the liberalization of trade in goods in the subregion, the adoption of a common external tariff, among others.

The progress of integration and the emergence of new challenges stemming from global economic change brought to the fore the need for both institutional and policy reforms in the Cartagena Agreement. These were accomplished by the Protocols of Trujillo and Sucre, respectively. The institutional reforms gave the process political direction and created the Andean Community and the Andean Integration System. The policy reforms extended the scope of integration beyond the purely trade and economic areas.

The Andean Community started operating on 1 August 1997 with a General Secretariat, with headquarters in Lima, Peru. The Council of Presidents and the Council of Foreign Ministers were formally established as new policy-making and leadership bodies. The legislative role of the Commission, comprised of the trade ministers, was broadened by including ministers of other sectors. Now the Andean Community includes five countries with a population of more than 109 million people and an area of 4.7 million square kilometres. The Andean Community's website is *www.comunidadandina.org* and it can be e-mailed at *contacto@comunidadandina.org*. The General Secretariat's address is Avenida Paseo de la Republica 3895, Lima 27, Perú. The phone number is +511 221 2222 and the fax is +511 221 3329.

Andean Development Corporation: The Corporación Andina de Fomento (CAF), a legal entity in public international law, is the main promotional and financial institution of the Andean Community of Nations. Its constituent agreement was signed on 7 February 1968 and entered into force on 30 January 1970. The first shareholders' meeting was held in June 1970 and the corporation began operations in June 1970. The total authorized capital of the corporation is $3 billion. Its paid-in capital and reserves amount to $1.4 billion, its loan portfolio is $4.2 billion and total assets amounted to $5.4 billion at the end 1999.

CAF's mandate is to promote sustainable development and regional integration, by attracting capital resources for financial services to the public and private sectors of the shareholders' countries. CAF's primary line of business, either directly or through financial intermediaries, is long, medium and short-term lending to both the public and private sectors. It finances expansion and modernization of companies in several economic sectors such as in the textile, paper and chemical industries. The corporation makes funds available to private-sector banks to be used to finance small and medium-sized company projects in a wide range of industries, from agribusiness to tourism. CAF also works as a partner and lender in a variety of co-financing activities with multilateral institutions such as the World Bank, Inter-American Development Bank, (IADB) International Fund for Agricultural Development (IFAD), and International Finance Corporation

(IFC). It also works with financial institutions such as the export-import banks of the United States and Japan.

The CAF has 12 shareholder countries: the five Andean Community nations – Bolivia, Colombia, Ecuador, Peru and Venezuela – and Brazil, Chile, Jamaica, Mexico, Panama, Paraguay, Trinidad & Tobago, as well as 22 private banks based in the region. The Andean Development Corporation's website is *www.caf.com* and its address is Avenida Luis Roche, Torre CAF, 69011 Altamira, Caracas 1060, Venezuela.

Association of Latin American Trade Partners: ALADI was established after a new agreement known as the 1980 Montevideo Treaty, was signed in Montevideo, Uruguay, on 12 August 1980 by the ministers of foreign affairs of 11 Latin American countries (Argentina, Bolivia, Brazil, Chile, Colombia, Ecuador, Mexico, Paraguay, Peru, Uruguay and Venezuela). Cuba became the 12th member on 26 August 1999.

The 1980 Montevideo Treaty is a commitment to advance the economic integration process begun in 1960 with the establishment of the Latin American Free Trade Association (ALALC) under its predecessor, the Montevideo Treaty of 1960. Member countries have established an area of economic preferences, comprising a regional tariff preference, regional and partial scope agreements, and conditions favouring the participation of countries at a relatively less advanced stage of economic development into the integration process, based on principles of non-reciprocity and community co-operation. An agreement establishing a Multilateral Compensation and Reciprocal Credit Mechanism (CPCR) was signed by the ALALC member countries' central in 1965 and came into effect on 1 June 1966. The Dominican Republic joined the CPCR in 1973. A new Reciprocal Payments and Credit Agreement was signed on 25 August 1982, adjusted to ALADI's new guidelines but maintaining the general features of the previous pact.

The main features of the agreement are: (a) establishment of bilateral lines of credit denominated in US dollars between each pair of central banks; (b) four-month paid multilateral compensation of balances accumulated in the bilateral accounts and the outstanding balances paid in US dollars, usually through the Federal Reserve Bank of New York; (c) channelling of payments through the system is voluntary, although if convenient or necessary members' central banks may make them mandatory, as was recently the case with Venezuela. During 1997 the volume of payments handled through this clearing mechanism reached $7.864 million; in 1998 it fell to $5.570 million; in 1999 it fell to $3.93 million. Since 1966, the settlement of payments channelled through the agreement has amounted to a total of $207.418 million, actually paying $61.3 million, which represented an average saving of 70 per cent in the use of convertible foreign exchange.

As of 1 May 1991 a transitory financing mechanism of the credits due to the multilateral compensation balances (Automatic Payment Programme) was incorporated in the agreement. The programme tries to foresee occasional liquidity difficulties that member countries' central banks might face at the end of their multilateral compensation periods. This mechanism is multilateral and automatic and consists of postponing payments for four months.

The Santo Domingo Agreement is another credit programme signed by the central banks of the ALALC member countries and the Dominican Republic in 1969. This agreement, which was amended on 22 September 1981, consists of credit lines provided by the members' central banks up to a combined total of nearly $700 million. This fund is earmarked for the temporary relief of member countries experiencing liquidity problems in cases of (a) deficits in the payments clearance of intra-regional trade; (b) deficits in the overall balance of payments; and (c) deficits caused by natural disasters. This agreement was last used in 1984. The Banco Central de Reserva del Perú is the agent bank of both systems.

ALADI's website is *www.aladi.org* and its e-mail is *sgaladi@aladi.org*. The address is Casilla de Correos 577, Calle Cebollatí 1461, C.P. 11200, Montevideo, Uruguay. The phone number is +598 2400 1121.

Association of South East Asian Nations: The ASEAN Regional Forum (ARF) consists of 10 ASEAN members – Brunei, Burma, Cambodia, Indonesia, Laos, Malaysia, Philippines, Singapore, Thailand, Vietnam – and one observer – Papua New Guinea. ASEAN was founded in 1967 and its aim is to encourage regional economic, social and cultural co-operation among the non-communist countries of southeast Asia. Russia and China are consultative partners and ASEAN has eight dialogue partners: Australia, Canada, the European Union, India, Japan, South Korea, New Zealand and the United States.

The address is 70 A Jalan Sisingamangaraja, Jakarta 12110, Indonesia. The phone number is +62 21 7262991 and fax is +62 21 7398234.

Balance of payments: A country's balance of payments is the difference between the amount it receives for its exports and the amount it pays to other countries for its imports. The balance of payments is divided into goods and services.

Bank for International Settlements: The BIS was established under the Young Plan under the Hague Agreements of 20 January 1930 for the purpose of facilitating German reparation payments after World War I. The BIS was founded by a group of six central banks and a financial institution of the United States and established in Basel, Switzerland where it began operations on 17 May 1930, making it the world's oldest international financial organization and meeting place.

The Bank for International Settlements is an international organization that promotes international monetary and financial co-operation and acts as a bank for central banks. The banking department carries out a wide range of banking operations to assist central banks in the management of their external reserves. The bank is not permitted to make advances to governments or open current accounts in their name. About 120 central banks and international financial institutions from around the world place deposits with the BIS. The currency deposits placed with the BIS amounted to about $128 billion at the end of March 2000, representing around 7 per cent of world foreign exchange reserves. Most of these funds are placed in the market, mainly in the form of investments with top-quality commercial banks and purchases of short-term government securities. In accordance with two collateral pledge agreements, the BIS acts in the capacity of collateral agent to hold and invest collateral for the benefit of the holders of certain US dollar-denominated bonds issued by Brazil under the rescheduling arrangements and maturing in either 15 or 30 years. The BIS has undertaken similar functions for Peru since March 1997.

The Bank for International Settlements' website is *www.bis.org* and it can be e-mailed at *emailmaster@bis.org*. The address is 2 Centralbahnplatz, Basel, Switzerland CH-4002. The phone number is +41 61 280 8080.

Bonds: Bonds are issued by governments and private companies. They are loans which are meant to be traded. Bond prices are expressed as a percentage of the face or par value. There are three components to the interest rates set on bonds: the time value or opportunity cost; compensation for inflation in order to retain the investment's purchasing power over time; and credit risk. A coupon yield is the original percentage level set on a bond. A current yield is the percentage level you will get from buying a bond on a secondary market. A yield to maturity is the interest rate paid out if you hold the bond until its due date.

Cartagena Group: Please see Group of 11.

Central bank: A bank for banks, the central bank can lend other banks money in the last resort. It can also exercise some control over other banks' activities and supervises the functioning of a nation's financial services system.

Coca: A bush with leaves that contain the stimulant used to make cocaine. Coca is not to be confused with cocoa, which comes from cacao seeds and is used in making chocolate, cocoa and cocoa butter. Cocaine is a stimulant derived from chemically leaching certain properties from the leaves of the coca bush.

Consumer Price Index: A measurement of how much money can buy in terms of a basket of goods and services typically consumed by the average household. If there has been inflation, a unit of currency will buy less than it did previously.

Deflation: A fall in the general level of prices resulting in the contraction in the size of gross domestic product.

Deregulation: The abolition or reduction of state controls and supervision over economic activities.

Devaluation: A reduction in the value of a currency against that of other currencies.

Dredging: Deepening an existing waterway. It is a technique used for collecting bottom-dwelling marine life such as shellfish or harvesting coral which often causes significant destruction of reef and ocean-floor ecosystems.

European Union: The EU evolved from the European Community and took effect in November 1993. It has 15 member nations and co-ordinates regional policy in three areas: economics, building on the European Economic Community's (EEC) efforts to establish a common market and a common currency called the 'euro'; defence, under the Common Foreign and Security Policy (CFSP); and justice and home affairs, including immigration, drugs, terrorism, and improved living and working conditions. Member nations are: Austria, Belgium, Denmark, Finland, France, Germany, Greece, Ireland, Italy, Luxembourg, Netherlands, Portugal, Spain, Sweden and the United Kingdom. Thirteen countries have applied to become members: Bulgaria, Cyprus, Czech Republic, Estonia, Hungary, Latvia, Lithuania, Malta, Poland, Romania, Slovakia, Slovenia, Turkey. The address is European Commission, Rue de la Loi 200, B-1049 Bussels, Belgium. The phone number is +32 2299 1111 and the fax is +32 2295 0138.

Exchange rate: The price at which one currency can be exchanged for another currency. To prevent fluctuations in the rate of exchange, exchange rates can be fixed or controlled. Exchange rates which are left free to market forces are known as floating exchange rates.

Financial Fund for the Development of the River Plate Basin: Fondo Financiero para el Desarrollo de la Cuenca del Plata (Fonplata) was created as a result of the River Plate Treaty of 1969 for the development and integration of the subregion. Member nations are Argentina, Bolivia, Brazil, Paraguay and Uruguay. Fonplata is a regional financial institution having an independent juridical personality. Its functions are to finance studies, projects, programmes, and works with the end of promoting development and physical integration of the River Plate Basin and its surroundings.

The authorized capital of Fonplata is $308 million, of which 87 per cent is paid in and 13 per cent is callable. Argentina and Brazil each contributed the equivalent of $205.4 million; Bolivia, Paraguay and Uruguay contributed the equivalent of $102.6 million. Paid-up capital, as of 31 December 1998, was $268 million.

Fonplata's website is *www.fonplata.org* and its address is Espana 74, Sucre, Bolivia, Casilla Correo 47. The phone number is +591 646 0207.

Fiscal policy: This is the government's plan for taxation and government spending. Fiscal policy is one way in which a government can attempt to control the economy. Another way is through monetary policy which attempts to guide the economy by controlling the money supply.

General Agreement on Tariffs and Trade: The GATT was created on 30 October 1947 to promote the expansion of international trade on a non-discriminatory basis and was later subsumed by the World Trade Organization (WTO) on 1 January 1995. (Also see World Trade Organization.) The address is Centre William Rappard, 154 Rue de Lausanne, CH-1211 Geneva 21, Switzerland. The phone number is +4122 739 5111.

Gold standard: A system in which the value of a currency is legally fixed in terms of how much gold it is worth.

Gross domestic product: The total market value of final goods and services produced by a country in one year. GDP is only an estimate because illegal activities are not measured. Intermediate goods such as steel are not included until they become final goods such as a car part in a vehicle bought by a consumer. The basic components of GDP are domestic consumption, investment, government spending (but not social welfare which is considered a transfer payment) and net exports.

Group of 11: The G11 is also known as the Cartagena Group and includes 11 nations: Argentina, Bolivia, Brazil, Chile, Colombia, Dominican Republic, Ecuador, Mexico, Peru, Uruguay and Venezuela. Created in June 1984 the G11's objective is to provide a forum for Latin America's largest debtor nations.

Household income: Data on household income or consumption come from household surveys, the results adjusted for household size. Nations use different methodology in collecting and adjusting the data. Surveys based on income will normally show a more unequal distribution than surveys based on consumption.

Inflation: A rise in the general level of prices. **Hyperinflation** is an inflation that proceeds at a high rate but perhaps for only a brief period of time. **Creeping inflation** is an inflation that lasts for a long time at a fairly steady pace.

Institute for the Integration of Latin America and the Caribbean: INTAL was created by an agreement between the Inter-American Development Bank (IADB) and the government of Argentina in 1964. Institutionally, INTAL is part of the Integration and Regional Programs Department of the IADB. INTAL's activities include research on all aspects about regional integration and co-operation, subjects related to international trade, hemispheric integration and international relations with other regions and countries of the world. All activities are channelled through four lines of action: (1) Regional and national technical co-operation projects on integration; (2) Policy forums; (3) Integration forums; and (4) Journals and information. Documentation and information services are channelled through its Documentation Center and comprise 80,000 documents, 10,000 books, and 400 titles of periodicals.

The institute's database (INTEG) is available through its website *www.iadb.org/intal* and its e-mail is *gloriapr@iadb.org* or *irisc@iadb.org*. The address is Esmeralda 130, Casilla de Correo 39, 1035 Buenos Aires, Argentina. The phone number is +5411 4320 1850.

Interest: A payment by a borrower for the use of a sum of money.

Inter-American Development Bank: The IADB, the oldest and largest regional multilateral development institution, was established in December 1959 to help accelerate economic and social development in Latin America and the Caribbean. bank membership totals 46 nations. In addition to the bank, the IDB Group consists of the Inter-American Investment Corporation (IIC) and the Multilateral Investment Fund (MIF). The IIC, an autonomous affiliate of the bank, was established to promote the economic development of the region by financing small and mid-sized private enterprises. The MIF was created in 1992 to promote investment reforms and to stimulate private-sector development.

The bank's charter states that its principal functions are (1) to use its own capital, funds raised by it in financial markets, and other available resources, for financing the development of the borrowing member countries; (2) to supplement private investment when private capital is not available on reasonable terms and conditions; and (3) to provide technical assistance for the preparation, financing and implementation of development plans and projects. In carrying out its mission, the bank has mobilized financing for projects that represent a total investment of $240 billion. Annual lending has grown dramatically from the $294 million in loans approved in 1961 to $10 billion in 1998. The bank has borrowed funds for its operations from the capital markets of Europe, Japan, Latin America, the Caribbean and the United States. The Bank's debt is AAA rated by the three major rating services in the United States, and is accorded equivalent status in the other major capital markets.

The IADB's website is *www.iadb.org* and its address is 1300 New York Avenue, N.W., Washington, D.C. 20577 U.S.A. The phone number is 1 202 623 1000.

International Centre for the Settlement of Investment Disputes (ICSID): See World Bank Group.

International Chamber of Commerce: The ICC has 62 member nations. Founded in 1919, the ICC's objective is to promote free trade and private enterprise as well as lobby for business interests at the national and international levels. The ICC's address is 38 Cours Albert 1er, F-75008 Paris, France. The phone number is +33 1 4953 2828 and fax is +33 1 4953 2942.

International Monetary Fund: The IMF is made up of 183 member countries. It was established at a conference held in Bretton Woods, New Hampshire, United States in July 1944 and came into official existence on 27 December 1945 when 29 countries signed its articles of agreement. Financial operations began on 1 March 1947.

The IMF's mandate is to promote international monetary co-operation; to facilitate the expansion and balanced growth of international trade; to promote exchange stability; to assist in the establishment of a multilateral system of payments; to make the general resources of the fund temporarily available to the members under adequate safeguards; and to shorten the duration and lessen the degree of disequilibrium in the international balances of payments of its members.

The IMF website is *www.imf.org* and its e-mail is *communications@imf.org*. The address is 700–19th Street, N.W., Washington, D.C., 20431 U.S.A. and its phone number is 1 202 623 4661.

International Organization for Standardization: The ISO is a worldwide federation of national standards bodies from 110 countries. The ISO is a non-governmental organization which began operating in 1947. It's mission is to promote the development of standardization and related activities to ease international trade in goods and services, and to develop co-operation in the areas of intellectual, scientific, technological and economic activity. ISO's work results in international agreements which are published as international standards.

Latin American Reserve Fund: The Fondo Latinoamericano de Reservas (FLAR) has six member countries: Bolivia, Colombia, Costa Rica, Ecuador, Peru and Venezuela. The Latin American Reserve Fund was established in March 1991 as the successor to the Andean Reserve Fund (ARF) which was created by the Cartagena Agreement. At its seventh extraordinary meeting in Caracas, Venezuela in January 1988 the ARF decided to expand to include other Latin American countries.

The FLAR is a regional financial institution having an independent juridicial personality. Its functions are to assist in correcting payments imbalances through loans with terms of up to four years and guarantees extended to members, to co-ordinate their monetary, exchange and financial policies, and to promote the liberalization of trade and payments in the Andean subregion. Subscribed capital of the FLAR is $1.125 billion, to which Bolivia, Costa Rica and Ecuador each contribute $125 million, while Colombia, Peru and Venezuela each contribute $250 million. The paid-up capital up to December 2000 was US$1.034 billion.

The website is *www.flar.net* and e-mail is *flar@flar.net*. The address is Edificio Banco de Occidente, Apartado Aereo 241523, Carrera 13, No. 27-47, Piso 10, Santafe de Bogota, D.C., Colombia. The phone number is +571 241 9860 and fax is +571 241 8872.

Organization of American States: The OAS was created in April 1890 as the International Union of American Republics and adopted its current charter in April 1948. All 35 countries of the western hemisphere are members of the OAS. The agency's mandate is to promote regional peace and security as well as economic and social development.

Its address is 17th Street and Constitution Avenue NW, Washington, DC 20006, U.S.A. The phone number is 1 202 458 3000 and the fax is 1 202 458 3967.

Organization of the Petroleum Exporting Countries: OPEC was created in 1960 to co-ordinate and unify members' petroleum policies and to safeguard their interests. There are 11 member nations: Algeria, Indonesia, Islamic Republic of Iran, Iraq, Kuwait, Libya, Nigeria, Qatar, Saudi Arabia, United Arab Emirates and Venezuela.

The address is Obere Donaustrasse 93, A-1020 Vienna, Austria, 134474. The phone number is +431 21 1120 and fax is +431 216 4320.

Plan Colombia: The Government of Colombia developed'Plan Colombia' to promote the peace process, combat the narcotics industry, revive the Colombian economy, and strengthen its democratic institutions. Plan Colombia is a $7.5 billion programme. President Andres Pastrana has pledged $4 billion of Colombian resources and has called on the international community to provide the remaining $3.5 billion. The United States has offered $1.6 billion, about 80 per cent of which is military aid.

Quota: A limit on the amount of a good that can be imported into a country.

Rio Group: The Rio Group was formerly known as'Grupo de los Ocho', established in December 1986. Argentina, Bolivia, Brazil, Chile, Colombia, Ecuador, Mexico, Panama, Paraguay, Peru, Uruguay, Venezuela are members. The organization's aim is to consult member nations on regional Latin American issues.

The address is Ministerio de Relaciones Exteriores, Edificio AYFRA, Piso 10, Presidente Franco y Ayolas, Asuncion, Paraguay. The phone number is +595 21 448409 and fax number is +595 21 450911.

Shining Path: The Shining Path originated in 1959, when a group of young professors teaching at the university in the southern mountain city of Ayacucho joined the Peruvian Communist Party's regional committee. One of them, Abimael Guzman Reynoso (the Shining Path's future'President Gonzalo'), a philosophy professor, and later dean of the faculty, became chairman of the party regional committee. Guzman soon formed a secret group within the party, which called itself the 'Red Faction'. In 1964 the Peruvian party split, with a smaller group including the leadership supporting the Soviet party, and the larger part supporting the Chinese. The 'Red Faction' allied with the pro-China party. Guzman spent most of 1965 in China studying the Chinese Communist Party's political line at that time and military tactics before returning to Peru.

The name originates from a Communist Party of Peru slogan: 'Follow the Shining Path of Mariategui' in honour of Jose Carlos Mariategui, the founder of Peru's communist movement.

From 1968 to 1980 Peru was under a military dictatorship and Guzman was jailed briefly. He managed to expel Shining Path members opposed to armed conflict in 1979 and the movement has taken on violent guerrilla tactics since 1980. The military during the 1990–2000 rule of Alberto Fujimori rounded up most Shining Path members, including Guzman, and imprisoned them.

Southern Cone Common Market (Mercosur): The world's third-largest trade bloc was created by the signing of the Treaty of Asuncion on 26 March 1991. Argentina, Brazil, Paraguay and Uruguay are full members while Bolivia and Chile are associate members. The objective of Mercosur is to increase regional economic co-operation to eventually create an EU-like common market. The Common Market of the South aims to establish more productive and dynamic economies through the enlargement of the market and to promote harmonious and balanced socio-economic development through the effective use of indigenous natural and human resources, the preservation of the environment, the co-ordination of macro-economic policies, and the development of economic complementarity.

The address of the General Secretariat is Rincon 575, Piso 12, 11000 Montevideo, Uruguay. The phone number is +598 2916 4590 and fax number is +598 2916 4591.

Southern Cone of South America: As a geographical area, the Southern Cone of South America includes Argentina, Bolivia, Brazil, Chile, Paraguay, Peru and Uruguay covering a total area of more than 5.6 million square miles (15 million square kilometres) or an area larger than continental Europe.

Tariff: A tax on imports.

Tupac Amaru: The Movimiento Revolucionario Tupac Amaru (MRTA) is a traditional Marxist-Leninist revolutionary movement founded in 1983 and formed from remnants of the Movement of the Revolutionary Left, a Peruvian insurgent group active in the 1960s. Its objective is to establish a Marxist regime and rid Peru of US and Japanese influence. Peru's counter-insurgency programme has diminished the group's ability to carry out guerrilla attacks. MRTA has suffered from in-fighting, the imprisonment or deaths of senior leaders, and loss of leftist support. The MRTA used to conduct bombings, kidnappings, ambushes and assassinations, but its activities in recent years have fallen dramatically.

In December 1996, 14 MRTA members occupied the Japanese Ambassador's residence in Lima and held 72 hostages for more than four months. Peruvian forces stormed the residence in April 1997, rescuing all but one of the remaining hostages and killing most of the group's leaders. The group has not conducted a significant guerrilla operation since and appears more focused on obtaining the release of imprisoned MRTA members.

United Nations Conference on Trade and Development: Unctad is the principal organ of the United Nations General Assembly in the field of trade and development. It was established as a permanent inter-governmental body in 1964 in Geneva as a result of the first session of the conference, with a view to accelerating economic growth and development, particularly for the developing countries. Unctad undertakes policy analysis and intergovernmental debates, and monitors, implements and follows up on its policy proposals as well as providing technical co-operation.

UNCTAD's website is *www.unctad.org* and its address is Palais des Nations, CH-1211 Geneva 10, Switzerland. The phone number is +4122 907 1234 and fax is +4122 907 0057.

United Nations Development Programme: The UNDP was established in 1965 through a merger of the United Nations Expanded Programme of Technical Assistance and the United Nations Special Fund. The UNDP's mandate is to help countries realize sustainable human development through poverty elimination, the regeneration of the environment, employment creation and the empowerment of women. The UNDP is the United Nations' central co-ordinating organization.

For 1998, contributions to UNDP's core resources were more than $750 million. The UNDP has offices in 134 countries and helps people in more than 170 countries. Since 1990, the UNDP has commissioned a team of experts to produce its annual Human Development Report. This report represents the independent analysis of those experts and uses a new measure of development – the Human Development Index (HDI) – which combines three indices – life expectancy, educational attainment and purchasing power. The comparison of country ranking according to gross national product and HDI shows that economic growth, although vital to improved living conditions, is by itself no guarantee of human development.

The agency's website is *www.undp.org* and its address is One United Nations Plaza, New York, New York, U.S.A. 236286. The phone number is 1 212 906 5000 and fax is 1 212 826 2057.

United Nations Economic Commission for Latin America and the Caribbean: The Comision Economica para America Latina y el Caribe (CEPAL) has 41 member nations and seven associate members. The commission was founded in 1948. Member governments in 1996 updated the mission to increase the relevance of activities sponsored in the region. Under the new guidelines, the commission must act as a centre of excellence to aid member states in the analysis of development. This process includes drafting, evaluating, and following up on public policies as well as providing assistance in areas of specialized information. Experts also offer advice, training and support for regional and international co-operation and co-ordination.

The commission's website is *www.eclac.org* and its address is Edificio Naciones Unidas, Casilla 179-D, Avenida Dag Hammarskjold, Santiago, Chile. The phone number is +562 210 2000 and fax is +562 208 0252.

World Bank Group: The World Bank Group comprises five organizations: the International Bank for Reconstruction and Development (IBRD), the International Development Association (IDA), the International Finance Corporation (IFC), the Multilateral Investment Guarantee Agency (MIGA), and the International Centre for the Settlement of Investment Disputes (ICSID).

The IBRD was founded in 1944 at the Bretton Woods Conference. It is the World Bank Group's main lending organization. It lends to developing countries with relatively high per capita incomes. The money the IBRD lends is used to pay for development projects, such as building highways, schools and hospitals, and for programmes to help governments change the way they manage their economies. IBRD has 181 member countries.

The International Development Association has 161 member countries and was established in 1960 to provide assistance on concessional terms to the poorest developing countries – those that cannot afford to borrow from the IBRD. IDA loans, known as 'credits', are provided mainly to countries with annual per capita incomes of $800 or less.

The International Finance Corporation (IFC) was established in 1956 to help strengthen the private sector in developing countries. The IFC lends directly to the private sector, while the IBRD and IDA lend to governments. The IFC aids the private sector by providing long-term loans, equity investments, guarantees and 'stand-by financing', risk management and 'quasi-equity instruments', such as subordinated loans, preferred stock and income notes. The IFC has 174 member countries.

The International Center for the Settlement of Investment Disputes (ICSID) was founded in 1966 to promote increased flows of international investment by providing facilities for the conciliation and arbitration of disputes between governments and foreign investors. ICSID also provides advice, carries out research, and produces publications in the area of foreign investment law. Some 131 countries are members of ICSID.

The World Bank Group's website is *www.worldbank.org* and its address is 1818 H Street, NW, Washington, D.C., U.S.A. 20433. The phone number is 1 202 477 1234 and fax is 1 202 477 6391.

World Trade Organization: The WTO succeeded the General Agreement on Tariff and Trade (GATT) on 1 January 1995. The GATT was created on 30 October 1947 to promote the expansion of international trade on a non-discriminatory basis. The address is Centre William Rappard, 154 Rue de Lausanne, CH-1211 Geneva 21, Switzerland. The phone number is +4122 739 5111.

Index